History and International Law

History and International Law

An Intertwined Relationship

Edited by

Annalisa Ciampi

Professor of International Law, University of Verona, Italy

Edward Elgar
PUBLISHING

Cheltenham, UK • Northampton, MA, USA

© Annalisa Ciampi 2019

All rights reserved. No part of this publication may be reproduced, stored in a retrieval system or transmitted in any form or by any means, electronic, mechanical or photocopying, recording, or otherwise without the prior permission of the publisher.

Published by
Edward Elgar Publishing Limited
The Lypiatts
15 Lansdown Road
Cheltenham
Glos GL50 2JA
UK

Edward Elgar Publishing, Inc.
William Pratt House
9 Dewey Court
Northampton
Massachusetts 01060
USA

A catalogue record for this book
is available from the British Library

Library of Congress Control Number: 2019951075

This book is available electronically in the Elgaronline
Law subject collection
DOI 10.4337/9781788977494

ISBN 978 1 78897 748 7 (cased)
ISBN 978 1 78897 749 4 (eBook)

Printed and bound in Great Britain by TJ International Ltd, Padstow

Contents

List of contributors		vii
Acknowledgements		viii
Foreword by Giorgio Gaja		ix

PART I   HISTORY AND INTERNATIONAL LAW: AN INTRODUCTION

1   Creative forces and institution building in international law   2
Rolf Einar Fife

2   Eastern Europe's imprint on modern international law   22
Stefan Troebst

PART II   HISTORY AND INTERNATIONAL HUMAN RIGHTS LAW

3   History, isolation and effectiveness of human rights   44
Annalisa Ciampi

4   EU human rights law and history: a tale of three narratives   82
Sionaidh Douglas-Scott

PART III   HISTORY, INTERNATIONAL HUMANITARIAN LAW AND INTERNATIONAL CRIMINAL LAW

5   'Treaty after trauma': 'protection for all' in the Fourth Geneva Convention   103
Gilad Ben-Nun

6   History and core international crimes: friends or foes?   135
Olympia Bekou

| 7 | The legacy of the ICTY in Croatia, Bosnia and Serbia
Katarina Ristić | 168 |
| 8 | The rise and demise of the ICC relationship with African states and the AU
Erika de Wet | 191 |

Index   213

Contributors

Olympia Bekou is Professor of Public International Law and Head, International Criminal Justice Unit, Human Rights Law Centre, School of Law, University of Nottingham.

Gilad Ben-Nun is Senior Scholar in Residence and EEGA Fellow, Centre for Area Studies, Leipzig University and Former EU Marie Curie Individual Fellow, University of Verona, 2016–2018.

Annalisa Ciampi is Professor of International Law, University of Verona, Visiting Professor of European Human Rights law, Monash University, and formerly UN Special Rapporteur on the Rights to Freedom of Peaceful Assembly and of Association.

Sionaidh Douglas-Scott is Anniversary Chair in Law, Queen Mary University of London, Honorary Research Fellow, Lady Margaret Hall, University of Oxford and Leverhulme Major Research Fellow, 2018–2021.

Rolf Einar Fife is Ambassador of Norway to the European Union, formerly Director General for Legal Affairs and Legal Adviser of the Norwegian Ministry of Foreign Affairs 2002–2014.

Katarina Ristić is Researcher Associate, Global and European Studies Institute, Leipzig University.

Stefan Troebst is Professor of East European Cultural History, Leipzig University.

Erika de Wet is SARChI Professor of International Constitutional Law, Faculty of Law, University of Pretoria; Honorary Professor, Faculty of Law, University of Bonn.

Acknowledgements

I am grateful to Elgar external anonymous reviewers for their comments and advice. My associate editor and friend, Gilad Ben-Nun, has encouraged and supported me in many ways, and Amber Watts and Fiona Todd have skilfully and patiently guided me through the production process. The book would not have been possible without the hard work of the contributors, whom I thank for agreeing to participate.

Annalisa Ciampi

Foreword
Giorgio Gaja

The present collection of essays intends to address both the impact of history on international law and the contribution that international law makes to history. The subject is clearly huge and may be considered only under some limited aspects. These are mainly from the areas of international human rights law and international humanitarian law, but, notwithstanding the absence of an essay devoted to methodology, the book offers reflections that cover a wider ground.

This is in particular true of the introductory study by Rolf Einar Fife. He examines some significant moments in the development of international law. The stress is on the influence played by certain international lawyers on the elaboration and consolidation of some significant concepts. His first example is taken from the principle of the stability of frontiers, as applied in Latin America and in Africa and more recently in Europe. He then examines the elaboration of the concept of the self-determination of peoples and finally the emergence of the concept of a supranational organ (High Authority) with regard to the European Communities and later the European Union. The references to these developments are meant to illustrate how concepts may influence the course of history.

Stefan Troebst's essay is dedicated to the impact that events and scholarly work in Eastern Europe had on the development of international law. He considers in particular the so-called 'Brezhnev Doctrine' on intervention and the evolution of practice through the application of the principle that intervention should not take place outside one state's sphere of influence. He further stresses the erosion of the *uti possidetis* principle over Kosovo and the development from a policy of exchanges of population to the configuration of ethnic cleansing as a crime against humanity.

The concepts taken as examples have certainly had great significance. Their elaboration was one of the main reasons for their impact. However, what contributed greatly to their influence is the fact that the political context provided a favourable ground to their reception when their application was sought. For instance, when the concept of self-determination was successfully applied in the 1960s to non-self-governing territories, several administering powers found it expedient to replace colonialism with neo-colonialism, which implied the formal independence of the former colonial people.

Annalisa Ciampi's essay provides an ample survey of the development of international human rights law. The main focus is on the divide between civil and political rights, on the one hand, and economic, social and cultural rights, and later the right to development, on the other. One of her points is that, while human rights are often described as 'indivisible', their protection hardly follows a unitary approach. She stresses the need for a greater integration of human rights in development and economic activities.

The analysis emphasizes the gaps in the protection of human rights as they result from practice. Ratification of human rights treaties and adoption of instruments proclaiming rights rarely lead to a higher protection. Moreover, states are reluctant to pursue the settlement of international disputes in this field. While there is much truth in these propositions, one may suggest that the survey could have given greater weight to the role that human rights bodies play with regard to individual applications and in making general comments.

Sionaidh Douglas-Scott examines the development of the protection of human rights within the European Union. The analysis is centred on the relations between human rights and free market rights. The author notes that the pursuit of the objectives of progressing towards an ever closer Union and of defending the supremacy of European Union law do not provide an exhaustive explanation of the development of the protection of human rights within the Union. She underlines also the importance of discontinuities, giving weight to economic rights in a free and equal market society. One may agree with the author's remark that institutions of the European Union are reluctant to expand their role with regard to the protection of human rights in the Union. However, the institutional system would not be able to take on new tasks, such as providing a judicial remedy against violations of human rights, and would risk collapsing.

The next section consists of four contributions that concern specific issues of international humanitarian law or of international criminal law.

Gilad Ben-Nun makes an in-depth analysis of the preparatory work to common Article 3 of the 1949 Geneva Conventions, in particular the Fourth Convention on the Protection of Civilians. This study is based on some unpublished material relating to the discussions that took place at Stockholm before the Geneva Conference and that led to the scope of the protection of civilians being extended to include nationals targeted by the government of a state involved in a conflict not of an international character. In this regard, the author underlines the shift in the position of the International Committee of the Red Cross and the role played by the Soviet Union.

The following contributions address the repression of international crimes. Olympia Bekou examines how some historical events led to drafting the repression of genocide, crimes against humanity and war crimes in the Statute of the International Criminal Court (ICC). She outlines how the definition of crimes against humanity has moved away from the requirement of a connection with war, which was implied in the Charter of the Nuremberg Tribunal, and has included apartheid. This is described as a 'regime of systematic oppression and domination by one racial group over any other racial group or groups' (Article 7(2)(h) of the ICC Statute), reflecting the situation prevailing in South Africa until 1994. The author then considers the developments in Rwanda and former Yugoslavia that led to the inclusion of 'forced pregnancy' among the crimes against humanity (Article 7(1)(g) and (2)(f) of the ICC Statute). She advocates that for both crimes, and also for genocide, a wider definition be adopted in order to take more recent events into account. She suggests that for that purpose the ICC Statute be considered a 'living instrument'. However, this approach conflicts with the need not to widen retroactively conduct that is punishable.

Katarina Ristić analyses the attitude taken in Bosnia, Croatia and Serbia towards the International Criminal Tribunal for the former Yugoslavia (ICTY). She recalls that victims' organizations in Bosnia criticized the leniency of certain sentences and the dismissal of charges of genocide for events other than those of Srebrenica. In Croatia there was an outright rejection of the view that Croat leaders, including President Tuđman and General Gotovina, could be considered war criminals. There was also strong criticism of the ICTY's failure to recognize that genocide had been committed by Serbia in Vukovar. Serb public opinion considered the ICTY a politically biased entity and insisted on the symmetry between crimes committed by Serbs and Bosnians in what was defined a civil war; the genocide in Srebrenica was downgraded to a massacre. The impact of public opinion explains the failure of the prosecution of war crimes by national courts. Notwithstanding the predominant narratives, some non-governmental organizations and certain media argued in favour of justice for victims, including in the criticism of some questionable acquittals. With regard to the findings of the ICTY concerning genocide in Srebrenica, in other parts of Bosnia and in Vukovar, one may add that they have all been endorsed by the International Court of Justice.

Erika de Wet examines the criticism voiced by several African states about the International Criminal Court (ICC), which they had originally supported. The indictment of African leaders, especially President Bashir of Sudan and the future President of Kenya, Uhuru Kenyatta, have been considered as an expression of bias. Moreover, self-referrals by African states have led to unsatisfactory results. For the time being, the threat of some African states to withdraw from the ICC Statute has had very limited impact. The author advocates the strengthening of the prosecution of international crimes through national and regional courts, such as the African Criminal Chamber under the 2014

Malabo Protocol. However, financial considerations may well be an obstacle to regional developments, as shown by the events concerning the prosecution in Senegal of the former President of Tchad, Hissène Habré.

The variety of issues examined in the contributions to the present volume and the brevity of the considerations generally dedicated to the legal implications of political events do not point to specific conclusions, which are therefore not offered by the editor. However, the book offers several examples of interesting analysis which may be taken as paradigms and should stimulate further research.

PART I

History and international law: an introduction

1. Creative forces and institution building in international law
Rolf Einar Fife[1]

INTRODUCTION

The phrase 'the end of history' was the euphoric title of an article by the American political scientist Francis Fukuyama in the summer of 1989, before the dismantling of the Berlin Wall and the dissolution of the Soviet Union.[2] Taking a largely Hegelian approach to the philosophy of history, the phrase came to signify that with the collapse of the Soviet Union the last ideological alternative to liberalism would be eliminated.[3] This would entail a number of consequences for the evolution of world order. Irrespective of a largely critical reception of the phrase, the 1990s saw a quantum leap in the development of new international legal norms and institutions, notably with the establishment of the World Trade Organization, the United Nations Conference on Environment and Development in Rio de Janeiro, the entry into force of the United Nations Convention on the Law of the Sea, and the establishment of institutions of international criminal justice.

Following the end of the Cold War, unprecedented patterns of cooperation emerged also within the United Nations Security Council (UNSC). After the liberation of Kuwait in 1991 based on an authorization of use of force under Chapter VII of the Charter, the Council convened an extraordinary summit of Heads of State and Government in January 1992.[4] It tasked the new

---

[1] The author is alone responsible for the contents of this chapter, which does not represent a statement of positions of the Government of Norway.

[2] F. Fukuyama, 'The End of History', *The National Interest*, no. 16, Summer 1989, pp. 3–18. This was followed by the author's best-selling book *The End of History and the Last Man*, New York: Free Press, 1992.

[3] L. Menand, 'Francis Fukuyama postpones the end of history', *The New Yorker*, 27 August 2018, available at https://www.newyorker.com/magazine/2018/09/03/francis-fukuyama-postpones-the-end-of-history.

[4] UNSC Statement concerning the Council's Responsibility in the Maintenance of International Peace and Security, 3046th meeting, 31 January 1992, *International Legal Materials*, vol. 31(3), 1992, pp. 758–62.

Secretary-General of the United Nations, Boutros Boutros-Ghali, to issue an 'analysis and recommendations on ways of strengthening and making more efficient within the framework and provisions of the Charter the capacity of the United Nations for preventive diplomacy, for peace-making and for peace-keeping'.[5]

The resulting report *An Agenda for Peace* acknowledged the collapse of an 'immense ideological barrier that for decades gave rise to distrust and hostility' and called for a common 'will to take the hard decisions demanded by this time of opportunity'.[6] The report couched fundamental challenges in international legal terms:

> The foundation-stone of this work is and must remain the State. Respect for its fundamental sovereignty and integrity are crucial to any common international progress. The time of absolute and exclusive sovereignty, however, has passed; its theory was never matched by reality. It is the task of leaders of States today to understand this and to find a balance between the needs of good internal governance and the requirements of an ever more interdependent world. Commerce, communications and environmental matters transcend administrative borders; but inside those borders is where individuals carry out the first order of their economic, political and social lives. The United Nations has not closed its door. Yet if every ethnic, religious or linguistic group claimed statehood, there would be no limit to fragmentation, and peace, security and economic well-being for all would become ever more difficult to achieve.[7]

The report spoke of the need for a 'balanced design', ensuring at the same time the stability of frontiers, the principle of self-determination for peoples and respect for democratic principles:

> The sovereignty, territorial integrity and independence of States within the established international system, and the principle of self-determination for peoples, both of great value and importance, must not be permitted to work against each other in the period ahead. Respect for democratic principles at all levels of social existence is crucial: in communities, within States and within the community of States. Our constant duty should be to maintain the integrity of each while finding a balanced design for all.[8]

---

[5] Statement by the President of the Council, section entitled 'Peace-making and peace-keeping', UN Doc. S/23500.

[6] *An Agenda for Peace: Preventive Diplomacy, Peace-Making and Peace-Keeping*, Report of the Secretary-General pursuant to the statement adopted by the Summit Meeting of the Security Council on 31 January 1992, UN Doc. A 47/247, at para. 6.

[7] Ibid., at para. 17.

[8] Ibid., at para. 19.

The expression 'established international system' referred to the consolidation of a universal legal system after decades of decolonization, including wars of national liberation, the Cold War and other centrifugal challenges to its unity. This body of law accumulated over time might have been seen by some as a mere consequence of irresistible winds of history. In ways unforeseen by Fukuyama in 1989 or 1992, this legal architecture and its institutions appear however, yet again, to be challenged.[9] In this chapter I will reflect on three entirely disparate moments in the history of international law that have contributed to consolidating this 'established international system'. My focus will be on key mechanisms and creative forces for reception of international legal norms, concepts or patterns of thought.

HOW STABILITY OF FRONTIERS IN THE FACE OF STATE SUCCESSION BECAME A BEDROCK OF MODERN INTERNATIONAL LAW

Part of this *acquis* of international law is the coming of age and universalization of the objective of stability and finality of boundaries.[10] While a sustained historical focus has been dedicated to other developments of international law, including human rights and international criminal law, less attention has been devoted to how the stabilization of frontiers came about, and to its contributions to the maintenance of international peace and security. Arguably, no phenomenon reflects this general thrust better than the gradual maturing and ultimately universal reception of the principle of *uti possidetis juris*, requiring newly independent states to respect inherited frontiers.

This principle was generated in Latin America in the nineteenth century, at a time when several European powers were engaged in colonial policies in Africa.[11] A century later, it gained extraordinary momentum with the accept-

---

[9] F. Fukuyama, *Identity: The Demand for Dignity and the Politics of Resentment*, New York: Farrar, Straus & Giroux, 2018.

[10] The expression 'stability and finality of frontiers' stems from a case concerning *The Temple of Preah Vihear* (*Cambodia v. Thailand*), Merits, Judgment of 15 June 1962, *ICJ Reports* 1962, p. 6, p. 34 ('In general, when two countries establish a frontier between them, one of the primary objects is to achieve stability and finality'). See M. G. Kohen, 'L'influence du temps sur les règlements territoriaux', in Société française pour le droit international, *Colloque de Paris: Le droit international et le temps*, Paris: Editions A. Pedone, 2001, p. 150; G. Abi-Saab, 'La pérennité des frontières en droit international', *Relations Internationales*, vol. 64, 1990, pp. 345–6.

[11] T. Pakenham, *The Scramble for Africa: The White Man's Conquest of the Dark Continent from 1876 to 1912*, London: Weidenfeld & Nicolson, 1991. In the following I am particularly indebted to Marcelo Kohen for his analysis, see in particular footnotes 10, 16, 18 and 28.

ance of inherited colonial boundaries by the Organization of African Unity (OAU) in Cairo in 1964.[12] In 1986, it was coined by the International Court of Justice as a general principle with universal validity.[13] In the 1990s it was also applied in Europe, notably in the former Yugoslavia.[14]

A description of the content and origins of *uti possidetis juris* was given in 1922 by the Swiss Federal Council acting as arbitrator in the Boundary Dispute between Colombia and Venezuela:

> When the Spanish colonies of Central and South America proclaimed their independence in the second decade of the nineteenth century, they adopted a principle of constitutional and international law to which they gave the name of *uti possidetis juris* of 1810. The principle laid down the rule that the boundaries of the newly established republics would be the frontiers of the Spanish provinces which they were succeeding. This general principle offered the advantage of establishing the absolute rule that in law no territory of old Spanish America was without an owner. [. . .] Encroachments and ill-timed efforts at colonization beyond the frontiers, as well as occupations in fact, became invalid and ineffectual in law. This principle also had the advantage, it was hoped, of doing away with boundary disputes between new states. Finally it put an end to the designs of colonizing states of Europe against lands which otherwise they could have sought to proclaim as *res nullius*. The international status of Spanish America was from the very beginning quite different from that of Africa for example. This principle later received general sanction under the name of the Monroe Doctrine, but had long before been the basis of South American public law.[15]

The principle setting out the permanence of former colonial territorial divisions to promote territorial integrity and counter colonialism represents the most famous Latin American contribution to international law.[16] Spanish

---

[12] P. Daillier, M. Forteau and A. Pellet, *Droit international public*, 8th ed., Paris: LCDJ, 2009, p. 521.

[13] International Court of Justice, *Frontier Dispute (Burkina Faso v. Republic of Mali)*, Judgment of 22 December 1986, *ICJ Reports* 1986, p. 554, p. 565, at para. 205.

[14] *Conference on Yugoslavia, Arbitration Commission*, Opinion No. 3, 11 January 1992, *International Legal Materials*, vol. 31, 1992, pp. 1497–9; Daillier et al., *Droit international public*.

[15] J. B. Scott, 'The Swiss Decision in the Boundary Dispute between Colombia and Venezuela', *American Journal of International Law*, vol. 16(3), 1922, pp. 428–31. The quoted paragraph is translated from the French language; *Sentence arbitrale du Conseil Fédéral Suisse sur diverses questions de limites pendants entre la Colombie et le Vénézuéla*, Berne, 24 March 1922, Neuchâtel, Imprimerie Paul Attinger, 1922, pp. 5–6; RSA, vol. I, p. 228.

[16] M. G. Kohen, 'La contribution de l'Amérique Latine au développement progressif du droit international en matière territoriale', *Relations internationales*, vol. 139, 2009, p. 13, p. 14; E. J. de Aréchaga, 'Boundaries in Latin America: *Uti Possidetis* Doctrine', in R. Bernhardt (ed.), *Encyclopedia of Public International Law*, vol. 1,

South American territories had been the first to oppose royalist authorities in 1810, starting in Caracas and Buenos Aires, and developing thereafter as a chain reaction across the continent.[17] The Spanish Central American states refer, on their part, to the end of recognition of Spanish rule in 1821 and Brazil's declaration of independence from Portugal came in 1822, thus establishing later critical dates for the consideration of territorial state succession.[18]

The reception of the concept in international law proved a lengthy journey. Its semantic roots are to be found in Roman law, but the term reappeared with other meanings in other contexts, playing a specific function under the prevailing circumstances in order to resolve a given problem.[19] In Roman civic law, *uti possidetis* referred to an interdict against the interference with actual possession.[20] The term was borrowed and transplanted into an international legal context with the Peace Treaties of Westphalia at the end of the Thirty Years War in 1648. These have been considered as a bridge between Roman law as it had been perceived in the seventeenth century and modern international law.[21]

In an international legal context, as also used by prominent South American publicists, the expression denoted the maintenance of a territorial status quo after armed conflict, i.e. the legal effects of military occupation.[22]

Amsterdam: North-Holland, 1992, p. 449, p. 450; Luis Ignacio Sanchez Rodriguez, 'L'*uti possidetis* et les effectivités dans les contentieux territoriaux et frontaliers', *Collected Courses of the Hague Academy of International Law*, vol. 263, 1997, pp. 149–381.

[17] J. H. Elliott, *Empires of the Atlantic World: Britain and Spain in America 1492–1830*, New Haven, CT: Yale University Press, 2006, pp. 379–82.

[18] M. G. Kohen, *Possession contestée et souveraineté territoriale*, Paris: Presses Universitaires de France, 1997, p. 15.

[19] M. Troper, 'L'histoire du droit et la théorie générale du droit', in Bernardo Sordi (ed.), *Storia e diritto: esperienze a confronto, Atti dell'incontro internazionale di studi in occasione dei 40 anni dei Quaderni fiorentini, Firenze, 18–19 ottobre 2012*, Milano: Giuffrè, 2013, p. 387, p. 391. On reception of law, see A. Watson, 'Aspects of Reception of Law', American Journal of Comparative Law, vol. 44(2), 1996, pp. 335–51.

[20] References to Roman law in Kohen, *Possession contestée*, p. 426, note 1 and p. 427 note 3; E. Cantarella, V. Marotta, B. Santalucia, U. Vincenti, A. Schiavone and E. Stolfi, *Diritto privato romano – Un profilo storico*, Turin: Einaudi, 2003, pp. 278–80. See G. Nesi, '*Uti Possidetis* Doctrine', in *Max Planck Encyclopedia of Public International Law*, 2018, available at http://opil.ouplaw.com/view/10.1093/law:epil/9780199231690/law-9780199231690-e1125.

[21] L. Winkel, 'The Peace Treaties of Westphalia as an Instance of Reception of Roman Law', in R. Lesaffer (ed.), *Peace Treaties and International Law in European History: From the Late Middle Ages to World War One*, Cambridge: Cambridge University Press, 2004, p. 222, pp. 229–35 (in particular p. 232).

[22] C. Calvo, *Derecho Internacional Téorico y Práctico de Europa y América*, Paris: Amyot, Durand, Pedone-Lauriel, 1868, vol. II, p. 129.

This had remarkably little to do with respect for inherited title in the form of administrative boundaries after state succession.[23] Its use by Spanish American diplomats was decisive, albeit leading to some confusion.[24] For instance Arnold McNair made no use of the concept when, as late as in 1961, he described developments relating to the independence of new states in Spanish South America.[25] He appears only to have analysed *uti possidetis* in the context of Roman law, in which he incidentally was proficient.[26]

The current use of the term was introduced by diplomats in negotiations, referring to the inheritance of the administrative boundaries established by the former colonial power. Rather than signifying a subservience to the authority of colonial European powers or a legal crossover to colonial law, reliance on inherited boundaries became a rampart against foreign powers' intervention. As consecrated by the Swiss Federal Council acting as Arbiter in 1922, the term thus stemmed from Spanish American states referring to *uti possidetis juris*, with an emphasis on 'the Latin genitive juris'. This established that there was no *terra nullius* on the American continent, and thus no basis for occupation by non-American powers, and secondly, recognition of pre-existing administrative limits:

> There are several different aspects to this principle, in its well-known application in Spanish America. The first aspect, emphasized by the Latin genitive *juris*, is found in the pre-eminence accorded to legal title over effective possession as a basis of sovereignty. Its purpose, at the time of the achievement of independence by the former Spanish colonies of America, was to scotch any designs which non-American colonizing powers might have on regions which had been assigned by the former metropolitan State to one division or another, but which were still uninhabited or unexplored. However, there is more to the principle of *uti possidetis* than this particular aspect. The essence of the principle lies in its primary aim of securing respect for the territorial boundaries at the moment when independence is achieved. Such territorial boundaries might be no more than delimitations between

---

[23] Ibid.: 'El titulo de posesion del territorio conquistado se completa, bien por un tratado de paz, ya por provisiones expresas, bien en vertud del uti possidetis. Cuando la cesion se establece por pacto expecial, es costumbre muy general requerir las condiciones mas ventajosas posibles para los habitantes del territorio. Igual cumplida confirmacion recibe el titulo á poseer del conquistador si se fija en un tratado general de paz, porque como su base es el uti possidetis, á no ser que se exprese el contrario, el territorio conquistado permanece con él y no puede, en manera alguna, dudarse de la validez de un titulo adquirido así.'

[24] Kohen, *Possession contestée*.

[25] A. McNair, *The Law of Treaties*, Oxford: Oxford University Press, 1961, pp. 601–3, as opposed to, for instance, Herbert Briggs, *The Law of Nations: Cases, Documents and Notes*, 2nd ed., London: Stevens and Sons, 1953, p. 262.

[26] W. W. Buckland and A. D. McNair, *Roman Law and Common Law*, 2nd ed. (rev. by F. H. Lawson), Cambridge: Cambridge University Press, 1965, pp. 63, 141 and 394.

different administrative divisions or colonies all subject to the same sovereign. In that case, the application of the principle of *uti possidetis* resulted in administrative boundaries being transformed into international frontiers in the full sense of the term.[27]

This Spanish American conception has been contrasted with the Brazilian doctrine of *uti possidetis*, formulated without the Latin genitive *juris* (or sometimes referred to as *uti possidetis de facto*). However, it has been shown that this difference has been exaggerated.[28] Brazil did not negate *uti possidetis juris* as applicable to pre-existing or colonial administrative frontiers within the same empire or sovereign, i.e. to Spanish America. In other cases, applicable treaties might resolve the issue. In the absence of such legal title, including where Brazil had denied the continued existence of treaties in force, Brazil would then rely on evidence of effective possession. As Brazil's foreign minister José Maria da Silva Paranhos Jr., Baron of Rio Branco, explained to his Ecuadorian colleague Carlos Tobar:

> *Uti possidetis* is the rule that we observe in our conventional relations with neighbouring States, instead of the one known as *uti possidetis juris* which may only be applied in negotiations on limits between Spanish American states, as these correspond to the ancient territorial divisions and are drawn by the same authorities.[29]

Thus, Brazil and the Spanish American states shared in reality more than a few fundamental conceptions.[30] There was agreement that, at the beginning of the nineteenth century, no *terrae nulliae* existed in South America. No such territories could therefore be occupied by non-American colonial powers. Moreover, new states had succeeded to the territorial sovereignty of Spain and Portugal. Furthermore, where frontier treaties concluded with colonial powers were still in force, these would be applied to define the borders with the newly independent states, as was the case for instance with France as regards French Guyana.[31] There are therefore few fundamental differences as to the theoretical

---

[27] *ICJ Reports* 1986, p. 566, at para. 23.
[28] M. G. Kohen and K. Del Mar, 'Decolonization in Latin America: Its Trail-Blazing Role for Decolonization in Other Parts of the World', in C. Auroi and A. Helg, *Latin America 1810–2010: Dreams and Legacies*, London: Imperial College Press, 2012, p. 43, p. 50; Kohen, 'La contribution de l'Amérique Latine', p. 18.
[29] Rio Branco, 'Letter to Ecuador's Foreign Minister Carlos Tobar, Antônio A. Cançado Trindade', *Repertório da Prática Brasileira do Direito Internacional Público* (Período 1899–1918), Brasilia: Fundaçao Gusmão, 1986, vol. I, p. 265, quoted in French by Kohen, 'La contribution de l'Amérique Latine', p. 18, note 12.
[30] Kohen, 'La contribution de l'Amérique Latine', p. 18.
[31] Arbitral Award relating to the *question of the boundaries between Brazil and French Guyana*, RIAA, 1 December 1900, vol. XXVIII, pp. 349–78, 2007.

underpinnings of the legal approach taken in South America.[32] In this context, the role of the baron of Rio Branco (1845–1912) stands out.[33] As a diplomat and later foreign minister of Brazil (1902–12), he was a key architect of Brazil's peaceful settlement of a considerable number of outstanding border issues through treaty negotiations and arbitration.[34]

A deep undercurrent in the modern history of international law has been the consolidation of the principle of stability of borders after state succession, thus contributing to maintain international peace and security. Rosalyn Higgins, quoting Judge Ad hoc Abi Saab, has also observed that without the stability of frontiers, the exercise of self-determination is in reality a mirage.[35] The maintenance of territorial status quo by the Organization of African Unity in 1964 was a major step in this direction as confirmed by the International Court of Justice:

> At first sight this principle conflicts outright with another one, the right of peoples to self-determination. In fact, however, the maintenance of the territorial *status quo* in Africa is often seen as the wisest course, to preserve what has been achieved by peoples who have struggled for their independence, and to avoid a disruption which would deprive the continent of the gains achieved by much sacrifice. The essential requirement of stability in order to survive, to develop and gradually to consolidate their independence in all fields, has induced African States judiciously to consent to the respecting of colonial frontiers, and to take account of it in the interpretation of the principle of self-determination of peoples.[36]

The dynamics behind these momentous developments and the role of actors that influence state action and production of norms in this context may deserve

---

[32] Kohen and Del Mar, 'Decolonization in Latin America', p. 51; Kohen, *Possession contestée*, pp. 448–49.

[33] A. G. de A. Jorge, *Rio Branco e as Fronteiras do Brasil (Uma introdução às obras do Barão do Rio Branco)*, Brasília: Senado Federal, 1999. On the role of the Brazilian lawyer Ruy Barbosa de Oliveira (1849–1923) and his relations with Rio Branco, see J. Fischel de Andrade and D. Limoeiro, 'Rui Barbosa e a política externa brasileira: considerações sobre a Questão Acreana e o Tratado de Petrópolis (1903)', *Revista Brasiliera de Politica Internacional*, vol. 46(1), 2003, pp. 94–117.

[34] There appears to be a discrepancy between Brazil's celebration of this diplomat, and the limited analysis in the history of international law of his contributions, including to the peaceful resolution of disputes and the maintenance of international peace and security. The Diplomatic Institute of the Brazilian Foreign Ministry is incidentally also named Instituto Rio Branco, http://www.institutoriobranco.itamaraty.gov.br/historia.

[35] R. Higgins, *Problems and Process: International Law and How We Use it*, Oxford: Clarendon Press, 1994, pp. 122–4.

[36] *ICJ Reports* 1986, p. 567, at para. 26.

further scrutiny. So does the role of legal concepts in negotiations and their evolution within a given legal context.

The Latin expression *uti possidetis* projects semantically the idea of preserving something inherited from the past, with the aim of contributing to stability and predictability. As such, it may be vaguely related to *rebus sic stantibus*, i.e. as things stand. There are rich traditions of utilizing phrases stemming from the language of Roman law in various receptions of patterns of thought in the history of law and utilizing them in a different legal context with adaptations.[37] With Roman law's aspirations as a universal legal order, later inherited by the canonic legal order, also using Latin, it may come as no surprise that problem-solving in international law often attempted to draw legitimacy through such authority. Prominent examples of international law pioneers who relied heavily on historical analysis with use of Roman legal concepts, adapted to their ongoing work as problem-solving practitioners, include Hugo Grotius and Carlos Calvo.[38]

Critical analysis has drawn on history, deconstructing legal norms and process, leading to a discussion of the determinacy of international law.[39] There may, however, also be scope for studying further the process of construction of legal concepts within a legal system, which is something different than undertaking a history of evolution of concepts in international law.[40] It may reveal the creative forces, institution building and actors that contribute to

---

[37] M. Stolleis, 'Il Quadro Europeo', in B. Sordi (ed.), *Storia et Diritto, Esperienze a Confronto*, Atti dell'incontro internazionale di studi in occasione dei 40 anni dei Quaderni Fiorentini, Florence, 18–19 October 2012, Milan: Giuffrè, 2013, pp. 36–8; F. Calasso, *Introduzione al Diritto Comune*, Milan: Giuffrè, 1951; F. Calasso, *I Glossatori e la Teoria della Sovranità, Studio di diritto comune pubblico*, 2nd ed., Milan: Giuffrè, 1951.

[38] Both the Dutch and the Argentinian theorists were also practitioners, incidentally, having served in different centuries in diplomatic postings in Paris. The two following works are heavily influenced by historical analysis: Hugo Grotius, *Mare Liberum* (1609) (translated into English by Richard Hakluyt as *The Free Sea*, in D. Armitage (ed.), *Natural Law and Enlightenment Classics*, Indianapolis: Liberty Fund, 2004); C. Calvo, *Derecho Internacional Téorico y Práctico de Europa y América*, Paris: D'Amyot, 1868 (§1. 'La importancia del derecho internacional en la ciencia general del derecho se reflecha también en la historia del mismo derecho internacional [. . .]'; §2. 'En esta primera época el derecho internacional se nos ofrece dominado por la idea religiosa ó por las formulas del derecho romano [. . .]').

[39] M. Koskenniemi, *From Apology to Utopia: The Structure of International Legal Argument* (Cambridge: Cambridge University Press, 1989), and *The Gentle Civilizer of Nations: The Rise and Fall of International Law 1870–1960* (Cambridge: Cambridge University Press, 2001) provide two examples.

[40] Troper, 'L'histoire du droit et la théorie générale du droit', p. 391. See his references, including M. Bloch, *Apologie pour l'histoire du métier d'historien*, Paris: Armand Colin, 1949, p. 12.

such determinacy of law. The cursory references made to the notion of *uti possidetis* may provide ammunition to the assessment made by Quentin Skinner, inspired notably by Wittgenstein and J. L. Austin, that:

> one of the most important of the many injunctions contained in Wittgenstein's *Philosophical Investigations* is that we ought not to think in isolation of 'the meanings of words'. We ought rather to focus on their use in specific language-games and, more generally, within particular forms of life.[41]

The famous sentence 'the meaning of a word is its use in the language' is an inspiration to identify and document actual uses of terms in the specific language-games utilized between states, on the basis of their ordinary use in the relevant contexts.[42] This links up perfectly with the general rule of interpretation set out in the Vienna Convention on the Law of Treaties in 1969 article 31, as regards the 'ordinary meaning' to be given to the terms of a treaty and other accepted means of interpretation of the treaty. In the context of *uti possidetis juris*, as highlighted by Judge Ad hoc Abi Saab in the 1986 judgment of the International Court of Justice:

> this principle, like any other, is not to be conceived in the absolute; it has always to be interpreted in the light of its function within the international legal order.[43]

The generic content and the stability of key components of this principle were thus provided primarily by Latin American and then by African states.

FROM OUTRIGHT REJECTION OF INTERNATIONAL LAW AS A MERE CAPITALIST AND IMPERIALIST TOOL TO GRADUAL ADAPTATION TO THE INTERNATIONAL LEGAL SYSTEM

As noted by Crawford, since the mid-nineteenth century the only serious attempt on the part of a major state to reject and abandon international law was that of the Russian Socialist Federative Soviet Republic after the Bolshevik

---

[41] Q. Skinner, *Visions of Politics: Regarding Method*, vol. I, Cambridge: Cambridge University Press, 2002, p. 103; L. Wittgenstein, *Philosophische Untersuchungen. Philosophical Investigations*, translated by G. E. M. Anscombe, Oxford: Blackwell Publishing (first published 1958), 3rd ed., 2001, pp. 46–7, at paras. 138–9, and p. 68, at paras. 197–8; J. L. Austin, *How to Do Things with Words*, 2nd ed. (ed. J. O. Urmson and M. Sbisà), Cambridge, MA: Harvard University Press, 1980, pp. 94–8. It is enlightening to consider translations, as they may denote approaches to interpretation.

[42] Wittgenstein, *Philosophical Investigations*, p. 18, at para. 43.

[43] *ICJ Reports* 1986, Separate Opinion of Judge Abi-Saab, p. 111, at para. 13.

Revolution of 1917 and, after its foundation in 1922, that of the early Soviet Union.[44] This rejection was, in the words of Anand, based on a 'conflicting and aggressive ideology which sought to repudiate many of the values and institutions shared by the Western countries'.[45] Early Soviet lawyers had largely dismissed international law as a part of the superstructure of law, an attribute of the foreign policy of states and an expression of the will of the ruling class.[46] They were inspired by the international law theorist Evgeny Pashukanis (1891–1937), who provided the main theoretical underpinnings of this Marxist critique.[47] Influential Soviet protagonists later included Andrey Vyshinsky (1883–1954) and Evgeny A. Korovin (1892–1964), who came to represent a strict positivist approach based on new treaties, dismissing the universal roots and architecture of international law.[48]

However, Soviet formal legal positions were not static. They evolved from initial rejection of a universal system of international law to a gradual engagement in its codification and progressive development, albeit to be mustered to promote Soviet political goals. As opposed to common reduction of Soviet schools of international law to one of the 'most important historical examples of regional approaches to international law',[49] a neglect of Marxist and Soviet theories in the wake of the dismantlement of the Berlin Wall has rightly been ascribed to a limited knowledge of these theories in the West.[50]

---

[44] J. Crawford, 'Chance, Order, Change: The Course of International Law', *Collected Courses of the Hague Academy of International Law*, vol. 365, 2013, pp. 407–8 and 235–6.

[45] R. P. Anand, *Confrontation or Cooperation? International Law and the Developing Countries*, New Delhi: Banyan Publications, 1986, p. 33.

[46] Higgins, *Problems and Process*, p. 11.

[47] E. B. Pashukanis, 'The General Theory of Law and Marxism', in P. Beirne and R. Sharlet (eds.), *Evgeny Pashukanis: Selected Writings on Marxism and Law*, London and New York: Evgeny Pashukanis, 1980; V. Vereschetin and R. Mullerson, 'International Law in an Interdependent World', *Columbia Journal of Transnational Law*, vol. 28(1), 1990, p. 291; Crawford, 'Chance, Order, Change', p. 408.

[48] E. Korovin, 'La république des Soviets et le droit international', *Revue générale de droit international public*, vol. 32, 1925, p. 292. E. McWhinney, 'Soviet Bloc Publicists and the East–West Legal Debate', *Canadian Yearbook of International Law*, vol. 2(1), 1964, pp. 172–83. B. Bowring, 'Positivism Versus Self-Determination: The Contradictions of Soviet International Law', in S. Marks (ed.), *International Law on the Left: Re-examining Marxist Legacies*, Cambridge: Cambridge University Press, 2008, pp. 133–68.

[49] A. Peters, 'International Scholarship under Challenge', in J. D'Aspremont, T. Gazzini, A. Nollkaemper and W. Werner (eds.), *International Law as a Profession*, Cambridge: Cambridge University Press, 2017, p. 120.

[50] A. Bianchi, *International Law Theories: An Inquiry into Different Ways of Thinking*, Oxford: Oxford University Press, 2016, p. 74. See also T. Långström, *Transformation in Russia and International Law*, Leiden: Martinus Nijhoff, 2003;

Grigorii I. Tunkin (1906–93) played a particular role in this context.[51] He was born in Archangelsk in the Russian Arctic in 1906, distinguished himself academically, and served as a diplomat, notably in Iran during the Second World War and on the Korean Peninsula at the end of hostilities in the Korean War. As the legal adviser of the Soviet foreign ministry (1952–65), he incarnated Soviet international legal argument during large parts of the Cold War. He represented the Union of Soviet Socialist Republics at the United Nations, in bilateral intergovernmental negotiations, as an influential teacher for a generation of Russian and other socialist students and a prolific publicist quoted in most treatises describing competing world views of international law. Significantly, he became an active member of the International Law Commission, becoming its president in 1961 and participating notably in the codification of the law of treaties and a broader international discourse of sources of international law.[52] The evolution in Soviet formal legal positions, as expressed by Tunkin, cannot merely be dismissed as a function of changing political circumstances. It also denoted an increased role and refinement of formal legal argument in international policy formulation by the Soviet Union, arguably influenced by considerations of utility as regards diplomatic multilateral persuasion, but also by an ambition of individuals to better satisfy criteria of scientific method. Tunkin may thus be said to have contributed to a turn in Soviet legal argument, including through his course at The Hague Academy of

---

J. Quigley, 'Perestroika and International Law', *American Journal of International Law*, vol. 82(4), 1988, pp. 788–9; J. Quigley, 'The New Soviet Approach to International Law', *Harvard International Law Club Journal*, vol. 7(1), 1965, pp. 1–2; L. Mälksoo, *Russian Approaches to International Law*, Oxford: Oxford University Press, 2015.

[51] Grigorii Ivanovich Tunkin (1906–93). From 1939 with the Ministry of Foreign Affairs. Soviet consul in Gorgan (Iran). 1948–51 and 1951–52 Minister-Counsellor of the Soviet Embassy in the Korean People's Democratic Republic. Doctoral dissertation in 1954: 'The Korean Problem After the Second World War in the Light of International Law'. From 1952 to 1965 head of the legal section of the Ministry of Foreign Affairs. See G. I. Tunkin, *Theory of International Law* (translated with an introduction by W. E. Butler and edited by W. E. Butler, L. N. Shestakov, The Vinogradoff Institute, University College London), 2nd ed., London: Wildy, Simmonds and Hill Publishers Ltd., 2003. *Theory of International Law* was published in an English version in 1974, based on the Russian 1970 edition, and reissued in 2003.

[52] R. Mullerson, 'Obituary: Professor Grigory Tunkin', *The Independent*, 28 August 1993. Mullerson's obituary contrasts with the book review by M. Akehurst, Theory of International Law. By G. I. Tunkin (translated from the Russian, with an introduction, by William E. Butler). London: George Allen & Unwin, 1974, *British Yearbook of International Law*, vol. 47(1), 1976, p. 496, which referred to a 'strange mixture of first-rate legal argument and crude propaganda'.

International Law in 1956 and a treatise of international law that appeared in different editions and was translated into other languages.[53]

After the thaw following Stalin's death in 1953, he opposed Korovin's and Vyshinsky's approaches, unequivocally recognizing the existence of a separate international legal system:

> For thousands of years jurists have debated about definitions of law, but notwithstanding this law has existed. States, politicians, and jurists of different countries can hold various theories relating to the nature of international law, but this difference of opinion does not create insuperable obstacles to achieving agreements relating to the acceptance of specific rules of conduct as international legal norms.[54]

He enlisted the authority of Pashukanis, when recalling '[s]ince States have no higher authority above them which would establish norms of conduct for them, the sources of international law in the technical juridical sense of the word are custom and treaty'. On this basis, he took as did other Soviet lawyers a restrictive positivist approach to international law, recognizing treaties and customary international law, emphasizing however the integrity of this legal system. In so doing, he advocated a strictly voluntarist approach to international law, both as regards treaties and customary law:

> The process of concluding an international treaty is the process of bringing the wills of States into concordance, the result of which is an agreement that is embodied in the norms of the treaty.
> It should be pointed out that the process of forming a customary norm of international law, just as a treaty norm, is the process of the struggle and cooperation of States. The formulation of a customary rule occurs as a result of the intercourse of States, in which each State strives to consolidate as norms of conduct those rules which would correspond to its interests.
> A rule of conduct which is the result of general practice [. . .] becomes a customary norm of international law only when it is accepted or recognized by States as legally binding, as a norm of law.[55]

Confirming an allegiance to a superior system of international law, based on a principle of *pacta sunt servanda*, he served Soviet foreign policy interests by paving the way for a legal basis for the elaboration of the concepts of

---

[53] Långström, *Transformation in Russia and International Law*, p. 92. See also Bianchi, *International Law Theories*. G. Tunkin, 'Co-Existence and International Law', *Collected Courses of The Hague Academy of International Law*, vol. 95(1), 1956, pp. 5–78.

[54] G. I. Tunkin, *Theory of International Law* (translated by William E. Butler), Cambridge, MA: Harvard University Press, 1974, p. 48.

[55] Ibid., pp. 214, 114 and 127.

peaceful coexistence and self-determination of peoples.[56] As noted by Higgins, there was 'an operational agreement on the existence of international law as a system' and '[w]here the will of the ruling classes of the socialist and capitalist systems coincided, international law could exist'.[57] As a member of the International Law Commission from 1957 to 1966 Tunkin was involved in the deliberations leading to the adoption of the Vienna Convention on the Law of Treaties in 1969. Characteristically for his approach, he is for instance quoted as stating:

> 14. Mr. TUNKIN said that the *pacta sunt servanda* rule should be stated concisely and in precise terms [. . .] The rule was, in his opinion, of much wider application than the law of treaties, as agreement between States underlay every norm of international law.[58]

Acknowledging the role of foreign policy in international law, he also referred to the influence of international law on foreign policy and diplomacy:[59] 'International law, just as national law, influences the social relations which it regulates'. He disputed McDougal's and other realists' conception that international law merely merges into politics. Tunkin spoke in favour of law as a social phenomenon, distinct from politics.[60] His participation in the formulation of the rules of treaty law contributed to consolidating international law as a grammar for international relations, advocating its codification and

---

[56] Bowring, 'Positivism Versus Self-Determination'; N. S. Khrushchev, 'On Peaceful Coexistence', *Foreign Affairs*, vol. 38(1), 1959, pp. 1–18; S. B. Krylov, 'Les notions principales du droit des gens: la doctrine soviétique du droit international', *Collected Courses of The Hague Academy of International Law*, vol. 70(1), 1947, pp. 415–74; V. P. Karpov, 'The Soviet Concept of Peaceful Coexistence and its Implications for International Law', in H. W. Baade (ed.), *The Soviet Impact on International Law*, New York: Oceana Publications, 1965, pp. 14–20; W. Lerner, 'The Historical Origins of the Soviet Doctrine of Peaceful Coexistence', *Law and Contemporary Problems*, vol. 29(4), 1964, pp. 865–70; R. St. J. Macdonald, 'The Idea of Peaceful Co-Existence: Then and Now', in E. Yakpo and T. Boumedra (eds.), *Liber Amicorum: Mohammed Bedjaoui*, The Hague: Kluwer Law International, 1999, pp. 201–10.

[57] Higgins, *Problems and Process*, p. 11.

[58] International Law Commission, Summary records of the sixteenth session 11 May–24 July 1964, Law of Treaties, 727th meeting of 20 May 1964, *Yearbook of the International Law Commission*, vol. I, 1964, p. 27, at para. 14 (UN Docs. A/CN.4/167 and A/CN.4/SERA/1964).

[59] Tunkin, *Theory of International Law*, pp. 304–18.

[60] G. I. Tunkin, *Droit international public, Problèmes théoriques* (translated into French on the basis of the Russian 1962 edition), Paris: Editions A. Pedone, 1965, p. 190. G. I. Tunkin (ed. Theodor Schweisfurth), *Völkerrechtstheorie* (translated into German on the basis of the 1970 Russian edition), Berlin: Verlag, 1972, p. 336.

progressive development. At the same time, he 'enlisted' international law also to play a role in international relations, including combating colonialism.[61]

Tunkin personifies an important moment of political consolidation of international law, which might also be studied from the perspective of a phenomenon of broader reception of international law. He contributed to formulating a grammar that changed the Soviet legal discourse embracing established international law, while linking it to a socialist and Soviet political programme of action. It promoted the principle of self-determination of peoples, first as a reference advanced by the Soviet Union in 1945 and included in the United Nations Charter, and later included on a Soviet initiative in the Decolonization resolution 1514 (XV) of 14 December 1960.[62]

Broadening the scope of reflection, one can detect here broader phenomena of reception of international law. These have arguably come at a time that largely coincided with decolonization and choices made by newly independent states embracing, while criticizing the content of, international law. Thus, Higgins has found it striking that there is no suggestion by emergent countries that they are not bound upon independence by international law as a whole, even if its formation owed much to Western European history.[63]

THE EMERGENCE OF 'SUPRANATIONAL' INSTITUTIONS

The Schuman plan of 9 May 1950 established the vision of European integration to build peace in Europe. As a first step it envisaged the establishment of a High Authority for coal and steel. The plan was announced by foreign minister Robert Schuman in the *Salon de l'horloge* of the French foreign ministry, almost to the day, five years after the armistice on 8 May 1945 of the Second World War. Inspired and coordinated by the visionary Jean Monnet, it is widely referred to as the Monnet plan.[64] Setting the foundations for sharing sovereign powers through a common supranational organ, the High Authority, it provided the institutional origins, or the keystone, of the future European Commission and European integration.[65]

---

[61] Tunkin, *Theory of International Law*, p. 259.
[62] Bowring, 'Positivism Versus Self-Determination', p. 135.
[63] Higgins, *Problems and Process*, p. 12, with reference to B. Verzijl, 'Western European Influence on the Foundation of International Law', *International Relations*, vol. 1(4), 1955, pp. 137–46.
[64] E. Roussel, *Jean Monnet 1888–1979*, Paris: Fayard, 1996, pp. 528, 553.
[65] C. Blumann and L. Dubouis, *Droit institutionnel de l'Union européenne*, 6th ed., Paris: LexisNexis, 2016, p. 5, at para. 10; G. Bebr, 'The European Coal and Steel

Monnet himself, however, credited the lawyer Paul Reuter (1911–90) not only for conceiving the institutional mechanism of the authority, but also for its name.[66] André Gros who was elected to the International Court of Justice in 1964, has described Reuter's key role in the team of advisers assembled round Jean Monnet 'at the stage of a white page' or of a 'legal vacuum'.[67] The Frenchman Reuter was born in 1911 in the city of Metz, then under German administration, five years after the birth of Grigorii Tunkin. He became a member of the International Law Commission in 1964, towards the end of Tunkin's membership, contributing notably to the codification of the law of treaties.

His contributions to the development of new international institutions coincided with the launch of the debate on the concept of 'supranational' organs.[68] Reuter set out the three essential elements for such organs. They had to be independent in respect of national governments, which was not something new, but the independence encompassed a broader scope of competencies. The transfer of such competencies, combined with the setting in common of them, could be seen as the result of a partial fusion of national powers, thereby making it possible to talk of a 'Community'.[69] The third element is the emergence of direct relations between the Community's organs and individuals, contrary to traditional international law.[70]

Community: A Political and Legal Innovation', *Yale Law Journal*, vol. 63(1), 1953, p. 1.

[66] 'Toujours est-il que Paul Reuter fut à l'origine de la Haute Autorité, du mot comme de la chose.' J. Monnet, *Mémoires*, Paris: Fayard, 1976, p. 431.

[67] A. Gros, 'Hommage au professeur Paul Reuter', in *Le droit international, unité et diversité: mélanges offerts à Paul Reuter*, Paris: Pedone, 1981, p. 6. See similarly F. Roth, *Robert Schuman 1886–1963. Du Lorrain des frontières au père de l'Europe*, Paris: Fayard, 2008, pp. 383–6 and 528. A critical analysis is provided by A. Cohen, 'Le plan Schuman de Paul Reuter. Entre communauté nationale et fédération européenne', *Revue française de science politique*, vol. 48(5), 1998, pp. 645–63.

[68] P. Reuter, *La Communauté européenne du charbon et de l'acier*, Paris: LGDJ, 1953, pp. 138–40, at paras. 140–143.

[69] Ibid., p. 139, at para. 142.

[70] P. Reuter, *Les interventions de la Haute autorité. Rapport présenté au Congrès international d'études sur la Communauté européenne du charbon et de l'acier, IVème commission scientifique internationale, Centre italien d'études juridiques*, Milan: Giuffrè, 1957, pp. 72–5. R. Monaco, 'Le Comunità Sopranazionali nell'Ordinamento Internazionale', in R. Monaco, *Scritti di diritto europeo*, Milan: Giuffrè, 1972, pp. 47–75.

THE DANGER OF ANACHRONISMS

Having considered three moments of the history of international law that marked periods of deep consolidation or transformation, a first word of caution concerns transposition of legal terms or concepts out of their legal context. In his classic introduction to Roman law, Barry Nicholas reminded us for example that:

> The Romans often declare that possession is a fact, and this has given rise to some debate among modern jurists, who commonly prefer to see it as a right. There is, however, a danger of being bemused by words unless one inquires first what the Romans meant by possession as a fact. And one should perhaps begin with what they did not mean.[71]

This type of caution could be applicable to the interpretation of concepts in international law, and reflects issues of method relating to interpretation and identification of context, as shown by the International Court of Justice in 1986, and supported by Quentin Skinner's reflections concerning the history of ideas.

Both the historian and the lawyer may benefit from the admonition of Marc Bloch, and his comparison with the investigative magistrate:

> Before interpreting a phenomenon, the latter must be discovered. [. . .] [Someone may ask maybe,] is there really a need to go to all this trouble to 'discover' historic facts? They are only known to us and recognizable through documents; [. . .] isn't it sufficient to read texts or documents? Undoubtedly, but on condition that one is able to read them. A document is like a witness; as most witnesses, it won't speak unless interrogated. The challenge is thus to formulate the right questions. This is where comparisons provide precious support to the ceaseless investigative magistrate that a historian actually is.[72]

CHALLENGES RELATING TO SOURCES

A basic dependence on *primary sources* and their *interpretation* is common to both history and international law. The two disciplines' success criteria and legitimacy are in large part linked to this double dependence.

---

[71] B. Nicholas, *An Introduction to Roman Law*, Oxford: Clarendon Press, 1962, p. 114.
[72] M. Bloch, 'Pour une histoire comparée des sociétés européennes', in M. Bloch, *L'Histoire, la Guerre, la Résistance*, Paris: Quarto Gallimard, 2006, pp. 353–4 (translation from the French into English by the author). See also M. Bloch, *The Historian's Craft*, New York: Vintage Books, 1954.

Interpretation is the central mode of understanding in both disciplines. As such, these involve different hermeneutical processes, but often overlap, without being absorbed into each other. The development of international law has gone along with historical narratives leading to the identification of authoritative sources and derived chains of authority. This has contributed to the construction of legitimacy.

As opposed to historians, international lawyers take decisions to ensure finality and determinacy as regards legal questions (*pacta sunt servanda, res judicata*, etc.). In so doing, they rely on *authority* as regards interpretation, based on formal criteria and a definition of relevant sources, and they build on a relationship between concepts of law and legal institutions.[73] Moreover, in some cases, international lawyers may create new primary sources and negotiate the creation of new institutions. Historians cannot do either. On the other hand, they are thoroughly unconstrained by formal *authority* in terms of past interpretation. Being mainly bound by the authenticity of original primary sources or data, historians are instead engaged in a ceaseless reappraisal, reformulation and redefinition of questions, premises and perspectives. Where the international lawyer strives for justice relying on rule-based impartial determination and predictability, the historian is engaged in Sisyphean uncovering of meaning, either as 'parachutists' or as 'truffle hunters', to quote Le Roy Ladurie.[74] Or, as suggested by Berlin, either as a 'fox that knows many things' or 'the hedgehog that knows one big thing'.[75]

While the historian's endeavours may lead to interpretive pluralism, the international lawyer puts emphasis on continuity and authority.[76] Thus, contemporary international law strives for coherence and order in a complex world with an increasing variety of recognized institutions and stakeholders.[77] This

---

[73] N. MacCormick, *Legal Reasoning and Legal Theory*, Oxford: Oxford University Press, 1978; N. MacCormick, *Institutions of Law: An Essay in Legal Theory*, Oxford: Oxford University Press, 2007.

[74] E. Le Roy Ladurie, *Paris-Montpellier PC-PSU 1945–1963*, Paris: Gallimard, 1982, pp. 207–8, as quoted by J. H. Elliot, *History in the Making*, New Haven, CT: Yale University Press, 2012, p. 197.

[75] In philosophy, an analogy may be drawn to the distinction between the working methods of a hedgehog and a fox. See I. Berlin, *The Hedgehog and the Fox: An Essay on Tolstoy's View of History*, London: Weidenfeld & Nicolson, 1953.

[76] J. Raz, *Between Authority and Interpretation: On the Theory of Law and Practical Reasons*, Oxford: Oxford University Press, 2009, pp. 231–2.

[77] R. Dworkin, *Justice for Hedgehogs*, Cambridge, MA: Harvard University Press, 2011.

may be described as a reason-driven striving against fragmentation, including through systemic integration.[78]

History may, at all stages, contribute particular insights into international law, its emergence, context and sometimes contents, and vice versa.[79] The history of international relations may have underestimated the role of international law, as regards development of international politics on a variety of levels.[80]

Moreover, the exercise of a variety of roles in the context of international law may require high-intensity identification and interpretation of historical facts, which often relies on documentary evidence and a critical approach to primary sources. This may not least be an important feature of legal process in the resolution of territorial issues, whether through treaty negotiations or third-party settlement. Different questions arise in judicial fact-finding in the context of armed conflict or atrocities, where the mapping of social and political structures, chains of civil or military command or knowledge, may require collection and assessment of vast amounts of evidence. Those examples differ from the roles of the historian.

REFLECTIONS ON HISTORY AND INTERNATIONAL LAW: REASONS TO TAKE AN INTEREST

There is a variety of different reasons to take an interest in history when dealing with international law. And, inversely, international law ought to interest historians, albeit for a range of different reasons.[81] A third issue concerns the questions raised in history of international law, which has matured into a distinct discipline, mushrooming in different directions often under the influence of broader philosophical approaches, including critical theory. I have in this chapter attempted to take the long view reflecting on particular moments of change or consolidation of international law, where legal argument inter-

---

[78] M. Koskenniemi, 'Fragmentation of International Law: Difficulties arising from the Diversification and Expansion of International Law', *Report of the Study Group of the International Law Commission*, UN Doc. A/CN.4/L.682, 13 April 2006.

[79] An example is the historical analysis of constitutional and international law in the case *Legal Status of Eastern Greenland (Denmark v. Norway)*, Judgment of 5 April 1933, Permanent Court of International Justice, Series A/B, No. 53. See R. E. Fife, '*Legal Status of Eastern Greenland (Denmark v Norway)* (1933)', in E. Bjørge and C. Miles, *Landmark Cases in Public International Law*, London: Hart Publishing, 2017, pp. 133–57.

[80] Fife, '*Legal Status of Eastern Greenland (Denmark v Norway)* (1933)', pp. 133–4.

[81] L. Schapiro, 'The Importance of Law in the Study of Politics and History', in E. Dahrendorf (ed.), *Russian Studies*, New York: Penguin Books, 1986, pp. 29–44.

acted in a decisive manner with political change, and in so doing influenced in depth the further course of events.

Of particular interest are situations where international legal arguments as such may have proved decisive at political levels, and had lasting influence on the course of history. A key question may be how acceptance or actual endorsement of legal rules or institutions established by other states came to be perceived to be in the national interest – and how they in fact were taken on board, contributing to what with hindsight may be considered a systemic shift. Consequentialist arguments may play a decisive role at the stage of drafting or negotiating new legal instruments or approaches.[82]

Historians of law are familiar with the concept of 'reception' of legal systems, norms, concepts or patterns of thought – which could mean adopting a broader concept or drawing ideas from a different legal system. The three moments described shed light on how broader reception, in a historical sense, may take place. Might this provide a different lens to situate future issues or trends in the history of international law?

---

[82] On consequentialist arguments, see MacCormick, *Legal Reasoning and Legal Theory*, pp. 129–51.

2. Eastern Europe's imprint on modern international law

Stefan Troebst

INTRODUCTION

For quite some time now, historians have been confronted with a significant paradigm shift in their trade. In the nineteenth century, historical discipline focused predominantly on the 'state'. And while twentieth-century historians were predominantly captivated with 'society', for twenty-first century historians, a key disciplinary shift has taken place towards 'memory'.[1] This shift was triggered by the global caesura of 1989, which saw democratization in Eastern Europe and parts of Eurasia, and a new focus on dictatorial pasts in Southern Europe, Latin America and South Africa.[2] Not coincidentally, the journal *History & Memory*, published by Indiana University Press in Bloomington, USA, was founded in 1989.

This means that historians continue, of course, to look into the past, to go to archives, to decipher ego-documents, and to interview contemporary witnesses. Yet in addition, these days, they also analyse present-day cultures of remembrance, and occasionally even counsel directors of historical TV series, as part of their daily professional chores. They are often required to carefully monitor the use of historical arguments and references in the public realm by political actors, media, civil society and others – and, where necessary, to correct them. In short, historians today are routinely applying both diachronic as well as synchronic approaches to their work – often in tandem.

These developments in the historical profession provide for an interesting reverse parallel to the field of study of international law, which has recently

---

[1] D. Diner, 'Von "Gesellschaft" zu "Gedächtnis". Über historische Paaradigmenwechsel', in D. Diner (ed.), *Gedächtniszeiten. Über jüdische und andere Geschichten*, Munich: C. H. Beck, 2003, pp. 7–15.

[2] V. Tismaneanu and B. C. Iacob (eds.), *Remembrance, History, and Justice: Coming to Terms with Traumatic Pasts in Democratic Societies*, Budapest: Central European University Press, 2015.

experienced a 'historiographic turn'.[3] Nowadays, and in stark contrast to the past, the development of international law is no longer perceived as an endogenous and teleological legal process of a success story pointing towards a brighter future for mankind. Rather, the development of modern international law seems more attuned to a thorny meandering path, the red thread of which has been critically shaped by conflicts, aggression, intervention, secession, war, occupation, ethnic cleansings and genocides. Accordingly, modern international law can be described by the metaphor of a storage medium of conflict memory.[4] To the historian, international legal treaties seem like a glass aquarium, in which – as one looks through them – one observes the ruptures, wars and events that brought about the drafting of this or that treaty's clauses, or determined the specific geographical path of an existing given borderline between states.

In the following pages, I wish to provide an initial and general sketch of how the history of Eastern Europe has shaped modern international law as we know it today. I use the concept of 'Eastern Europe' as a historical meso-region in the sense of the German term '*Osteuropa*', i.e. Russia/Soviet Union, East Central Europe, Northeastern Europe and Southeastern Europe – the Balkans.[5] While a full and comprehensive survey of Eastern Europe's impact is far beyond the scope of this chapter, I wish, nevertheless, to highlight the primordiality of the Eastern European experience to modern international law's historical unfolding. Looking to the origins of human rights law in the late nineteenth and early twentieth centuries, a special place shall be dedicated to the development of

---

[3] G. R. Bandeira Galindo, 'Martti Koskenniemi and the Historiographical Turn in International Law', *European Journal of International Law*, vol. 16(3), 2005, pp. 539–59. See also M. Koskenniemi, *The Gentle Civilizer of Nations: The Rise and Fall of International Law 1870–1960*, Cambridge: Cambridge University Press, 2001.

[4] S. Troebst, 'Speichermedium der Konflikterinnerung. Zur osteuropäischen Prägung des modernen Völkerrechts', *Zeitschrift für Ostmitteleuropa-Forschung*, vol. 61(3), 2012, pp. 404–31.

[5] K. Zernack, *Osteuropa. Eine Einführung in seine Geschichte*, Munich: C. H. Beck, 1977. In its voluminous section on 'Regions' a recent authoritative handbook does not make a difference between Eastern and Western Europe but covers next to 'Africa and Arabia', 'Asia' and 'The Americas and the Caribbean', all with regional sub-chapters, just 'Europe' and that in chronological subchapters: B. Fassbender and A. Peters (eds.), *The Oxford Handbook of the History of International Law*, Oxford: Oxford University Press, 2012, pp. 381–810. See, however, in a subdivision on 'Encounters', L. Mälksoo, 'Russia – Europe', in the same volume, pp. 764–86. Obviously, 'Russia' is here not considered to be part of 'Europe', but is also not listed under 'Asia' or under 'Eurasia', a term not contained in the index. Here only 'Western Europe' figures (including 'The Baltic States', p. 1226) while there is no entry on 'Eastern Europe'.

minority rights – so distinctly associated with the legal workings of Eastern Europe and its jurists and probably more so than for any other world region.

TWO GENERAL OBSERVATIONS: EASTERN VS. WESTERN EUROPE AND THE ROLE OF MEMORY IN HISTORY

During the early modern period, the two halves of Europe – West and East – developed in very different directions. In the West, states like Portugal, Spain, France, the Netherlands and Britain grew rich due to their colonial empires, and at the same time adopted an increasingly national character. In Europe's East, territorial warfare with its human losses and military devastations was far more endemic than in the West – with the ensuing result of the decline of great powers such as Sweden–Finland, Poland–Lithuania and the Ottoman Empire, which was coupled with the rise of new great powers as in Muscovite Russia and Brandenburg–Prussia, later known as unified Germany. Subsequently, nineteenth-century Eastern Europe witnessed the region-wide triumph of nationalism and national movements. This in turn triggered the emergence of a dozen or so small and medium-sized nation-states, spread across the territory hitherto maintained by the former multi-ethnic empires (Habsburg and Ottoman) – a process which lasted up to the end of the twentieth century, and arguably even into the beginning of the twenty-first.[6] This turbulent epoch in the history of Eastern Europe coincided almost entirely with the development of modern international law. It is thus not surprising that the latter was so heavily shaped by Eastern Europe's tumultuous path from, say, the partitions of Poland at the end of the eighteenth century to the proclamation of the Republic of Kosovo in 2008.

In the almost two centuries since 1830, in Western, Southern and Northern Europe, in addition to the already existing states, altogether seven new states were founded.[7] In contrast, in Eastern Europe, the number of newly formed states – twenty-five – was almost four times higher. The same phenomenon

---

[6] For the nineteenth and twentieth centuries, see E. D. Weitz, 'From the Vienna to the Paris System: International Politics and the Entangled Histories of Human Rights, Forced Deportations, and Civilizing Mission', *American Historical Review*, vol. 113(5), 2008, pp. 1313–43; M. M. Payk, 'Institutionalisierung und Verrechtlichung. Die Geschichte des Völkerrechts im späten 19. und frühen 20. Jahrhundert', *Archiv für Sozialgeschichte*, vol. 52, 2012, pp. 861–84; and M. M. Payk, *Frieden durch Recht? Der Aufstieg des modernen Vökerrechts und der Friedensschluss nach dem Ersten Weltkrieg*, Munich: De Gruyter, 2018.

[7] Belgium, Italy, Norway, Finland, Ireland, Vatican City State, and – temporarily – German Democratic Republic. The German Empire founded in 1871 can to a considerable degree be perceived as a 'Bismarckian' enlargement of Prussia.

can be observed with regard to the number of international congresses held by the European pentarchy, between the Congress of Vienna of 1815 and the outbreak of the First World War in 1914. Out of twenty-seven international congresses in total, more than half were devoted to Eastern Europe alone. All through this period, the main target of European international humanitarian interventions was the Ottoman Empire, with its still large territories in the Balkans.[8]

During the nineteenth century – the very formation period of modern international law – international action was predominantly geared towards Europe's East, resulting in the significant imprint of this region on modern international law. Notwithstanding the fact that Europe's Eastern half formed an unequivocal part of the geographical region of Europe, to Arnulf Becker Lorca's mind it was nevertheless 'non-Western' and 'semi-peripheral', like Latin America, China, Japan and other parts of the world. Correspondingly, Becker Lorca's perception of modern international law was one of a mixture of 'European' and 'non-Western' elements, for which he duly coined the term 'mestizo international law'.[9]

The second general observation draws from Jean Carbonnier's article on the *Code civil* in the second volume of Pierre Nora's famous collection *Les lieux de mémoire*. In this study, Carbonnier stresses 'the responsibility of law for memory', as he defines customary law as 'a manifestation of collective memory'.[10] Other authors label the Peace of Westphalia of 1648 as 'a realm of memory of European dimension',[11] and without second thought recall

---

[8] D. Rodogno, *Against Massacre: Humanitarian Interventions in the Ottoman Empire, 1815–1914 – The Emergence of a European Concept and International Practice*, Princeton, NJ: Princeton University Press, 2012; G. Bass, *Freedom's Battle: The Origins of Humanitarian Intervention*, New York: Knopf, 2008. See also A. Th. Skordos, *Interdependenzen regionaler und globaler Prozesse: Die Prägung des modernen Völkerrechts durch die Konfliktgeschichte Südosteuropas (19.–20. Jahrhundert)*, Vienna: Böhlau, forthcoming.

[9] A. B. Lorca, *Mestizo International Law: A Global Intellectual History 1842–1933*, Cambridge: Cambridge University Press, 2014. See also A. Th. Skordos, 'Geschichtsregionale Völkerrechtsforschung: Der Fall Südosteuropa', Zeitschrift für Ostmitteleuropa-Forschung, vol. 61(3), 2012, pp. 433–73.

[10] J. Carbonnier, 'Le Code civil', in P. Nora (ed.), *Les Lieux de mémoire*, vol. 2 (Le territoire, l'État, le patrimoine), Paris: Gallimard, 1986, pp. 293–315, p. 293.

[11] B. Klesmann, 'Kalkül – Transfer – Symbol: Europäische Friedensverträge der Vormoderne. Arbeitsgespräch in der Herzog August Bibliothek Wolfenbüttel vom 14. bis 16. März 2005', *Wolfenbütteler Bibliotheksinformationen*, vol. 30(1), 2005, pp. 33–5, p. 33. See also C. Gantet, 'Der Westfälische Frieden', in É. François and H. Schulze (eds), *Deutsche Erinnerungsorte*, vol. 1, Munich: C. H. Beck, 2001, pp. 86–104; H. Duchhardt, 'Der Westfälische Friede', in P. den Boer et al. (eds), *Europäische Erinnerungsorte*, vol. 2, Munich: R. Oldenbourg, 2012, pp. 491–9.

Courtroom no. 600 in the Palace of Justice at Nuremberg, where between 1945 and 1946 the International Military Tribunal tried the political and military elite of Nazi Germany – a first-rate *lieu de mémoire* in Nora's sense of this term.[12] Tellingly, nowadays, a part of this museum in Nuremberg is called '*Memorium* Nuremberg Trials'.

And it is most probably not entirely coincidental that Henri Dunant's book, which triggered both the founding of the International Committee of the Red Cross (ICRC) and the signing of the First Geneva Convention 'for the Amelioration of the Condition of the Wounded in Armies in the Field', was entitled *A Memory of Solferino*.[13] Dunant described the misery of the wounded on that battlefield in northern Italy, who did not receive medical attention and were left to die from their wounds, an experience which might be compared – in the metaphorical sense – to a tiny insect in a gem of amber: in its historical dimension it is a minutely small event, yet one which back in its time caused a major innovation in international law. As with the insect, so with this treaty, it is inscribed into the subsequent unfolding of this innovation (today's ICRC); yet by now, it is hardly recognizable and can only be observed when backlit by historical scholarship of modern international law's diachronic development.

EASTERN EUROPE AND THE ORIGINS OF HUMAN RIGHTS LAW: 1917 AND ITS CONSEQUENCES

A particularly prominent example for the impact of Eastern Europe's conflict history on modern international law can be observed in the so-called 'Wilsonian moment'. Following the weakening of Tsarist Russia in the First World War, the right of peoples to their own self-determination was propagated by a variety of different political actors: from US President Woodrow Wilson all the way to the leader of the Russian Bolsheviks, Vladimir Ilyich Lenin.[14] Almost simultaneously to its proclamation, this new doctrine was first put into force in Eastern Europe, when Finland split off from Russia and gained its independence in 1917. In 1918, Estonia, Latvia, Lithuania, Poland, Ukraine, Georgia and Armenia followed suit. At the world's other end, the

---

[12] E. Dietzfelbinger and H.-C. Täubrich, 'Der Schwurgerichtssaal 600. Vom Welt-Gericht zum Erinnerungsort', *Einsichten und Perspektiven. Bayerische Zeitschrift für Politik und Geschichte*, vol. 4(1), 2007, pp. 48–61.

[13] H. Dunant, *Un souvenir de Solférino*, Genève: Imprimerie Jules-Guillaume Fick, 1862.

[14] E. Manela, *The Wilsonian Moment: Self-Determination and the International Origins of Anticolonial Nationalism*, Oxford: Oxford University Press, 2007.

hopes of the anti-colonial movements in Asia and Africa were, in contrast, bitterly disappointed.[15]

In addition to the propagation of self-determination in Eastern Europe, the Bolshevik *coup d'état* of 1917 had a number of other consequences for international law. First there was the huge wave of refugees from Russia to Central and Western Europe, which brought Frithjof Nansen, the High Commissioner for Refugees of the new League of Nations, to issue in 1922 a new type of ID card for 'personnes d'origine russe', labelled *Passport Nansen – Certificat d'identité et de voyage*. Soon, this new identification document for stateless people was also issued to refugees from the now-disintegrated Ottoman Empire.[16]

A second consequence of 1917 was the rise of new Soviet Russia. From 1922 onwards, the Soviet Union developed its own 'revolutionary' perception of international law.[17] This was based on the assumption that there were three so-called circles of international law: a 'socialist international law', a 'bourgeois international law' and an 'inter-systemic international law' – the latter to be applied in situations of contact, overlap or friction between the formers: 'socialist' and the 'bourgeois' ones.[18]

With the emergence of a 'socialist community' after the Second World War, 'socialist international law' was applied also in the relationship between the Moscow centre and the East Central and Southeast European peripheries' respective satellite states. In this context, the 'socialist international law' now implied a limitation of the sovereignty of 'socialist states' due to the mandatory concept of a 'proletarian internationalism' imposed by force by the Soviet Union.[19] What in the context of the invasion of Czechoslovakia by Soviet and

---

[15] J. Fisch, *Das Selbstbestimmungsrecht der Völker. Domestizierung einer Illusion*, Munich: C. H. Beck, 2010, pp. 51–6 and 148–57.

[16] J. Torpey, *The Invention of the Passport: Surveillance, Citizenship and the State*, Cambridge: Cambridge University Press, 2000, pp. 124–31; H. Arendt, 'Die Nation der Minderheiten und das Volk der Staatenlosen', in H. Arendt,, *Elemente und Ursprünge totaler Herrschaft. Antisemitismus, Imperialismus, totale Herrschaft*, Munich, Zurich: Piper, 1986 (1st ed. 1955), pp. 564–601.

[17] M. Geistlinger, *Revolution und Völkerrecht. Völkerrechtsdogmatische Grundlegung der Voraussetzungen und des Inhalts eines Wahlrechts in bezug auf vorrevolutionäre völkerrechtliche Rechte und Pflichten*, Vienna: Böhlau, 1991, pp. 151–271.

[18] E. A. Korowin, *Das Völkerrecht der Übergangszeit. Grundlagen der völkerrechtlichen Beziehungen der Union der Sowjetrepubliken*, Berlin: W. Rothschild, 1929.

[19] G. I. Tunkin, *Theory of International Law* (translated with an introduction by W. E. Butler and edited by W. E. Butler, L. N. Shestakov, The Vinogradoff Institute, University College London), 2nd ed., London: Wildy, Simmonds and Hill Publishers, 2003. See also H. Kelsen, *The Communist Theory of Law*, New York: Frederick A. Praeger, 1955; T. Schweisfurth, *Sozialistisches Völkerrecht? Darstellung – Analyse*

other Warsaw Pact troops in 1968 was termed the Brezhnev Doctrine, was first tested during the upheavals in East Germany in 1953 and in Hungary in 1956. Only during the late Perestroika period under Gorbachev, and mainly due to Soviet military overstretch, was this doctrine given up. In the autumn of 1989, a Soviet diplomat proclaimed a new doctrine:

> The Brezhnev Doctrine is dead. You know the Frank Sinatra song 'My Way'? Hungary and Poland are doing it their way. We now have the Sinatra Doctrine.[20]

In the new Russian Federation post-1989, the short-lived Sinatra Doctrine of the late Soviet period was replaced by a new-old concept labelled the 'Near Abroad'. Paraphrasing Carl Schmitt's formula of an *'Interventionsverbot für raumfremde Mächte'* (a 'prohibition of intervention by powers outside of one's own space of influence'), Russia imposed its own right of intervention, as in Georgia in 2008 and in Ukraine 2014. Its non-withdrawal of formerly Soviet (now Russian) troops from the already independent states of Moldova and Georgia was a mere extension of the Russian application of Schmitt's first principle. In short: the 'Brezhnev Doctrine' never really died in the first place. It only altered its pattern of justification – 'Putin Doctrine'. Back in 1919, Eastern Europe continued to give birth to the principles of minorities protection and peoples' right to self-determination. A century later, in the name of the protection of Russian minorities in South Ossetia, Abkhazia, Crimea, the Dniester Valley and eastern Ukraine, Tsarist Russia's reawakened *Geist*, now in the shape of Putinist Russia, could dress its geo-strategic interests with an international-legal argumentative garb (minorities' protection) that had originally stemmed from this region one hundred years earlier.

– *Wertung der sowjetmarxistischen Theorie vom Völkerrecht 'neuen Typs'*, Berlin: Springer, 1973; L. Mälksoo, *Russian Approaches to International Law*, Oxford: Oxford University Press, 2015; F. Hirsch, 'The Soviets at Nuremberg: International Law, Propaganda, and the Making of the Post-war Order', *American Historical Review*, vol. 113(3), 2008, pp. 701–30; S. Troebst, 'Sozialistisches Völkerrecht und die sowjetische Menschenrechtsdoktrin', in N. Frei and A. Weinke (eds.), *Toward a New Moral World Order? Menschenrechtspolitik und Völkerrecht seit 1945*, Göttingen: Vandenhoeck and Ruprecht, 2013, pp. 94–104; J. Quigley, *Soviet Legal Innovation and the Law of the Western World*, Cambridge: Cambridge University Press, 2007.

[20] Quoted after William F. Buckley Jr., 'The Sinatra Doctrine', *National Review*, 26 May 2004, available at www.nationalreview.com/2004/05/sinatra-doctrine-william-f-buckley-jr. See also M. J. Ouimet, *The Rise and Fall of the Brezhnev Doctrine in Soviet Foreign Policy*, Chapel Hill: University of North Carolina Press, 2003; R. A. Jones, *The Soviet Concept of 'Limited Sovereignty' from Lenin to Gorbachev: The Brezhnev Doctrine*, Basingstoke: Macmillan, 1990.

EASTERN EUROPE AS A LEGAL AMPLIFIER

In addition to the genuine innovations in international law which were born as a response to Eastern Europe's conflicts, this historical-geographic meso-region also functioned as an amplifier for international legal concepts which originated in other parts of the world, yet which came to be applied within this area. A striking example is the principle of *uti possidetis juris*. As the Swiss historian Jörg Fisch has observed, this concept

> was developed in the context of the independence of the Ibero-American states and taken over in the 20th century first of all in the decolonization of Africa and the dissolution of the Soviet Union and Yugoslavia.[21]

Briefly put, *uti possidetis* (Latin for 'as you possess') implies the application of territorial attribution and sovereign title to the longstanding possessor of a territory, and the demarcation of territorial boundaries according to the previously recognized boundaries. In this sense, one could certainly add Czechoslovakia to Fisch's list, given the 1992 experience of the drawing of the Czech–Slovak border according to *uti possidetis*. Nevertheless, a mere return to older and seemingly universally recognized borders does not, in and of itself, ensure a frictionless international evolvement. In the case of theYugoslavia's breakup into independent states, the strict adoption of *uti possidetis* by the Badinter Arbitration Committee in 1992, and the ensuing recognition by the European Community of the boundaries of six of the former Yugoslav republics (albeit *not* for the two autonomous provinces of Vojvodina and Kosovo), considerably exacerbated the ongoing Serb–Albanian conflict in the former Socialist Autonomous Province of Kosovo.[22] Conversely, and notwithstanding the fact that the Kosovo case was internationally declared to be *sui generis*, it is arguable that the recognition of the Republic of Kosovo in 2008

---

[21] Fisch, *Das Selbstbestimmungsrecht der Völker*, p. 43. On Latin America as another potent regional case in the development of modern international law see A. Rodiles, 'The Great Promise of Comparative Public Law for Latin America: Toward *Ius Commune Americanum*?', in A. Roberts et al. (eds.), *Comparative International Law*, Oxford: Oxford University Press, 2018, pp. 501–23.

[22] S. Terret, *The Dissolution of Yugoslavia and the Badinter Arbitration Commission: A Contextual Study of Peace-Making Efforts in the Post-Cold War World*, London: Routledge, 2017; S. Troebst, *Conflict in Kosovo: Failure of Prevention? An Analytical Documentation, 1992–1998*, Flensburg: European Centre for Minority Issues, 1998.

by most EU member states has considerably eroded the international validity of the *uti possidetis* rule.[23]

Here then, a spin in the reverse direction can be observed. The term 'Balkanization', which was coined in the wake of the retreat of the Ottoman Empire from Southeastern Europe, and which also embodied the emergence of small Christian nation-states there,[24] had become, from the 1960s onwards, a popular metaphor for analysis of the outcomes of decolonization in Africa.[25]

THE PROSOPOGRAPHIC DIMENSION: JURISTS FROM MINORITIES FOR THE PROTECTION OF MINORITIES

The East European dimension in the shaping of modern international law becomes particularly obvious with regard to some of its prominent protagonists. East European jurists such as Hersch Lauterpacht[26] or Raphael Lemkin,[27] hold the copyright for the concepts of 'crimes against humanity' and 'genocide'. Both were born in Tsarist Russia's Pale of Settlement. Both received their education at the Austro-Hungarian and then Polish University of Lemberg (respectively Polish Lwów and today L'viv in Ukraine). The international lawyer Philippe Sands, author of the recent bestseller *East West Street: On the Origins of Genocide and Crimes against Humanity*, has labelled the East Galician capital 'the Mecca of modern international law'.[28]

---

[23] P. Hilpold (ed.), *Kosovo and International Law: The ICJ Advisory Opinion of 22 July 2010*, Leiden: Brill, 2012.

[24] P. S. Mowrer, *Balkanized Europe: A Study in Political Analysis and Reconstruction*, New York: E. P. Dutton and Co., 1921.

[25] B. Neuberger, 'The African Concept of Balkanisation', *Journal of Modern African Studies*, vol. 14(3), 1976, pp. 523–9; J. L. Pallister, 'Balkanization and Neo-Colonialism: Obstacles to an Independent Africa', *Africa Today*, vol. 24(4), 1977, pp. 95–6.

[26] There is no scholarly biography of Hersch Zvi Lauterpacht. See, however, the biographical sketch by A. Carty, 'Hersch Lauterpacht: A Powerful East European Figure', *Baltic Yearbook of International Law*, vol. 7(1), 2007, pp. 1–28, and a biographical book by Lauterpacht's son: Elihu Lauterpacht, *The Life of Sir Hersch Lauterpacht, QC, FBA, LLD*, Cambridge: Cambridge University Press, 2010.

[27] See the most recent biography by Douglas Irvin-Erickson, *Raphaël Lemkin and the Concept of Genocide*, Philadelphia: University of Pennsylvania Press, 2017; and, for the rediscovery of Lemkin in East Central Europe: A. Bieńczyk-Missala and S. Dębski (eds.), *Rafał Lemkin: A Hero of Humankind*, Warsaw: The Polish Institute of International Affairs, 2010; A. Bieńczyk-Missala (ed.), *Civilians in Contemporary Armed Conflicts: Rafał Lemkin's Heritage*, Warsaw: Wydawnictwo Uniwersytetu Warszawskiego, 2017.

[28] P. Sands, 'The Memory of Justice: The Unexpected Place of Lviv in International Law – A Personal History', *Case Western Reserve Journal of International Law*, vol. 43(3), 2011, pp. 739–58; P. Sands, *East West Street: On the Origin of Genocide*

Lo and behold, many other theoreticians and practitioners of international law indeed stemmed from Eastern Europe, predominantly from Tsarist Russia. This goes not only for Friedrich Fromhold von (Fëdor F.) Martens (the convener of the 1899–1907 Hague Conventions),[29] but also for Leonid A. Kamarovskij,[30] Paul Vinogradoff,[31] Leo Motzkin,[32] Paul Schiemann,[33] Bohdan Winiarski,[34] André Mandelštam,[35] Carl Bergbohm,[36] Shimshon Rosenbaum[37] and Jacob Robinson.[38] Born as Austro-Hungarian Eastern Europeans were

---

and Crimes against Humanity, London: Weidenfeld and Nicolson, 2016. See also S. Troebst, 'Lemkin and Lauterpacht in Lemberg and Later: Pre- and Post-Holocaust Careers of Two East European International Lawyers', *Tr@nsit-Online*, August 2013, available at www.iwm.at/read-listen-watch/transit-online/lemkin-and-lauterpacht-in-lemberg-and-later-pre-and-post-holocaust-careers-of-two-east-european-international-lawyers.

[29] M. Aust, 'Völkerrechtstransfer im Zarenreich. Internationalismus und Imperium bei Fedor F. Martens', *Osteuropa*, vol. 60(9), 2010, pp. 113–25; M. Aust, 'Das Zarenreich in der Völkerrechtsgeschichte 1870–1914', in M. Aust (ed.), *Globalisierung imperial und sozialistisch. Russland und die Sowjetunion in der Globalgeschichte 1851–1991*, Frankfurt: Campus, 2013, pp. 166–81; V. V. Pustogarov, *Our Martens: F. F. Martens, International Lawyer and Architecht of Peace*, Alphen aan den Rijn: Kluwer, 2000. See also P. Holquist, 'The Laws of War: From the Lieber Code to the Brussels Conference', *The Berlin Journal: A Magazine from the American Academy in Berlin*, vol. 32(1), 2018, pp. 68–70; and P. Holquist, *The Laws of War and Their Russian Origin*, forthcoming.

[30] A. B. Belobratov, 'Leonid Alekseevič Kamarovskij', in W. Böttcher (ed.), *Klassiker des europäischen Denkens*, Baden-Baden: Nomos, 2014, pp. 427–30.

[31] W. E. Butler (ed.), *On the History of International Law and International Organization: Collected Papers of Sir Paul Vinogradoff*, Clark: The Law Book Exchange, 2009.

[32] F. Nesemann, 'Leo Motzkin (1867–1933): Zionist Engagement and Minority Diplomacy', *Central and Eastern European Review*, vol. 1(1), 2007, pp. 32–54.

[33] J. Hiden, *Defender of Minorities: Paul Schiemann, 1876–1944*, London: C. Hurst, 2004.

[34] K. Skubiszewski, 'Sir Hersch Lauterpacht and Poland's Judges at the International Court: Judge Bohdan Winiarski', *International Community Law Review*, vol. 13(1), 2011, pp. 87–91.

[35] H. P. Aust, 'From Diplomat to Academic Activist: André Mandelstam and the History of Human Rights', *European Journal of International Law*, vol. 25(4), 2014, pp. 1105–21.

[36] V. E. Grabar, 'Karl Magnus Bergbohm 1849–1927', *Zeitschrift für Völkerrecht*, vol. 14(4), 1928, pp. 559–563.

[37] E. Bendikaitė, 'One Man's Struggle: The Politics of Shimshon Rosenbaum (1859–1934)', *Simon Dubnow Institute Yearbook*, vol. 13(1), 2014, pp. 87–109; E. Bendikaitė, 'Mittler zwischen den Welten. Shimshon Rosenbaum: Jurist, Zionist, Politiker', *Osteuropa*, vol. 58(8), 2008, pp. 295–302.

[38] O. Kaplan-Feuereisen, 'Im Dienste der jüdischen Nation: Jacob Robinson und das Völkerrecht', *Osteuropa*, vol. 58(8), 2008, pp. 279–294; O. Kaplan-Feuereisen,

Egon Schwelb,[39] Ludwik Ehrlich,[40] Michał Jan Rostworowski,[41] Louis B. Sohn,[42] Louis Henkin,[43] Rudolf Laun,[44] Manfred Lachs,[45] Hans Kelsen,[46] Charles Henry Alexandrowicz (Karol Aleksandrowicz)[47] and Ernő (Ernst) Flachbarth[48] – to name just a few.

That many of them were Jews (and Zionists) is no coincidence: contemporary anti-Semitism and Russian pogroms were a strong motivation for these jurists to embrace the career path of an international lawyer.[49] The same goes

---

'Geschichtserfahrung und Völkerrecht – Jacob Robinson und die Gründung des Institute of Jewish Affairs', *Leipziger Beiträg zur jüdischen Geschichte und Kultur*, vol. 2, 2004, pp. 307–27.

[39] M. Siegelberg, 'Egon Schwelb and the Human Rights via media', in J. Loeffler and M. Paz (eds.), The Law of Strangers: Jewish Lawyers and International Law in the Twentieth Century, Cambridge: Cambridge University Press, 2019; S.A., 'Egon Schwelb, Ex-Aide of UN Rights Division', *The New York Times*, 22 March 1979, p. 13, available at www.nytimes.com/1979/03/22/archives/egon-schwelb-exaide-of-un-rights-division.html.

[40] S. Rudnicki, 'Ehrlich, Ludwik', *The YIVO Encyclopedia of Jews in Eastern Europe*, available at www.yivoencyclopedia.org/article.aspx/Ehrlich_Ludwik.

[41] A. Wyrozumska, 'Count Rostworowski as an International Lawyer and Judge', *International Community Law Review*, vol. 13(1), 2011, pp. 59–79.

[42] D. F. Vagts, 'Louis Sohn', *Harvard Journal of International Law*, vol. 48(1), 2007, pp. 19–21.

[43] W. Grimes, 'Louis Henkin, Leader in Field of Human Rights Law, Dies at 92', *The New York Times*, 16 October 2010, available at www.nytimes.com/2010/10/17/us/17henkin.html.

[44] L. Wildenthal, 'Rudolf Laun and the Human Rights of Germans in Occupied and Early West Germany', in Stefan-Ludwig Hoffmann (ed.), *Human Rights in the Twentieth Century*, Cambridge: Cambridge University Press, 2019, pp. 25–144.

[45] E. McWhinney, 'Manfred Lachs and the International Court of Justice as Emerging Constitutional Court of the United Nations', *Leiden Journal of International Law*, vol. 8(1), 1995, pp. 41–52.

[46] T. Olechowski, 'Über die Herkunft Hans Kelsens', in T. Chiusi, T. Gergen and H. Jung (eds.), *Das Recht und seine historischen Grundlagen. Festschrift für Elmar Wadle zum 70. Geburtstag*, Berlin: Duncker and Humblot, 2008, pp. 849–63.

[47] D. Armitage and J. Pitts, 'This Modern Grotius: An Introduction to the Life and Thought of C. H. Alexandrowicz', in C. H. Alexandrowicz, *The Law of Nations in Global History* (ed. David Armitage and Jennifer Pitts), Oxford: Oxford University Press, 2017, pp. 1–31.

[48] S.A., 'Flachbarth Ernő', *Hungarian Wikipedia*, 15 November 2018, available at https://hu.wikipedia.org/wiki/Flachbarth_Ern%C5%91.

[49] J. Loeffler, *Rooted Cosmopolitans: Jews and Human Rights in the Twentieth Century*, New Haven, CT: Yale University Press, 2018; R. Y. Paz, *A Gateway between a Distant God and a Cruel World: The Contribution of Jewish German-Speaking Scholars to International Law*, Boston: Martinus Nijhoff, 2013; C. Fink, *Defending the Rights of Others: The Great Powers, the Jews, and International Minority Protection, 1878–1938*, Cambridge: Cambridge University Press, 2004; J. Loeffler and M. Paz

for the fact that they experienced the inversion of their status from that of an 'imperial' minority within the Romanov and Habsburg empires to the status of a 'national' minority in one of the newly established Eastern European nation-states. Dominated within these new states by a titular nation which more often than not strove for ethno-national homogeneity, these lawyers found themselves continuously combatant in favour of their (and others') minority's rights. This at the same time explains why many of them, like their Baltic-German or Bohemian-German colleagues, focused their research and practice upon topics associated with minorities' protection, human rights and group rights in general. Up to 1933, Jewish and German jurists from the new states in East Central Europe even cooperated with each other within the framework of the Congress of European Nationalities.[50] Most of Nazi Germany's Jewish Holocaust-surviving jurists did not stay in, nor did they return to their East European regions of origins. Overwhelmingly, they either pursued careers in their countries of exile such as Israel, the UK and the USA, or joined the emerging world of international organizations such as the United Nations. These jurists carried their theoretical legal baggage and substantive experiences from Lemberg, Vilna, Prague and Warsaw to their respective destinations.

In addition to the former Habsburg and Russian realms, the post-Ottoman Balkans also generated a disproportionately high number of leading international legal experts. Greeks such as Stefanos-Etienne Carathéodory, Michel Stavro Kebedgy, Nikolaos Saripolos and the Hellenized Bavarian Georgios Streit were particularly engaged with the 'Eastern Question' (the unfolding of the now-defunct Ottoman Empire).[51] The next generation of Balkan jurists who followed suit, which included Antoine F. Frangulis[52] and Nikolaos Politis,[53] gained prominence in the League of Nations. In the new post-First World War Yugoslavia, Slobodan Jovanović[54] – an early critic of Kelsen –

(eds.), *The Law of Strangers: Jewish Lawyers and International Law in the Twentieth Century*, Cambridge: Cambridge University Press, 2019.

[50] S. Bamberger-Stemmann, *Der Europäische Nationalitätenkongress 1925 bis 1938. Nationale Minderheiten zwischen Lobbyistentum und Großmachtinteressen*, Marburg: Herder-Institut, 2000; H. Glass, 'Ende der Gemeinsamkeit: Zur deutsch-jüdischen Kontroverse auf dem Europäischen Nationalitätenkongress 1933', *Leipziger Beiträge zur jüdischen Geschichte und Kultur*, vol. 2, 2004, pp. 259–82.

[51] For all of them, see B. Lorca, *Mestizo International Law*, passim.

[52] S.A., 'Antoine-F. Frangulis (1888–1975)', *Bibliothèque nationale de France*, available at https://data.bnf.fr/fr/11007376/antoine-f__frangulis.

[53] M. Papadaki, 'Nicolas Politis, une approche biographique', *Monde(s)*, vol. 7, 2015, pp. 45–64.

[54] A. Pavković, *Slobodan Jovanović: An Unsentimental Approach to Politics*, New York: Columbia University Press, 1993.

Milovan Dj. Milovanović,[55] Toma Živanović[56] and Juraj Andrassy[57] gained international reputation. Bulgaria's Nisim Mevorah, who drafted substantial parts of the Fourth Geneva Convention 'relative to the Protection of Civilian Persons in Time of War',[58] and the Romanian Vespasian Pella who untiringly endeavoured for an international criminal court, would be two of the Balkan jurists to impact the international legal scene after the Second World War.[59]

Back during the interwar period, Pella was one of the driving forces behind the idea of a League of Nations Convention against International Terrorism. The backdrop to this was a truly Balkan one: in 1934, two terrorist underground organizations, the *Internal Macedonian Revolutionary Organization* and the *Ustasha-Croatian Revolutionary Movement*, teamed up to assassinate the Yugoslav king Aleksandar I. Karadjordjević. They did so successfully, and on the occasion also killed the French Foreign Minister Louis Barthou. Pella's definition of terrorism in the 1937 draft Convention for the Prevention and Punishment of Terrorism was subsequently adopted by the United Nations during the 1980s. In Article 1(2) of Pella's proposed text international terrorism is defined as:

> all criminal acts directed against a State and intended or calculated to create a state of terror in the minds of particular persons or a group of persons or the general public.[60]

---

[55] D. MacKenzie, *Milovan Milovanovic: Talented and Peaceloving Diplomat*, Boulder, CO: East European Monographs, 2009.

[56] I. Janković, 'Prilozi za biografiju Tome Živanovića', *Pravni Zapisi*, vol. 7(1), 2016, pp. 68–116.

[57] Z. Pokrovac, 'Juraj Andrassy', in M. Stolleis (ed.), *Juristen: ein biographisches Lexikon. Von der Antike bis zum 20. Jahrhundert*, 2nd ed., Munich: C. H. Beck, 2001, p. 35.

[58] B. Mevorah, 'Professor Nissim Mevorah's Bulgarian-Jewish Way of Life', *East-European Quarterly*, vol. 19(1), 1985, pp. 75–80. For Mevorah's decisive role in drafting the Fourth Geneva Convention see G. Ben-Nun, *The Fourth Geneva Convention for Civilians: The History of International Humanitarian Law*, London: Bloomsbury Books & I. B. Tauris, 2019, Chapter 3 ('The Final Act: The Soviets Come on Board – Geneva 1949').

[59] P. Kovács, 'La Société des Nations et son action après l'attentat contre Alexandre, roi de Yougoslavie', *Journal of the History of International Law*, vol. 6(1), 2004, pp. 65–78. On the actual assassination and its immediate international consequences, see S. Clissold, 'Murder in Marseille. Chapter 3: Marseille', *The South Slav Journal*, vol. 7(1), 1984, pp. 18–26; and B. Kovrig, 'Mediation by Obfuscation: The Resolution of the Marseille Crisis, October 1934 to May 1935', *Historical Journal*, vol. 19, 1976, pp. 191–221.

[60] *Convention for the Prevention and Punishment of Terrorism*, 16 November 1937, reproduced in League of Nations (LoN), International Conference Proceedings on the Repression of Terrorism, Geneva, 1–16 November 1937, LoN Doc. C.94.M.47.1938.V.

The origins of Pella's focus on fighting terrorism could be found in 1920s Bulgaria where another national-revolutionary formation strove for a revision of the Versailles system: the *Internal Dobrujan Revolutionary Organization*, which operated and carried out its assaults cross-border from Bulgaria to Romania. Even before the 1934 murders in Marseille, Pella had already established contacts with Raphael Lemkin in the latter's campaign in the League of Nations in favour of an international criminal court – a demand which Pella outlined in his book *La criminalité collective des états et le Droit Pénal de l'avenir* of 1925. To Pella, the punishment of irredentism and revisionism by military means did not go far enough. Political, propagandistic and material support for terrorist underground movements also deserved criminalization and punishment in his eyes.[61]

A PARADIGM SHIFT: FROM MINORITIES PROTECTION TO EXPULSION AND POPULATION EXCHANGE

Arguably, in no area of international law was the impact of Eastern Europe and the Balkans as prominent for world affairs as in the paradigm shift which events in this region triggered concerning what once was known as 'population exchange' or the 'unmixing of peoples'. Considered as a sustainable solution to inter-ethnic tensions and ethno-political warfare, the forced population exchange executed under the League of Nations' auspices, pursuant to the terms of the Lausanne Convention Concerning the Exchange of Greek and Turkish Populations of 1923, quickly became the international legal go-to solution for the resolution of problems concerning ethno-religious minorities within majoritarian nation-states.[62]

See also B. Saul, 'The Legal Response of the League of Nations to Terrorism', *Journal of International Justice*, vol. 4 (1), 2006, pp. 78–102; and O. Ditrych, '"International Terrorism" as Conspiracy: Debating Terrorism in the League of Nations', *Historical Social Research*, vol. 38(1), 2013, pp. 200–210.

[61] D. Müller, 'Zu den Anfängen des Völkerstrafrechts. Vespasian Pella und Raphael Lemkin', in D. Müller and A. Skordos (eds.), *Leipziger Zugänge zur rechtlichen, politischen und kulturellen Verflechtungsgeschichte Ostmitteleuropas*, Leipzig: Leipziger Universitätsverlag, 2015, pp. 27–39.

[62] R. Hirschon (ed.), *Crossing the Aegean: An Appraisal of the 1923 Compulsory Population Exchange between Greece and Turkey*, New York: Berghahn, 2003; A. Th. Skordos, 'Die Konvention von Lausanne (1923) als völkerrechtliche Blaupause für Bevölkerungstransfers in Ostmitteleuropa, Asien und im Nahen Osten', in A. Th. Skordos (ed.), *Griechenland im Kontext des östlichen Europa. Geschichtsregionale, kulturelle und völkerrechtliche Dimensionen*, Leipzig: Leipziger Universitätsverlag, 2016, pp. 252–322.

Back in 1923, the 'Lausanne Accord' offered the international legal sanctioning for the forced displacement of some 1.8 million people. Seven decades later, in the Dayton Agreement for Peace in Bosnia and Herzegovina of 1995, forced migration became both *politically* and *legally* banned by the international community. The twentieth century, which began with the legalization of the uprooting of peoples in the Balkans, ended with the securement of their right of return as expellees and refugees, and obliged the domestic authorities to guarantee the safety of the returnees.[63] This landslide change in international legal thinking becomes evident when one compares the two core paragraphs of both treaties:

> As from the 1st May 1923, there shall take place a compulsory exchange of Turkish nationals of the Greek Orthodox religion established in Turkish territory, and of Greek nationals of the Moslem religions established in Greek territory.[64]
> All refugees and displaced persons have the right freely to return to their homes of origin.[65]

In 1995, coerced uprooting as enforced by state actors, which in 1923 had been considered *both* politically correct *and* perfectly legal, acquired the *moral* status of ethnic cleansing and the *international legal* status of a war crime, a crime against humanity, and – arguably, with regard to the Srebrenica massacre of 8000 Bosnian men and boys by Bosnian Serbs – genocide. Not only were the perpetrators tried, the expelled were also recognized the right to safe return. Soon after, the expulsion of some 900 000 Albanians from Kosovo into the neighbouring countries by regular and irregular Serbian armed forces in 1999 even triggered a forced international military intervention on behalf of the expellees, thus enabling their swift return. Thomas Franck labelled NATO Airstrike Operation Allied Force against rump-Yugoslavia technically illegal

---

[63] H. Adelman and E. Barkan, *No Return, No Refuge: Rites and Rights in Minority Repatriation*, New York: Columbia University Press, 2011; S. Troebst, 'Vom Bevölkerungstransfer zum Vertreibungsverbot – eine europäische Erfolgsgeschichte?', *Transit: Europäische Revue*, vol. 36, 2008/9, pp. 158–82.

[64] Convention Concerning the Exchange of Greek and Turkish Populations, Lausanne, 30 January 1923, *League of Nations Treaty Series*, vol. 32, pp. 76–87.

[65] Art. 1 of Annex 7 to the General Framework Agreement for Peace in Bosnia and Herzegovina, Agreement between the Republic of Bosnia and Herzegovina, the Federation of Bosnia and Herzegovina, and the Republika Srpska on Refugees and Displaced Persons, Paris, 21 November 1995, available at www.ohr.int/?page_id=63261.

but morally legitimate.[66] And even for a reluctant Antonio Cassese, under certain conditions '*ex iniuria ius oritur*'.[67]

The question remains, however, of what prompted between 1923 and the second half of the 1990s this 180-degree turnaround. Already in December 1922, shortly before the Lausanne Convention entered into force, the British foreign minister Lord Curzon had spoken of the idea of forced population exchange as recently propagated in Lausanne as a:

> thoroughly bad and vicious solution for which the world would pay a heavy penalty for a hundred years to come.[68]

Still, however, population exchange, be it based either on a formal treaty *à la Lausanne*, or more tacitly sanctioned by the international community as in the case of forced migrations in the second half of the 1940s, was legitimately considered by the international community as a meaningful measure of defusing ethno-political conflict. The decisions of the 'Big Three' in 1945 at the Potsdam Conference, with regard to the expulsion of some 12 million Germans from East Central Europe, the case of Slovenes and Croats in Trieste, and the 15 million Hindu–Muslim exchange between Pakistan and India in 1947, merely confirm this trend. To many jurists, including the current president of the OSCE's Court of Conciliation Christian Tomuschat, even the events in Cyprus as late as 1974 amounted to 'an exchange of population'.[69] And UN General Assembly Resolution 194(III) of 1948 on Palestine, which provided that 'refugees wishing to return to their homes, and live at peace with their neighbours, should be permitted to do so at the earliest practicable date', was merely 'hortatory', and 'did not contain the phrase right of return'.[70] Correspondingly, it had no consequences, not least thanks to the *deliberate* number of legal loopholes for the governmental actors involved.[71]

---

[66] T. M. Franck, *Recourse to Force: State Action against Threats and Armed Attacks*, Cambridge: Cambridge University Press, 2002, p. 70.

[67] A. Cassese, '*Ex iniuria ius oritur*: Are We Moving towards International Legitimation of Forcible Humanitarian Countermeasures in the World Community?', *European Journal of International Law*, vol. 10(1), 1999, pp. 22–44.

[68] Quoted after Stephen P. Ladas, *The Exchange of Minorities: Bulgaria, Greece, and Turkey*, New York: Macmillan, 1932, p. 341.

[69] C. Tomuschat, 'Prohibition on Settlements', in A. Clapham, P. Gaeta and M. Sassoli (eds.), *The Geneva Convention of 1949: A Commentary*, Oxford: Oxford University Press, pp. 1551–74, p. 1558.

[70] Adelman and Barkan, *No Return, No Refuge*, p. 203.

[71] R. Laipdoth, 'Israel and the Palestinians: Some Legal Issues', *Die Friedens-Warte*, vol. 76(2), 2001, pp. 211–40. On the deliberate murky wording of UNGA res. 194(III), 19 December 1948, see D. Forsythe, *United Nations Peacemaking: The Conciliation Commission for Palestine*, Baltimore: Johns Hopkins University Press, 1972, p. 29.

Lest one think that the international sanctioning of expulsion ended in 1974 in Cyprus, it should be mentioned that hardly any international protest took place when as late as 1989, the communist regime in Bulgaria (just a few months before its collapse) in the wake of a state-sponsored 'emigration hysteria' expelled some 370 000 of its own Turkish-speaking citizens of Muslim faith into neighbouring Turkey, in what would seem to be a massive violation of human rights, and most probably also a crime against humanity. The US Department of State and the Organization of Islamic Cooperation were virtually the only ones raising their voices in protest.[72]

And yet, merely six years after these events on the Turkish–Bulgarian border, an international paradigm shift seemed to have materialized in Bosnia – and another four years later in Kosovo. One possible answer as to the reasons behind the radical change between Lausanne and Dayton might have to do with the nexus between human rights and *realpolitik*. These of course are not always interlocking, but human rights might have had an impact on policy makers, because of two main factors: the bipolar world of the Cold War was very different from the multipolar one of the 1990s and due to technological progress of audio-visual media, the pictures from the concentration camps at Keraterm and Omarska run by Bosnian Serb forces surfaced around the world in no time.

BALKAN PERSPECTIVES ON INTERNATIONAL HUMANITARIAN LAW

To a historian of the Balkans what happened in 1998 and 1999 in Kosovo is not an entirely unknown scenario. The Kosovo Liberation Army's fight for independence from Belgrade quite obviously followed a conflict pattern developed by Greek and Macedonian insurgents against the Ottoman Empire during the nineteenth and early twentieth centuries. In this pattern, one can identify six stages:[73]

1. The emergence of a regional conflict of an asymmetric nature whose ideological bedrock lies in differences in ethno-political backgrounds.

---

[72] T. Kamusella, *Ethnic Cleansing During the Cold War: The Forgotten 1989 Expulsion of Turks from Communist Bulgaria*, London: Routledge, 2018; E. Kalinova, 'Remembering the "Revival Process" in Post-1989 Bulgaria', in M. Todorova, A. Dimou and S. Troebst (eds.), *Remembering Communism: Private and Public Recollections of Lived Experience in Southeast Europe*, Budapest: Central European University Press, 2014, pp. 567–93.

[73] S. Troebst, 'Von den Fanarioten zur UÇK: Nationalrevolutionäre Bewegungen auf dem Balkan und die "Ressource Weltöffentlichkeit"', in J. Requate and M. Schulze Wessel (eds.), *Europäische Öffentlichkeit. Transnationale Kommunikation seit dem 18.*

2. An appeal for help to the international public by the weaker party to the conflict.
3. An *overreaction* by the stronger party to the conflict in the form of massacres, ethnic cleansing, or even genocide, this reaction being invariably due to provocations by the weaker party, who supplies international media with harrowing reports and pictures.
4. Outrage by world public opinion and an increasing pressure on national and international political actors to intervene.
5. Intervention by national or international actors on behalf of the weaker side, with the result of a military solution (defeat, ceasefire, armistice), followed by a political solution (autonomy, protectorate, suzerainty, independence, etc.).
6. In the medium- or long-term: a change of norms of international law through the abolishment of previous norms, and the adoption of new ones.

The Kosovo War of 1999 and the earlier wars for Yugoslav succession from 1991 to 1995, together with the genocidal inter-ethnic conflict in Rwanda in 1994, triggered what Martti Koskenniemi has termed 'the turn to ethics in international law'. The adoption of the international principle of the Responsibility to Protect, the establishment of the International Criminal Tribunals for the former Yugoslavia (ICTY) and Rwanda (in 1993 and 1994, respectively), and the adoption of the Rome Statute establishing the International Criminal Court in 1998, all form part of this turn.[74] Accordingly, Theodor Meron, the Holocaust-surviving Polish-born president of the ICTY, could state:

> International humanitarian law has developed faster since the beginning of the atrocities in the former Yugoslavia than in the four-and-a-half decades since the Nuremberg Tribunals and the adoption of the Geneva Conventions for the Protection of Victims of War of August 12, 1949.[75]

A striking proof of this assessment is the fact that – based explicitly on the Bosnian experience – rape and other forms sexual violence in armed conflicts

---

Jahrhundert, Frankfurt: Campus, 2002, pp. 231–49; and T. Scheffler, 'Wenn hinten, weit, in der Türkei die Völker aufeinander schlagen . . .: Zum Funktionswandel "orientalischer" Gewalt in europäischen Öffentlichkeiten des 19. und 20. Jahrhunderts', in the same volume, pp. 205–30. See also D. D. Laitin, 'National Revivals and Violence', *Archives européennes de sociologie*, vol. 36(1), 1995, pp. 3–43.

[74] M. Koskenniemi, 'The Lady Doth Protest Too Much – Kosovo, and the Turn to Ethics in International Law', *Modern Law Review*, vol. 65(1), 2002, pp. 159–75.

[75] T. Meron, 'War Crimes Law Comes of Age', *American Journal of International Law*, vol. 92(3), 1998, pp. 462–8, p. 463.

are nowadays also considered as war crimes, crimes against humanity and even genocide.[76]

LOOKING THROUGH THE CONFLICT STORAGE MEDIUM'S HOURGLASS: EAST CENTRAL EUROPE'S INTERNATIONAL LEGAL LEGACY

With the body of today's modern international law so vast and wide, one might be excused for forgetting altogether where everything started. To return to the metaphor at the beginning of this chapter, Eastern Europe's experiences were the tiny insect around which the amber of today's international law began its development, yet can hardly be seen today. This merits a return to the point of departure.

For example, the European Commission on the Danube, a result of the Crimean War and in existence from 1856 to 1940, was the blueprint for a number of international organizations founded in later decades.[77] In 1930 the Permanent Court of International Justice provided for the first time the very definition of what it considered to be a legitimate 'minority' in its Advisory Opinion in the *Greco-Bulgarian Communities Case*.[78] Shortly after, that same Court set the rules for states to grant national minorities not only individual but also group rights in its 1935 Advisory Opinion on 'Minority Schools in Albania'.[79] To speak of minorities' rights is to speak firstly of the Balkans.

Similar path-breaking decisions in other branches of international law also stemmed from events in East Central Europe. The ICTY's judgment in the 1999 *Tadić* case, which established that the norms of international humanitarian law apply not only in international armed conflicts but also in

---

[76] A. M. L. M. de Brouwer, *Supranational Criminal Prosecution of Sexual Violence: The ICC and the Practice of the ICTY and the ICTR*, Antwerp: Intersentia, 2005; A. T. Skordos, 'Der Einfluss der postjugoslawischen Kriege auf die Ahndung sexualisierter Gewaltverbrechen im Völkerstrafrecht', in Müller and Skordos (eds.), *Leipziger Zugänge*, pp. 41–58.

[77] D. Müller, 'The Danube and the Danube Commissions in International Law', *Fifth European Congress on World and Global History, Ruptures, Empires, Revolutions*, Budapest 31 August – 3 September 2017 (on file with author).

[78] Permanent Court of International Justice, Advisory Opinion on the *Interpretation of the Convention Between Greece and Bulgaria Respecting Reciprocal Emigration, Signed at Neuilly-Sur Seine on November 27th, 1919 (Greco-Bulgarian 'Communities')*, 31 July 1930, PCIJ Series B, No. 17, 1930. The Court's definition can be found on p. 21. See also J. E. Nijman, 'Minorities and Majorities', in Fassbender and Peters (eds.), *The Oxford Handbook on the History of International Law*, pp. 95–119, p. 98, at note 7.

[79] Permanent Court of International Justice, Advisory Opinion on *Minority Schools in Albania*, 6 April 1935, PCIJ Ser. A./B., No. 64, 1935.

intra-state wars, is one example – this time from the branch of international humanitarian law.[80] The 1997 decision of the International Court of Justice in the *Gabčíkovo-Nagymaros* case concerning Hungary's refusal to stick to a 1977 treaty with Czechoslovakia on a dam across the Danube, where the Court clearly stressed that the principle of *clausula rebus sic stantibus* applies even after Hungary's regime change and the 'Velvet Divorce' of Slovakia from the Czech Republic, and this notwithstanding the negative effects on the economy and the ecology, is another example – this time concerning international procedural law.[81]

Of course, not all innovations originating in Eastern Europe were of lasting effect. This goes, for instance, for the temporary establishment of Free Cities. This was 'invented' at the Congress of Vienna in 1815 and applied to the West Galician capital of Cracow (till 1846), revitalized at the Paris Peace Conference of 1919/20 for Danzig (till 1939/45) and 'buried' in Osimo in 1975 when Italy and Yugoslavia sanctioned the 1954 division among themselves of the Free Territory of Trieste provided for in 1947.[82]

To come back to the metaphor of the provisions of international law as a storage medium of conflict memory, we return again to the amber gem enclosing an insect. In looking at this tiny insect through the magnifying glass, we often have difficulties even determining to which species it belongs, let alone the exact place on earth where it fell into the fossil resin in the first case. In the case of the history of international law, more often than not, this place was somewhere in Europe's 'other lung' in the East.

Thus a statement by Putin at the festive session on the occasion of the 60th anniversary of the International Court of Justice on 22 November 2005 contains more than a grain of truth:

> This innovative idea [of establishing a permanent international court] was born in our country and it was self-denyingly propagated by progressive representatives of the Russian legal science.[83]

---

[80] C. Greenwood, 'International Humanitarian Law and the *Tadic* Case', *European Journal of International Law*, vol. 7(2), 1996, pp. 265–83.

[81] International Court of Justice, *Gabčíkovo-Nagymaros (Hungary v. Slovakia)*, Judgment of 25 September 1997, *ICJ Reports* 1997, p. 7.

[82] T. Schweisfurth, *Völkerrecht*, Tübingen: Mohr Siebeck, 2006, pp. 27 and 290.

[83] V. V. Putin, 'Vystuplenie na zasedanii Meždunarodnogo Suda Organizacii Ob-edinennych Nacij', *Gaaga, Dvorec Mira*, 22 November 2005, available at http://kremlin.ru/events/president/transcripts/23247/audios. For the context, see L. Mälksoo, 'Case Law in Russian Approaches in International Law', in Roberts et al. (eds.), *Comparative International Law*, pp. 337–52, p. 342.

However, in April 2017 the ICJ as the principal judicial organ of the UN by thirteen votes to three, ordered that Russia

> [r]efrain from maintaining or imposing limitations on the ability of the Crimean Tatar community to conserve its representative institutions, including the Mejlis; refrain from imposing limitations on the ability of the Crimean Tatar community to conserve its representative institutions, including the *Mejlis*.[84]

The fact remains that this was ignored by the Russian occupation authorities on the Ukrainian peninsula of Crimea as well as by the president of the Russian Federation.

---

[84] International Court of Justice, *Application of the International Convention for the Suppression of the Financing of Terrorism and of the International Convention on the Elimination of All Forms of Racial Discrimination (Ukraine v. Russian Federation)*, provisional measures, Order of 19 April 2017, *ICJ Reports* 2017, p. 107, p. 40, at para. 106.

PART II

History and international human rights law

3. History, isolation and effectiveness of human rights

Annalisa Ciampi[*]

INTRODUCTION

Human rights, international trade law, international investment law, and international development law emerged, and largely developed, along separate paths. While historically interrelated, they have evolved in distinct, partly overlapping, partly conflicting regimes, consisting of norms and institutions independent of each other. Human rights rules and principles differ from those governing trade, investment or development assistance in their normative structure, legal framework, institutional settings, as well as their dispute settlement mechanisms.[1]

This chapter is about the intertwined relationship between history and human rights. From history to international law, it reconstructs the main phases that have led to the relative isolation of human rights law from international trade and investment law as well as international development law. From international law to history, it reflects on the 'power' of human rights norms

---

[*] This chapter builds upon an article originally published in volume 61 (2018) of the *German Yearbook of International Law*.

[1] A lot has been written about the history of these various areas of international law and their relative isolation from each other. See in particular M. Koskenniemi, 'A History of International Law Histories', in B. Fassbender and A. Peters (eds.), *The Oxford Handbook of the History of International Law*, Oxford: Oxford University Press 2012, p. 943. See also A. Becker Lorca, 'Eurocentrism in the History of International Law', in Fassbender and Peters (eds.), *The Oxford Handbook of the History of International Law*, p. 1034; I. De La Rasilla del Moral, 'The Shifting Origins of International Law', *Leiden Journal of International Law*, vol. 28(3), 2015, pp. 419–40; A. Orford, 'International Law and the Limits of History', in W. Werner, M. de Hoon and A. Galán (eds.), *The Law of International Lawyers: Reading Martti Koskenniemi*, Cambridge: Cambridge University Press, 2017, p. 297. Lastly see S. Moyn, *The Last Utopia: Human Rights in History*, Cambridge, MA and London: Harvard University Press, 2010, pp. 11–43.

and institutions to positively affect historical developments. It also accounts for recent normative and diplomatic efforts that aim to overcome the divide. The chapter considers that the particular historical evolution of human rights as distinct from other domains of global governance is at the origin of its current 'effectiveness' crisis. It thus argues for the desirability, and inquires into the feasibility, of bridging existing divides. History explains the relative isolation of human rights. International law should pave the way for more coherence between human rights and economic and development policies.

THE FAILURES OF THE UNITARY DESIGN OF THE UDHR AND THE HAVANA CHARTER IN THE AFTERMATH OF THE SECOND WORLD WAR

The Universal Declaration of Human Rights (UDHR) proclaimed by the UN General Assembly in Paris on 10 December 1948, under the heading 'International Bill of Human Rights',[2] is generally agreed to be a milestone document in the history of human rights and the foundation of international human rights law.[3] Drafted by representatives with different legal and cultural backgrounds from all regions of the world, the UDHR set out, for the first time, fundamental human rights to be universally protected.

Although it does not provide for democracy as a right in itself, the Declaration refers explicitly to democracy by way of limiting the purview of rights derogations.[4] And it recognizes the link between human rights and

---

[2] Universal Declaration of Human Rights (UDHR) 1948, United Nations General Assembly (UNGA) Res. 217A (III), 10 December 1948.

[3] As is well known, the Charter of the United Nations 1945, 15 UNCIO 335, envisaged respect for human rights protection as something to be encouraged and promoted. See Art. 1(3) ('The Purposes of the United Nations are: [. . .] To achieve international cooperation [. . .] in promoting and encouraging respect for human rights and for fundamental freedoms for all without distinction as to race, sex, language, or religion'), Art. 55(c) ('the United Nations shall promote: [. . .] universal respect for, and observance of, human rights and fundamental freedoms for all without distinction as to race, sex, language, or religion') and Art. 56 ('All Members pledge themselves to take joint and separate action in cooperation with the Organization for the achievement of the purposes set forth in Article 55'). These articles, with other provisions, have been called a 'golden thread' running through the Charter, which established human rights as a matter of international concern. D. L. Shelton, *Advanced Introduction to International Human Rights Law*, Cheltenham, UK and Northampton, MA, USA: Edward Elgar Publishing, 2014, pp. 31–2.

[4] Under Art. 29(2) UDHR, national limitations on the rights catalogued in the Declaration shall, *inter alia*, 'meet the just requirements of morality, public order and the general welfare *in a democratic society*' (emphasis added). In addition, Art. 21(1) UDHR proclaims an important element of democracy, namely, a right 'to take part in

economic and social conditions.[5] The UDHR thus encapsulated in a single document the progressive realization of democracy and development through the universal and effective recognition and observance of rights – with no distinction between mostly 'negative' classical civil and political rights, and essentially 'positive' economic, social and cultural rights (ESC), and collective rights. It was not, however, a treaty in the formal sense. While several authoritarian states (including the former Soviet Union and Yugoslavia, Poland, Czechoslovakia and Saudi Arabia) abstained, not even all liberal democracies were ready to bind themselves to its legal obligations.[6]

The ensuing *Cold War* significantly 'froze' possibilities for UN action. In turn, human rights became 'yoked to the ideological conflict' between the United States (US) (as leader of the Western countries) and the Soviet Union (along with its satellites).[7] Deep political disagreement and profoundly different conceptions of rights between the Western and non-Western worlds – which now included not only former socialist states but also the newly independent, developing states – led to the sub-division of human rights into three categories: the so called 'first generation' rights, known as civil and political rights, ESC as 'second generation' rights, and 'group rights' as 'third generation' rights.[8] It took eighteen years for the signature of the first universal

---

the government [. . .] directly or through freely chosen representatives'. Moreover, an explicit requirement of holding elections on the basis of equal and universal suffrage is contained in section 3, which proclaims that 'the will of the people shall be the basis of the authority of the government'.

[5] Art. 28 UDHR provides: 'Everyone is entitled to a social and international order in which the rights and freedoms set forth in this Declaration can be fully realized'.

[6] The resolution was adopted with – of the then 58 members of the United Nations (UN) – 48 members in favour and 8 abstaining. Two did not vote.

[7] E. A. Posner, *The Twilight of Human Rights Law*, New York: Oxford University Press, 2014, p. 18.

[8] See R. J. Vincent, *Human Rights and International Relations*, Cambridge: Cambridge University Press, 1986, p. 61. For a survey of the development of human rights during the Cold War era and the claim that the history of East–West relations was 'in an important sense the history of a dispute about human rights', see S. Soiffer and D. Rowlands, 'Examining the Indivisibility of Human Rights: A Statistical Analysis', *Journal of Human Rights*, vol. 17(1), 2018, p. 89, p. 103:

> The initial division of human rights was largely the result of Cold War politics. The Soviet bloc and developing states were in favour of a binding treaty that addressed what have come to be known as economic, social, and cultural rights but looked unfavourably on civil and political rights. The Anglo-American sphere, in contrast, took the opposite view.

For the opinion that Cold War politics were not the only factors that led to the division of UN recognized human rights into two distinct categories see C. Scott, 'Interdependence and Permeability Of Human Rights Norms: Towards Partial Fusion of the International Covenants on Human Rights', *Osgoode Hall Law*

instruments for the protection of a wide scope of international human rights – the International Covenant on Civil and Political Rights (ICCPR) and the International Covenant on Economic, Social and Cultural Rights (ICESCR) of 1966[9] – and then another decade for their entry into force.[10]

The adoption of the UN Covenants as two separate instruments marks the formal split between first and second generation of rights and the setting aside of collective rights. The first divide concerns both the substance of state obligations – ESC shall be progressively realized, rather than directly implemented[11] – and the supervisory mechanism, with only the ICCPR being endowed with a monitoring system which includes the right of individual complaint. Even after the entry into force of the recently adopted additional protocol to the ICESCR,[12] the systems are different, as are the numbers of ratifications of the Covenants themselves and the rate of acceptance of their optional protocols.[13] The vision of rights into 'generations' remains also at the regional level, particularly within the Council of Europe, which is considered to be the most advanced regional system for human rights protection.[14]

Journal, vol. 27(3), 1989, p. 769. For a challenge to the widespread belief that Western countries have been antagonistic to economic and social human rights, see D. Whelan and J. Donnelly, 'The West, Economic and Social Rights, and the Global Human Rights Regime', *Human Rights Quarterly*, vol. 29(4), 2007, p. 908.

[9] International Covenant on Civil and Political Rights (ICCPR) 1966, 999 UNTS 171; International Covenant on Economic, Social and Cultural Rights (ICESCR) 1966, 993 UNTS 3.

[10] The ICCPR was adopted by the UNGA Res. 2200A (XXI), 16 December 1966 and entered into force on 23 March 1976. The ICESCR was opened for signature in New York on 19 December 1966 and entered into force on 3 January 1976.

[11] In accordance with Art. 2(1) ICESCR: 'Each State Party to the present Covenant undertakes to take steps, individually and through international assistance and co-operation, especially economic and technical, to the maximum of its available resources, with a view to achieving progressively the full realization of the rights recognized in the present Covenant by all appropriate means, including particularly the adoption of legislative measures.'

[12] Optional Protocol to the ICESCR 2008, UN Doc. A/63/435, adopted by the UNGA on 10 December 2008 and opened for signature on 24 September 2009. It entered into force on 5 May 2013.

[13] As of 30 September 2019, the ICCPR has 173 state parties and its First Additional Protocol 116. The ICESCR has 170 parties, its Additional Protocol 24. In the literature, the generations of human rights narrative has been abandoned by S. L. B. Jensen, 'Putting to Rest the Three Generations Theory of Human Rights', *OpenGlobalRights*, 15 November 2017, available at www.openglobalrights.org/putting-to-rest-the-three-generations-theory-of-human-rights. See also P. Macklem, *The Sovereignty of Human Rights*, New York: Oxford University Press, 2015.

[14] The Council of Europe was established by ten Western European states in 1949. It has since expanded to include Central and Eastern European countries, bringing the total membership to 47 states. Membership in the Council is conditioned upon adher-

In parallel to this development of the human rights movement, the years immediately after the Second World War (itself partially the result of the economic recession of the 1930s) saw another setback – the failure of the Havana Charter for an International Trade Organization (Havana Charter).[15] The global inability to adopt this treaty resulted in a twofold split: the divide between international economic law and development and, within the first pillar, between trade and investment.

Under the leadership of the US and the United Kingdom who acted through their self-dominated United Nations Economic and Social Council, a Preparatory drafting Committee, which met between 1946 and 1947, produced a draft charter for the creation of an International Trade Organization. On 21 November 1947, fifty-seven states met in Cuba as part of the UN Conference on Trade and Employment, with the explicit aim of finalizing the drafting of the proposal which became the Charter for an International Trade Organization (ITO).[16] Because of the lack of ratification of the Charter by the US Congress, the ITO never came into existence. This resulted in the abandonment of the ITO altogether by the other states that had originally taken part in the negotiations.[17]

In addition to a chapter on commercial policy – the provisions of which already featured in the General Agreement on Tariffs and Trade (GATT, the forerunner of the World Trade Organization (WTO)) – the Havana Charter covered disciplines such as employment and economic activity and regulated a number of substantive matters. These included fair labour standards, economic development, and reconstruction (including cooperation for development and investment), restrictive business practices, procedures relating to services and commodity agreements.[18]

---

ence to the Convention for the Protection of Human Rights and Fundamental Freedoms (ECHR) 1950, 213 UNTS 221, the first human rights treaty of the post-war period, followed by the European Social Charter – which has a distinct monitoring mechanism – in 1961. See D. Shelton, *Advanced Introduction to International Human Rights Law*, p. 35.

[15] Havana Charter for an International Trade Organization 1948, UN Doc. E/CONF.2/78, 24 March 1948 (as explained in the text, the Havana Charter did not enter into force due to lack of instruments of acceptance within its prescribed time frame).

[16] R. N. Gardner, *Sterling–Dollar Diplomacy: Anglo-American Collaboration in the Reconstruction of Multilateral Trade*, Oxford: Clarendon Press, 1956, p. 42.

[17] S. Woolcock, 'The ITO, the GATT and the WTO', in N. Bayne and S. Woolcock (eds.), *The New Economic Diplomacy: Decision-Making and Negotiation in International Economic Relations*, Aldershot: Ashgate, 2003, p. 103, p. 112; S. Lester, B. Mercurio and A. Davies, *World Trade Law: Text, Materials and Commentary*, 3rd ed., Oxford: Hart Publishing, 2018, p. 57.

[18] For a comprehensive account, see G. Sacerdoti, 'The Havana Charter', in R. Wolfrum (ed.), *Max Planck Encyclopaedia of Public International Law*, 2014, available

Most notably, the Charter proclaimed that the avoidance of unemployment or underemployment was necessary for achieving the expansion of trade (Article 2). It required members to take into account workers' rights under international declarations, conventions, and agreements, and to eliminate unfair labour conditions 'through whatever action may be appropriate and feasible' (Article 7). The Charter also covered specific aspects of competition by addressing unfair business practices (Article 46). On international investment, it established that international investment can be of great value in promoting economic development and reconstruction, and consequent social progress (Article 12).[19]

GATT, which was originally to be a specific trade agreement within the broader institutional context of the Havana Charter, entered into force on 1 January 1948. It provided an alternative to realize the trade interests of the US and other countries, without having to make the concessions that had been requested under the ITO. Tariffs concessions and more generally the liberalization of trade relations were set as objectives distinct and separate from that of development and were regulated for almost fifty years under the GATT. Investment fell within the separate purview of a network of bilateral investment treaties (BITs).

The failure of the Havana Charter was thus at the origin of a twofold divide, the effects of which materialized during the Cold War: the separation between international economic law and what would later become international development law,[20] and the divide between trade and investment – the latter wholly internal to the international normative and institutional framework of economic relations.

The offshoots of these multiple divides of the aftermaths of the Second World War – that will be referred to in modern times as the 'fragmentation' of international law[21] – were multiple in turn.

---

at http://opil.ouplaw.com/view/10.1093/law:epil/9780199231690/law-9780199231690 -e1529.

[19] In anticipation of a debate that is still ongoing, however, these provisions were seen by developing states as overly protective of multinational enterprises, while developed states considered them too protective of host countries. Sacerdoti, 'The Havana Charter', at paras. 20–1.

[20] See the next paragraph.

[21] M. Koskenniemi, 'Fragmentation of International Law: Difficulties arising from the Diversification and Expansion of International Law', *Report of the Study Group of the International Law Commission*, UN Doc. A/CN.4/L.682, 13 April 2006.

DECOLONIZATION, THE FAILURE OF THE NIEO, THE EMERGENCE OF HUMAN RIGHTS AND THE END OF THE COLD WAR

The beginning of decolonization during the late 1950s, and its unfolding during the 1960s all through to the 1970s (and beyond) brought about the emergence of new international actors. This was the period of the rise and fall of the New International Economic Order (NIEO) and the emergence of human rights as a major force in international relations.

In 1964, the UN Conference on Trade and Development was set up as a counter to GATT and used by developing countries, particularly following the oil crisis of 1973, to press for changes in the management of the global economic system. The newly independent states in Africa and South America formed a new bloc of countries, the Non-Aligned Movement, apart from the largely developed Western states and the Soviet bloc.

Sponsored by these states that at the time formed the majority of the UN General Assembly, the NIEO was proclaimed unanimously by way of a Declaration and a Programme of Action on its establishment in May 1974.[22] It was to be founded on full respect of a set of principles, including: the broadest cooperation of all states based on equity, whereby the prevailing disparities in the world may be banished and prosperity secured for all, and full and effective participation on the basis of equality; the right of every country to adopt the economic and social system that it deems the most appropriate for its own development; and full permanent sovereignty of every state over its natural resources and all economic activities.

By way of these proclamations, the UN pledged to take action on inequities and injustices in the international system, eliminate the gap between developed and developing countries, ensure accelerating economic and social development, and secure peace and justice. International cooperation in economic

---

[22] UNGA Res. 3201 (S-VI), 1 May 1974 (Declaration on the Establishment of a New International Economic Order); UNGA Res. 3202 (S-VI), 1 May 1974 (Programme of Action on the Establishment of a New International Economic Order). For the view that 'these founding documents are mostly of historical interest for international relations', see G. Sacerdoti, 'New International Economic Order (NIEO)', in Wolfrum (ed.), *Max Planck Encyclopaedia of Public International Law*, 2015, at para. 19, available at

http://opil.ouplaw.com/view/10.1093/law:epil/9780199231690/law-9780199231690-e1542?prd=EPIL. On the NIEO see also H. W. Singer, 'The New International Economic Order: An Overview', *Journal of Modern African Studies*, vol. 16(4), 1978, p. 539. See also F. M. Gebremariam, 'New International Economic Order (NIEO): Origin, Elements and Criticisms', *International Journal of Multicultural and Multireligious Understanding*, vol. 4(3), 2017, p. 22.

matters and the furtherance of development were thus to proceed hand in hand. Developing countries had to be assisted by industrialized nations to achieve sustained development on terms chosen by developing countries themselves. At the same time, the latter should not be subject to reciprocal obligations and should be protected from external interference.[23] However, when the Charter of Economic Rights and Duties of States,[24] which was to turn into reality these proclamations of principles, was adopted, its approval was not unanimous. Among the developed states, six abstained and ten voted against. And for the most part, the general strategy of rich countries was to broadly reject the NIEO.

Some efforts were made to provide developing countries with additional trade preferences. While the original text of the General Agreement did not allow for preferences, Part IV of GATT on 'Trade and Development' (added in 1964) had dropped the reciprocity requirement for developing countries when developed countries negotiated (non-preferential) concessions with them. In 1979, the principle of non-reciprocal trade relations and the establishment of generalized systems of preferences accepted through a temporary waiver of the most-favoured nation treatment obligation in 1971, became a GATT permanent feature (the so-called 'Enabling Clause'). The International Monetary Fund created a trust fund to help developing countries by selling off a third of its gold holdings, particularly by the Europeans. A few agreements were also signed, for example in sugar and rubber, to ensure the stability of commodities prices for which developing countries were the main producers.

Trade preferences and non-reciprocity, however, remain the most important legacy of the NIEO. 'Abandoned' by the Western world, the furtherance of development became the remit of the developing countries, the UN and its specialized agencies. It took another decade for the UN General Assembly to proclaim the right to development as an inalienable 'third generation', solidarity human right, with the Declaration on the Right to Development (1986),[25] and

---

[23] Sacerdoti, 'New International Economic Order (NIEO)', at para. 14. See also M. Wionczek, 'The New International Economic Order: Past Failures and Future Prospects', *Development and Change*, vol. 10(4), 1979, pp. 647–71; P. S. Golub, 'From the New International Economic Order to the G20: How the "Global South" is Restructuring World Capitalism from Within', *Third World Quarterly*, vol. 34(6), 2013, p. 1000; X. Chongli, 'The Rise of Newly Emerging Countries and the Construction of a New International Economic Order: A Perspective from the Chinese Path', *Social Sciences in China*, vol. 34(1), 2013, p. 22; W. S. Thompson (ed.), *The Third World: Premises of US Policy*, San Francisco: Institute for Contemporary Studies, 1978, pp. 123–48.

[24] UNGA Res. 3281 (XXIX), 12 December 1974 (Charter of Economic Rights and Duties of States).

[25] UNGA Res. 41/128, 4 December 1986 (Declaration on the Right to Development). On the Declaration and its subsequent developments, see UN High Commissioner for

to call for the adoption of a strategy for sustainable development (1987).[26] The failure of the NIEO thus marked the definite separation between international economic law, in which market sector principles prevailed, and international development law, and paved the way to the duality of their respective regimes.

Because of the limited availability of official development assistance, and despite the rejection of a customary standard for investment liberalization and protection, developed states felt the need to attract foreign investment in order to meet their own economic development goals, especially after the debt crisis in the 1980s. They, therefore, undertook international commitments – mostly in the form of bilateral treaties – that guaranteed a minimum level of treatment, so as to protect foreign investors from the uncertainties of customary international law on the economic rights of aliens, weak governance in 'new' states and the only recent adoption by many of them of the market economy model. Hence the failure of the NIEO also relinquished the issue of protection of developed states' investors in developing states to BITs, which in a few decades became the truly global phenomenon that we know today.

In parallel to these developments, international human rights law began to exercise its influence. It is generally acknowledged that in the 1960s and more prominently in the 1970s and 1980s, human rights became a major force in international relations.[27]

1975 was the year of the Helsinki Accords and the beginning of the Helsinki process. Despite their lack of formal status as international treaties setting out binding commitments, the Helsinki Accords provided a framework for the scrutiny of human rights practice in the former Soviet Union and the states in

---

Human Rights (OHCHR), 'Development is a Human Right', available at www.ohchr.org/EN/Issues/Development/Pages/DevelopmentIndex.aspx.

[26] Report of the World Commission on Environment and Development: Our Common Future ('Brundtland Report'), UN Doc. A/42/427, 4 August 1987. On the multiple layers of international development law, which continue to shape the contemporary regime of development – the human rights dimension, the concept of sustainable development and the debates about development and good governance – see S. W. Schill, C. J. Tams and R. Hofmann, 'International Investment Law and Development: Friends or Foes?', in S. W. Schill (ed.), *International Investment Law and Development: Bridging the Gap*, Cheltenham, UK and Northampton, MA, USA: Edward Elgar Publishing, 2015, p. 3, p. 14.

[27] Moyn, *The Last Utopia*, pp. 176–211. See also S. L. B. Jensen, *The Making of International Human Rights: The 1960s, Decolonization, and the Reconstruction of Global Values*, New York: Cambridge University Press, 2016. Jensen here reinterprets the history of international human rights in the post-1945 era by documenting how pivotal the Global South – namely Jamaica, Liberia, Ghana and the Philippines – was for their breakthrough in the 1960s, laying the foundation – in profound and surprising ways – for the so-called human rights revolution in the 1970s, when Western activists and states began to embrace human rights.

its area of influence.[28] The Soviet Union ratified the ICCPR in 1973. In 1977, the US Congress passed a law conditioning certain types of aid to compliance with human rights.[29] The Convention on the Elimination of All Forms of Discrimination against Women was adopted in 1979, based on a General Assembly resolution sponsored by twenty-two developing countries and some East European states.[30] The Convention against Torture – which remains a milestone in the protection of the most fundamental human rights – was signed in 1984.[31] Following a proposal by Poland and other countries of the Soviet bloc, the Convention on the Rights of the Child was opened to signature in 1989.[32]

Yet, the end of the Cold War in 1989–91 was not a triumph of human rights or a direct result thereof. The collapse of the Soviet Union was not caused by its human rights violations, or by domestic or international opposition fuelled by those violations.[33] The real historical causes are of a socio-economic nature and lay in the failure of the Soviet system to deliver economic prosperity due to the inefficiencies of the Soviet command economy, which remained technologically backward and full of corruption, as well as the decline in the price of oil – one of the Soviet Union's assets, together with gold and natural gas.[34]

---

[28] On the impact of the Helsinki Accord on bringing about systemic change to the Cold War order, see D. C. Thomas, *The Helsinki Effect: International Norms, Human Rights, and the Demise of Communism*, Princeton, NJ: Princeton University Press, 2001. Thomas contends that the signing of the Helsinki Accord, for most of the Eastern bloc countries, opened up the floodgates of liberalization and democratization by providing the means for both domestically mobilized and transnational groups to work together.

[29] The Foreign Assistance Act promises that no financial assistance will be given to states engaging 'in a consistent pattern of gross violations of internationally recognized human rights' (United States (US) Code Title 21, § 2151n). The same will be true to a larger or smaller extent for practically all developed countries and for the European Community.

[30] Convention on the Elimination of All Forms of Discrimination against Women 1979, 1249 UNTS 13.

[31] Convention against Torture and Other Cruel, Inhuman or Degrading Treatment or Punishment 1984, 1465 UNTS 85.

[32] Convention on the Rights of the Child 1989, 1577 UNTS 3.

[33] Posner, *The Twilight of Human Rights Law*, p. 21: 'But with the collapse of the Soviet Union, the major ideological alternative to liberal democracy was gone, and so was the only country that could prevent the United States from imposing its values (for good or ill) on foreign countries.'

[34] R. Strayer, *Why Did the Soviet Union Collapse? Understanding Historical Change*, New York: Routledge, 2015, p. 56; P. Hanson, *The Rise and Fall of the Soviet Economy: An Economic History of the USSR from 1945*, New York: Routledge, p. 218.

THE DIVIDE BETWEEN THE THEORY AND PRACTICE OF INTERNATIONAL HUMAN RIGHTS

In the post-Cold War, post-decolonization era, the existence of an international human rights regime is well established. While not all countries have ratified all human rights treaties, most countries have ratified most of them. Moreover, some treaties – including the ICCPR and the Convention on the Rights of the Child – have been ratified nearly by all states and each of the six major human rights treaties have more than 150 parties.

The UN Office of the High Commissioner for Human Rights (OHCHR) was established in 1993, with the task of the coordination and leadership of the multiple human rights bodies existing at the universal level and established under the UN Charter and international human rights treaties. The OHCHR is guided in its work by UN General Assembly resolution 48/141,[35] the UN Charter, the UDHR and subsequent human rights instruments, the 1993 Vienna Declaration and Programme of Action,[36] and the 2005 World Summit Outcome Document.[37] Its mandate includes preventing human rights violations, securing respect for all human rights, promoting international cooperation to protect human rights, coordinating related activities throughout the UN, and strengthening and streamlining UN human rights work. In addition to its mandated responsibilities, the OHCHR should lead efforts to integrate a human rights approach within all work carried out by the UN system.[38]

Taking on human rights-related causes becomes one of the most important functions of non-governmental organizations (NGOs) around the world. In the 1990s, NGOs focusing on human rights issues increase in number and activities.[39] While the determination of what NGOs do best remains an area of continuing scholarly debate,[40] NGOs have influenced the human rights practices of governments and popular perceptions of human rights.

---

[35] UNGA Res. 48/141, 20 December 1993.

[36] World Conference on Human Rights, Vienna Declaration and Programme of Action, 25 June 1993, UN Doc. A/CONF.157/24.

[37] UNGA Res. 60/1, 24 October 2005.

[38] For the official policy of the Organization, see the OHCHR, official website, available at https://www.ohchr.org/EN/pages/home.aspx.

[39] For an overview of the most important human rights NGOs, see the database of NGOs with Consultative Status with ECOSOC, available at https://esango.un.org/civilsociety/login.do; the World Association of Non-Governmental Organizations, available at https://www.wango.org; and the Human Rights NGOs list from Duke University Library, available at https://library.duke.edu/research/subject/guides/ngo_guide/ngo_database.

[40] See e.g. C. E. Welch, Jr. (ed.), *NGOs and Human Rights: Promise and Performance*, Philadelphia: University of Pennsylvania Press, 2000. This volume

As advocacy organizations, human rights NGOs work with or against governments in developing agendas for action. Through treaty negotiations with governments, they seek to establish international standards for state behaviour. To mobilize public opinion, they investigate and report human rights abuses and offer direct assistance to victims of those abuses. They lobby political officials, corporations, international financial institutions, intergovernmental organizations, and the media. NGOs are also increasingly involved in providing services, such as holding training programmes for upholding the rule of law and providing humanitarian assistance in disaster areas.

While states remain the major protectors – and abusers – of human rights, NGOs such as Amnesty International and Human Rights Watch emerged as central players in the promotion of human rights around the world. Amnesty International – launched in 1961 by lawyer Peter Benenson through the 'Appeal for Amnesty' in the *Observer* newspaper, after two Portuguese students were jailed for raising a toast to freedom – evolved from seeking the release of political prisoners to upholding the whole spectrum of human rights: from abolishing the death penalty to protecting sexual and reproductive rights, and from combating discrimination to defending refugees and migrants' rights – 'for anyone and everyone whose freedom and dignity are under threat'.[41] Human Rights Watch, which began in 1978 with the creation of Helsinki Watch designed to support the citizens groups formed throughout the Soviet bloc to monitor government compliance with the 1975 Helsinki Accords,[42] formally adopted the all-inclusive name Human Rights Watch, in 1988. The new human rights challenges in the 1990s led to important innovations in, and further broadened and strengthened, its work.[43]

---

assesses the performance of NGOs by examining a number of significant organizations, including Amnesty International, Human Rights Watch and the International Commission of Jurists. The authors identify the goals of such organizations, analyse their strategies, and consider the resources necessary to implement those strategies effectively. They also look at some of the major financial supporters of NGOs and reveal evidence that transnational networks of organizations can both exert pressure on states and influence public opinion, resulting in the improved protection of human rights around the world.

[41] For a full historical account of Amnesty International's story and current campaigns see Amnesty International, available at www.amnesty.org/en.

[42] Helsinki Watch adopted a methodology of publicly 'naming and shaming' abusive governments through media coverage and through direct exchanges with policymakers. By shining the international spotlight on human rights violations in the Soviet Union and Eastern Europe, Helsinki Watch contributed to the dramatic democratic transformations of the late 1980s.

[43] In its reporting on the 1991 Persian Gulf War, Human Rights Watch for the first time addressed violations of the laws of war in bombing campaigns. In 1997, HRW

The 1990s was also the era when the legal theory of *jus cogens* emerged and permeated diplomatic intercourses (within the UN and in interstate relations), judicial arguments in national and international fora, and the academic debate.[44] As is well known, *jus cogens* refers to rules of customary international law that bind all states, irrespective of ratification of the relevant treaties, and cannot be derogated from under any circumstances.[45] They are generally held to include the prohibition of torture, genocide, and other serious breaches of human rights.[46] Moreover, according to the ensuing prevailing narrative, it is held that the absoluteness of these prohibitions would eventually prevent breaches, and ensure respect, of the most fundamental human rights. Events, however, would make a mockery of this view, notwithstanding the developments at the normative, institutional and operational level described above.

The European Union (EU) was established by the Maastricht Treaty 1992 (TEU),[47] bringing within one 'temple', i.e. under a single institutional framework, the European Communities and the activities of the member states in the

---

shared in the Nobel Peace Prize as a founding member of the International Campaign to Ban Landmines. See Human Rights Watch, available at www.hrw.org.

[44] In the extensive literature on the subject, see e.g. L. Hannikainen, *Peremptory Norms (Jus Cogens) in International Law*, Helsinki: Finnish Lawyers' Publishing Company, 1988; A. L. Paulus, 'Jus Cogens in a Time of Emergency and Fragmentation: An Attempt at a Re-appraisal', *Nordic Journal of International Law*, vol. 74(3), 2005, p. 297; C. Tomuschat and J. Thouvenin (eds.), *The Fundamental Rules of the International Legal Order*, Leiden and Boston: Koninklijke Brill, 2006; A. Orakhelashvili, *Peremptory Norms in International Law*, Oxford: Oxford University Press, 2008; B. Fassbender, *The United Nations Charter as the Constitution of the International Community*, Leiden and Boston: Martinus Nijhoff Publishers/Koninklijke Brill, 2009; J. A. Frowein, 'Jus Cogens', in Wolfrum (ed.), *Max Planck Encyclopaedia of Public International Law*, 2013, available at http://opil.ouplaw.com/view/10.1093/law:epil/9780199231690/law-9780199231690-e1437?prd=EPIL.

[45] According to the well-known definition of Art. 53 of the Vienna Convention on the Law of Treaties 1969, 1155 UNTS 331, a *jus cogens* norm is one which permits of no derogation and which can be modified only by a subsequent norm having that same character.

[46] See e.g. E. De Wet, 'The Prohibition of Torture as an International Norm of Jus Cogens and Its Implications for National and Customary Law', *European Journal of International Law*, vol. 15(1), 2004, p. 97; L. MacGregor, 'State Immunity and *Jus Cogens*', *International & Comparative Law Quarterly*, vol. 55(2), 2006, p. 437; O. Spiermann, 'Humanitarian Intervention as a Necessity and the Threat or Use of Jus Cogens', *Nordic Journal of International Law*, vol. 71(4), 2002, p. 523; J. Verhoeven, 'Droit des traités, réserves et ordre public (*jus cogens*)', *Journal des tribunaux*, vol. 13, 1994, p. 765; E. Kornicker, 'State Community Interests, *Jus Cogens* and Protection of the Global Environment', *Georgetown International Environmental Law Review*, vol. 11(1), 1998, p. 101.

[47] Treaty on European Union (TEU) 2002, OJ 2012 C 326/13 (Consolidated Version).

fields of Foreign and Security Policy and Justice and Home Affairs (the latter included at the time the areas of asylum, immigration, judicial cooperation in civil and criminal matters, and police cooperation). Human rights – long protected by the European Court of Justice as unwritten general principles – are formally recognized as a matter of EU domestic constitutional law (Article 6 TEU). Human rights acquire a prominent role as a limit to the legitimacy of acts by both the EU institutions and the member states (when acting within the scope of EU law).[48] They also officially enter the benchmarks to be met by new members before they obtain the economic benefits of the European Internal Market (Article 49 TEU). This, however, will be at the origin of the divide between requirements demanded from third states applying for membership to the EU and internal standards. The treaties provide that respect for human rights, democracy, and the rule of law lie at the foundation of the EU, but true enforcement mechanisms are conspicuously absent so as to ensure compliance by the member states.[49] Similarly, the promotion of human rights is confirmed as an objective of the Common Foreign and Security Policy, as well as of all other forms of cooperation with third countries, including development cooperation. As an external human rights actor, however, the EU fails to devote significant resources to advancing human rights outside Europe.[50]

These contradictions are but the tip of the iceberg of a larger scenario, where human rights acquire prominence in the dominant discourse, but human practices fall short of the proclamations of principles and the actual commitments of international organizations and their member states. Where the 1970s had seen the human rights movement acquiring prominence in international law, the 1990s set the beginning of a divide between *the theory* and *the practice* of human rights.

---

[48] See e.g., J. D. Dinnage and J. F. Murphy, *The Constitutional Law of the European Union*, 2nd ed., Newark: Lexis Nexis Matthew Bender, 2008, pp. 947–86; P. Craig and G. de Búrca, *EU Law: Text, Cases & Materials*, 6th ed., Oxford: Oxford University Press, 2015, pp. 362–406; R. Schütze, *European Constitutional Law*, 2nd ed., Cambridge: Cambridge University Press, 2016, pp. 429–70.

[49] The so-called 'Article 7 TEU procedure', which, at its most severe, allows for the suspension of voting rights in case of a 'serious and persistent breach' of EU values by an EU country, has never been resorted to. It was amended by the Treaty of Amsterdam to include in addition to a sanctioning mechanism, an 'early warning' (preventive) mechanism, i.e. a procedure to be triggered in case of a 'clear risk of a serious breach' – rather than a 'serious and persistent breach by a Member State' – of the common values of the EU. Both mechanisms are now enshrined in Art. 7 TEU and have been invoked against Poland and Hungary but have so far not been applied.

[50] See e.g., A. Egan and L. Pech, 'Respect for Human Rights as a General Objective of the EU's External Action', in S. Douglas-Scott and N. Hatzis (eds.), *Research Handbook on EU Law and Human Rights*, Cheltenham, UK and Northampton, MA, USA: Edward Elgar Publishing, 2017, p. 243.

At the door of Europe, the dissolution of the Soviet Union on 26 December 1991 and the establishment of the Russian Federation was marked by the First Chechen War – which broke out due to a rebellion by the Chechen Republic of Ichkeria against the Russian Federation, and which was fought from December 1994 to August 1996. The armed conflict set the prelude to the ten-year long Second Chechen War (1999–2009), with estimates of military and civilian casualties – while varying in the numbers – certainly exceeding tens of thousands of human lives lost.

As is well known, in the civil war that erupted in the former Yugoslavia in 1991, countless international crimes were committed by all sides to that conflict (see Ristić's contribution in this volume). In the 1994 Rwandan genocide, during the Rwandan Civil War, which had started in 1990, between 500 000 and 1 million Rwandans lost their lives, constituting an estimated 70 per cent of that country's Tutsi population. These atrocities prompted the establishment of the International Criminal Tribunal for the former Yugoslavia and the International Criminal Tribunal for Rwanda – which in turn paved the way to the creation of an International Criminal Court. As an independent permanent court, this international judicial instance would be tasked with putting an end to impunity for the most serious crimes of concern to the international community as a whole.[51] The Rome Statute of the International Criminal Court (ICC) was adopted on 17 July 1998 and entered into force on 1 July 2002.[52] Whatever its success, this can hardly be measured in terms of prevention and punishment of human rights and international humanitarian law breaches worldwide.

Another manifestation of this rising divide between human rights theory and practice is the Western response to human rights conditions in China. When the Soviet Union was in the throes of its collapse and the fall of the Berlin Wall was just a few months away, two events with human rights implications occurred in China: the Chinese government's armed repression of the political unrest in Tibet in 1987–9 and the violent suppression of the pro-democracy movement at Tiananmen Square in June 1989. Western countries imposed severe economic sanctions and arms embargoes on Chinese entities and officials, which led in turn to a spiral of harsher measures of suppression of other protests around China and heavier condemnation by the West. Initially, the US adopted strong measures against the Chinese government, including the

---

[51] See United Nations Security Council (UNSC) Res. 827, 25 May 1993; UNSC Res. 955, 8 November 1994; and Rome Statute of the International Criminal Court 1998, 2187 UNTS 90.

[52] Rome Statute of the International Criminal Court, 17 July 1998, UN Doc. A/CONF.183/9. An examination of the ICC alternative fortunes in the first decade of the twenty-first century (and its current uncertain future) is beyond the scope of this chapter.

suspension of military sales, the cancellation of high-level visits and regular meetings between the two countries, a request to stop all new loans from the International Monetary Fund and the World Bank, the revocation of China's most favoured nation status, and the connection of the issue of human rights with trade.[53] 'American bilateral monitoring' of Chinese human rights conditions, however, officially ended in 1994, when the Clinton administration decided not to link these two issues any longer.[54]

THE DIVIDE BETWEEN TRADE AND INVESTMENT

The WTO was established in 1995, after over seven years of the Uruguay Round negotiations between 127 countries (1986–94), to substitute the informal framework of GATT, of which it incorporated (in addition to the practice developed thereunder) most of the substantive and institutional components. The Preamble of the Marrakesh Agreement recognizes that interstate

> relations in the field of trade and economic endeavour should be conducted with a view to raising standards of living, ensuring full employment [. . .] while allowing for the optimal use of the world's resources in accordance with the objective of sustainable development, seeking both to protect and preserve the environment and to enhance the means for doing so in a manner consistent with their respective needs and concerns at different levels of economic development.

Yet, the main purpose of the Organization is 'to ensure that trade flows as smoothly, predictably and freely as possible'.[55] The word 'human rights' does not appear anywhere in the Agreement nor in its annexes (about sixty agree-

---

[53] D. D. A. Schaefer, 'US Foreign Policies of Presidents Bush and Clinton: The Influence of China's Most Favored Nation Status upon Human Rights Issues', *The Social Science Journal*, vol. 35(3), 1998, p. 407. See also R. Foot, *Rights beyond Borders: The Global Community and the Struggle over Human Rights in China*, Oxford: Oxford University Press, 2000; M. Wan, *Human Rights in Chinese Foreign Relations*, Philadelphia: University of Pennsylvania Press, 2001; R. L. Suettinger, *Beyond Tiananmen: The Politics of U.S.–China Relations 1989–2000*, Washington, DC: Brookings Institution Press, 2003; R. Foot and A. Walter, *China, the United States, and Global Order*, New York: Cambridge University Press, 2011.
[54] A. Kent, *China, the United Nations, and Human Rights: The Limits of Compliance*, Philadelphia: University of Pennsylvania Press, 1999, p. 233.
[55] See the World Trade Organization (WTO), official website home page, available at www.wto.org/index.htm.

ments and decisions totalling 550 pages), but for an indirect mention in one of the 'general exceptions' under Article XX GATT,[56] which allows for:

> the adoption or enforcement by any contracting party of measures [. . .] relating to the products of prison labour. (paragraph (e))[57]

Significantly, while Article XX is one of the most frequently invoked provisions in trade disputes, the 'prison labour' exception has never been invoked or applied.

Much has been written about the role of human rights within the WTO.[58] Whether one believes that trade liberalization advances human rights or not, the fact remains that the WTO's normative and institutional framework is set to advance trade and trade-related values. Human rights consistent practices can be a by-product of trade in so far as trade fosters economic development and this, in turn, raises living conditions for all.[59] When this happens, practices

---

[56] The General Agreement on Tariffs and Trade (GATT) 1994, 1867 UNTS 190, which must be read with GATT 1947, is in Annex 1A of the WTO Agreement.

[57] The very function of Art. XX GATT is to safeguard non-trade values even if this results in a restriction of trade. It cannot be excluded, however, that a challenge of a trade restrictive measure successfully brought under Art. XX GATT results in the adoption of a measure more restrictive than the one originally challenged, by way of implementation of the ruling which 'recommends' the withdrawal or modification of the measure to bring it into conformity with GATT requirements. This is typically the case when the measure complained of is found to be provisionally justified under one of the sub-paragraphs of Art. XX but fails to meet the requirement of impartiality and even-handedness of the *chapeau*.

[58] In the vast literature, see e.g. S. Joseph, *Blame it on the WTO? A Human Rights Critique*, Oxford and New York: Oxford University Press, 2011; T. Cottier, J. Pauwelyn and E. Bürgi (eds.), *Human Rights and International Trade*, Oxford: Oxford University Press, 2005; F. M. Abbott, C. Breining-Kaufmann and T. Cottier (eds.), *International Trade and Human Rights: Foundations and Conceptual Issues*, Ann Arbor: University of Michigan Press, 2006.

[59] The claim has also been advanced that there is (or should be) an individual 'right to trade'. R. McGee, 'The Moral Case for Free Trade', *Journal of World Trade*, vol. 29(1), 1995, p. 69; A. Sen, *Development as Freedom*, Oxford: Oxford University Press, 1999; E. Petersmann, 'Human Rights, Markets and Economic Welfare: Constitutional Functions of the Emerging UN Human Rights Constitution', in Abbott et al. (eds.), *International Trade and Human Rights*, p. 29:

> Absolutist claims in favour of a right to trade are indeed problematic, because trade liberalization can have harmful effects on human rights. These negative effects are of two main types. The first is that, in the short term, trade liberalization *ipso facto* harms inefficient producers, and can also be costly at the aggregate level, especially for developing countries. In principle, these costs can be compensated by the greater earnings produced by free trade, but this does not always happen in the short term, or in some cases at all. Second, some of the

consistent with human rights are not the result of human rights norms or policies but rather a side-effect, so to say, of norms and policies designed for another end: a predictable and stable international trade legal framework.

As to investment, its separation from trade which ensued from the failure of the NIEO, resulted in an outright divorce. Recognizing that certain investment measures can have trade-restrictive and distorting effects, the Agreement on Trade-Related Investment Measures, negotiated during the Uruguay Round, applies only to measures that affect trade in goods.[60] Any attempt to negotiate a Multilateral Agreement on Investment (MAI) was abandoned in 1998. In consequence thereof, while access of foreign investment to foreign markets remains under the full sovereignty of host countries, the bulk of rules concerning substantive standards of protection of foreign investment and procedural provisions on dispute settlement (both between the investor and the host state and between the latter and the state of nationality of the investor) continued to be negotiated bilaterally. The network of existing BITs expanded to include more and more complex treaties. At the end of the 1990s, but for the 'Brazilian exception',[61] no state was outside the investment treaty system.

These normative developments resulted in the emergence of two separate settings for the resolution of international disputes. While private traders have no possibility to vindicate their rights within the WTO, member states affected

---

rules imposed by trade regimes go beyond a simple reduction of protectionist measures, and can interfere with the ability of countries to pursue human rights objectives.
See also L. Bartels, 'Trade and Human Rights', in D. Bethlehem, D. McRae, R. Neufeld and A. Van Damme (eds.), *The Oxford Handbook of International Trade Law*, Oxford: Oxford University Press, 2009, p. 571, p. 573.

[60] Under the Agreement on Trade-Related Investment Measures 1994, available at https://www.wto.org/english/docs_e/legal_e/18-trims_e.htm, no Member shall apply a measure that is prohibited by the provisions of Art. III GATT (national treatment) or Art. XI GATT (quantitative restrictions).

[61] On the position that Brazil has assumed in the investment treaty system, not only as the sole major power never to have ratified a BIT, but also as the designer of a new model – the Cooperation and Facilitation Investment Agreement – which focuses on investment facilitation rather than investor protection, and alternative dispute resolution and state-to-state arbitration rather than investor-state arbitration, see H. Choer Moraes and F. Hees, 'Breaking the BIT Model: Brazil's Pioneering Approach to Investment Agreements', *AJIL Unbound*, vol. 112, 2018, p. 197. See also E. C. Schlemmer, 'Dispute Settlement in Investment-Related Matters: South Africa and the BRICS', *AJIL Unbound*, vol. 112, 2018, p. 212, on South Africa's recent decision to withdraw from the investment treaty system and to replace investment treaty protections with legislation and investor-state dispute settlement mechanisms with resort to domestic courts. These actions resulted from the shock South Africa experienced when early cases challenged South Africa's actions under its constitutional mandate to redress the historic injustices of apartheid.

by non-respect of rules and commitments by their trading partners can bring their claims under the Dispute Settlement Understanding (DSU).[62] With the newly established Appellate Body developing a largely consistent case-law and a climate of trust in trade disputes resolution, the DSU would long be considered the 'crown jewel'[63] of the entire multilateral trade system. It was mostly utilized by the US and the EU, but also by developing countries against other developing and developed countries as well; and it was effective also in terms of compliance with its final rulings.[64] In contrast, in the 1990s, investor-state dispute settlement mechanisms (ISDS) became standard provisions included in BITs, giving foreign investors private standing to invoke treaty breaches against the host state before an arbitral tribunal, thus avoiding the historical sensitive political implications of state-to-state dispute settlement in the exercise of diplomatic protection – something 'dramatically different from anything previously known in the international sphere'.[65] Arbitral awards – mostly pronounced at the initiative of investors from developed countries against host developing states – resulted in a sparse and fragmented case-law.

With these developments, the twofold divide between human rights and international economic law, and, within the latter, between the multilateral setting of trade and the extensive network of BITs unconnected to the WTO, was completed.

THE TURN OF THE CENTURY AND THE 'EFFECTIVENESS' CRISIS OF HUMAN RIGHTS

The beginning of the twenty-first century is indelibly marked by two events: the 11 September attacks of 2001 and the global financial shock of 2008, with the ensuing economic crisis. The distance between the theory and practice of human rights became more profound, posing dramatically the question of the 'effectiveness' of the international human rights regime, while both the WTO and the investment treaty system entered a period of crisis, which is also a 'legitimacy' crisis and continues to be ongoing.

---

[62] The Dispute Settlement Understanding (DSU) is Annex 2 of the WTO Agreement.
[63] J. Baccus, 'Inside the World Trade Organization', Special Keynote Address on 17 April 2002 at Columbia University, available at https://www8.gsb.columbia.edu/apec/sites/apec/files/files/discussion/bacchusdp.pdf.
[64] Lester et al., *World Trade Law*, p. 149.
[65] J. Paulsson, 'Arbitration Without Privity', *ICSID Review: Foreign Investment Law Journal*, vol. 10(2), 1995, p. 232, p. 256.

At the normative level, by the turn of the century most states had ratified the majority of the most important human rights treaties.[66] Institutionally, the Human Rights Council (HRC) was established in 2006 to replace the former UN Commission on Human Rights – long criticized for including among its members some of the most prominent human rights violators and for the uneven selection of situations to subject to the Commission's scrutiny.[67] The HRC is a global intergovernmental human rights body, made up of forty-seven UN member states elected by the UN General Assembly, responsible for strengthening the promotion and protection of human rights worldwide and for addressing situations of human rights violations and make recommendations on them. Among other procedures and mechanisms, the Council set up the Universal Periodic Review (UPR)[68] and continued to work with, and expanded, the so-called Special Procedures.[69] The UPR is a process to periodically assess the human rights situations in all 193 UN member states. UN member states are obliged to go through a review once every five years on all human rights issues – not just those enshrined in treaties to which they are parties.[70] It is

---

[66] The updated status of ratification of the nine core international human rights instruments – International Convention on the Elimination of All Forms of Racial Discrimination; ICCPR; ICESCR; Convention on the Elimination of All Forms of Discrimination against Women; Convention against Torture and Other Cruel, Inhuman or Degrading Treatment or Punishment; Convention on the Rights of the Child; International Convention on the Protection of the Rights of All Migrant Workers and Members of Their Families; International Convention for the Protection of All Persons from Enforced Disappearance; Convention on the Rights of Persons with Disabilities – is available at https://www.ohchr.org/EN/ProfessionalInterest/Pages/CoreInstruments.aspx.

[67] UNGA Res. 60/251, 15 March 2006. Little has been written about the HRC and its role in enforcing human rights law. See, however, M. C. Bassiouni and W. A. Schabas (eds.), *New Challenges for the UN Human Rights Machinery: What Future for the UN Treaty Body System and the Human Rights Council Procedures?*, Cambridge: Intersentia, 2011, pp. 239–478. On the first two successive terms of US membership on the HRC (2009–15), see M. P. Lagon and R. Kaminski, *Bolstering the UN Human Rights Council's Effectiveness*, Council on Foreign Relations Discussion Paper, January 2017, available at https://cfrd8-files.cfr.org/sites/default/files/pdf/2016/12/Discussion_Paper_Lagon_Kaminski_UNHRC_OR.pdf.

[68] See the UPR official website, available at www.ohchr.org/EN/HRBodies/UPR/Pages/UPRmain.aspx.

[69] See the Special Procedures official website, available at https://www.ohchr.org/en/hrbodies/sp/pages/welcomepage.aspx.

[70] E. McMahon and M. Ascherio, 'A Step Ahead in Promoting Human Rights? The Universal Periodic Review of the UN Human Rights Council', *Global Governance: A Review of Multilateralism and International Organizations*, vol. 18(2), 2012, p. 231. China was initially concerned that the UPR process might 'overlap with the work of human rights treaty bodies and special mechanisms, thus increasing report burdens for developing countries' (Permanent Mission of the People's Republic of China to the

thus the first human rights mechanism to ensure in principle that every state is equally represented and evaluated. Special procedures, established by the former Commission on Human Rights, are made up of special rapporteurs, special representatives, independent experts, and working groups that monitor, examine, advise, and publicly report on thematic issues or human rights situations in specific countries, as well as interact with a country's population on human rights concerns. They are appointed directly by the HRC, on the basis of open calls publicly available, for the purpose of assisting the Council in the discharge of its functions in relation to specific rights (thematic) or (country-specific) situations.[71] The Council also provides a forum for advancing human rights norms, including through the passage of thematic resolutions.

Human rights institutions also flourished and expanded at the regional level. The European Convention on Human Rights establishes itself as the most sophisticated and successful regional system of human rights protection in the world. Thanks to the automatic right of individual application introduced in 1998,[72] the European Court of Human Rights (ECtHR) holds to account forty-seven member states for violations of the rights and freedoms guaranteed by the Convention to over 800 million persons. The Inter-American Court of Human Rights, the African Court on Human and Peoples' Rights and the Arab Human Rights Commission are all functioning institutions that oversee compliance with their respective human rights charter.[73]

Law schools – where future generations of judges, lawyers and law-makers are formed – include in their curricula international human rights courses, not exclusively devoted to international careers. These developments in legal education in turn prompted private litigation, in the US and elsewhere, based upon human rights violations.[74]

UN, 2006). However, the UPR process was adopted as a complementary measure to the work of treaty bodies, emphasizing its 'cooperative nature' and suggesting that it should be 'constructive, non-confrontational and non-politicized' (M. Abraham, *Building the New Human Rights Council: Outcome and Analysis of the Institutional-Building Year*, Geneva: Friedrich-Ebert Stiftung, 2007, p. 36).

[71] Relatively little has been written also about the UN Special Procedures. For a rare exception, see H. Cantú Rivera, *The Special Procedures of the Human Rights Council*, Cambridge: Intersentia, 2015; and Bassiouni and Schabas (eds.), *New Challenges for the UN Human Rights Machinery*, pp. 387–478.

[72] See Protocol No. 11 to the ECHR, restructuring the control machinery established thereby 1994, ETS No. 155 (entry into force 1 November 1998).

[73] Shelton, *Advanced Introduction to International Human Rights Law*, pp. 61–73. See also D. Moeckli, S. Shah and S. Sivakumaran (eds.), *International Human Rights Law*, 3rd ed., Oxford: Oxford University Press, 2018.

[74] Posner, *The Twilight of Human Rights Law*, p. 26.

Human rights language is used everywhere and is routinely invoked to criticize governments in political and diplomatic discourse. Human rights NGOs continue to grow in the number and outreach of their reporting, lobbying and advocacy activities,[75] contributing to make both small and large-scale human rights breaches well-detected and documented. At no time in history has there been more information available to governments and the public about the state of human rights around the world.[76]

Yet, the 11 September attacks by the Islamic extremist group al-Qaeda against US targets exposed the fragility of fundamental rights and freedoms of the most powerful democracy and set the beginning of the most geographically and temporally undefined war in history, the war against international terrorism. While human rights law and institutions continue to look as healthy as ever, the severe economic downturn that followed the 2008 financial crisis, with low growth and rising unemployment and homelessness, brought significant additional challenges to the realization of human rights on the ground. This crisis of effectiveness and relevance is paralleled by a legitimacy crisis which invest both the multilateral regulation of trade within the WTO and the dispute settlement mechanism between states and foreign investors, under traditional BITs.

THE PARALLEL 'LEGITIMACY' CRISIS OF INTERNATIONAL TRADE AND INVESTMENT LAW

Notwithstanding the ever-closer link between international trade and international investment in the globalized economy of the early twenty-first century, '[t]he regulation of financial movements, trade in goods and services and of the making of direct investments remains subject [. . .] to *different regimes*'.[77]

---

[75] For an interesting empirical analysis of the human rights discourse in national constitutions and international agreements, see D. S. Law, 'The Global Language of Human Rights: A Computational Linguistic Analysis', *Law & Ethics of Human Rights*, vol. 12(1), 2018, p. 111. On new forms of civic activism, 'different from the familiar NGO model, being self-consciously shapeless, indeterminate and even nebulous in from, deed and vision', see R. Youngs, *Civic Activism Unleashed: New Hope or False Dawn for Democracy?*, Oxford: Oxford University Press, 2019 (quote at p. 4).

[76] B. A. Simmons, *Mobilizing for Human Rights: International Law in Domestic Politics*, Cambridge: Cambridge University Press, 2009, p. 9.

[77] 'Jürgen Kurtz has convincingly argued in favour of convergence in law-making, adjudication, and interpretation of relevant instruments between trade and investment law [J. Kurtz, *The WTO and International Investment Law: Converging Systems*, Cambridge: Cambridge University Press, 2016]. The close connection between these types of operations, more as complementarity than as substitution from an economic and business perspective, has not led to a significant approximation, merging or the

As a paradox or perhaps an irony of history, however, trade and investment become 'companions' in the multifaceted crisis that invests, in parallel, their respective institutional settings and adjudicatory mechanisms.

The Doha Development Round, the WTO trade negotiation round commenced in Qatar in 2001, to reduce subsidies for developed countries' agricultural industries and open up developing countries' markets to services, came to a halt in 2008. Neither developed economies like the US and the EU, nor developing countries like China or India were willing or able to make the fundamental needed concessions. In 2015, after repeated attempts to revive the talks, trade ministers from more than 160 countries formally acknowledged the divide on the future of the Doha Round. Failure to achieve Doha's ambitious agenda undermined the credibility of the multilateral trading system and hurt least-developed countries. But the failure also means that future multilateral trade agreements are probably doomed to fail for the same reasons as Doha.

Moreover, since late 2017, the US has been blocking new appointments to the Appellate Body,[78] which on 1 October 2018 was reduced to the minimum three members it needs to hear an appeal. If the stalemate is not overcome, on 11 December 2019 the WTO Appellate Body will be reduced to a single member and the WTO dispute settlement system will become non-operational.

The 2018 trade wars pose an even more serious threat to the WTO, where states respond to perceived WTO-inconsistent conduct by imposing equivalent tariffs in an escalation of reciprocal tariff increases. While WTO members adopting trade-restrictive measures on doubtful legal grounds is not a novelty, states imposing countermeasures based on their own assessment that the justifications put forward are ill-founded, break their key commitment under

---

bringing under a unitary "umbrella" of these different types of operations, institutionally and law making wise. Nor does it appear that we will witness such a movement in the near future.' G. Sacerdoti, 'Trade and Investment Law: Institutional Differences and Substantive Similarities', *Jerusalem Review of Legal Studies*, vol. 9(1), 2014, pp. 1 and 3.

[78] The US raises a number of objections to positions taken by the WTO Appellate Body. In the Annual Report issued by the US Trade Representative in 2017 an entire section is devoted to the tendency of the Appellate Body to 'Issu[e] Advisory Opinions on Issues Not Necessary to Resolve a Dispute' (Office of the United States Trade Representative, 2018 Trade Policy Agenda and 2017Annual Report of the President of the United States on the Trade Agreements Program, March 2018, available at https://ustr.gov/about-us/policy-offices/press-office/reports-and-publications/2018/2018-trade-policy-agenda-and-2017, at 27). This point has long been a concern of the US with regards to their participation in the WTO. See 'United States Blocks Reappointment of WTO Appellate Body Member', *American Journal of International Law*, vol. 110(3), 2016, p. 573; A. Sarvarian and F. Fontanelli, 'The USA and Re-Appointment at the WTO: A "Legitimacy Crisis"?', *EJIL: Talk!*, 27 May 2016, https://www.ejiltalk.org/the-usa-and-re-appointment-at-the-wto-a-legitimacy-crisis.

the DSU. WTO members should refrain from unilaterally interpreting the conduct of other Members as violations and reacting on the basis of their own interpretation.[79]

International investment law, now governed by over 3000 BITs, suffers from an analogous crisis which affects both the areas of substance (rights and obligations of the investor and the host state) and procedure (dispute resolution).[80] Although the number of investment disputes continues to grow, many states are withdrawing from, or re-examining, their commitments.[81]

THE 'POWER' OF INTERNATIONAL HUMAN RIGHTS LAW TO AFFECT HISTORICAL DEVELOPMENTS

The international regime of human rights is relatively weak compared to the regime of trade (or other regimes). No competitive market forces drive countries toward compliance, nor are states generally consistent in their application of human rights standards to their foreign policy, or employ sanctions

---

[79] For a thorough examination of the current combination of trade wars and a disappearing Appellate Body as signs of a deeper breakdown of the commitment that underpins the WTO Agreements, see G. Vidigal, *Westphalia Strikes Back: The 2018 Trade Wars and the Threat to the WTO Regime*, 2 October 2018, Amsterdam Law School Research Paper No. 2018-31, available at SSRN: https://ssrn.com/abstract=3259127.

[80] S. Shill, *The Multilateralization of International Investment Law*, Cambridge: Cambridge University Press, 2009; J. E. Alvarez and K. P. Sauvant (eds.), *The Evolving International Investment Regime: Expectations, Realities, Options*, New York: Oxford University Press, 2011; J. E. Alvarez, *International Investment Law*, Leiden and Boston: Brill Nijhoff, 2017; J. E. Alvarez, *The Public International Law Regime Governing International Investment*, The Hague: Hague Academy of International Law, 2011; J. Bonnitcha, L. N. Skovgaard Poulsen and M. Waibel, *The Political Economy of the Investment Treaty Regime*, Oxford: Oxford University Press, 2017; M. Sornarajah, *The International Law on Foreign Investment*, 4th ed., Cambridge: Cambridge University Press, 2017. See also C. Cai and A. Roberts (eds.), 'Symposium on the BRICS Approach to the Investment Treaty System', *AJIL Unbound*, vol. 112, 2018, p. 187; and F. C. Morosini and M. Ratton Sanchez Badin (eds.), *Reconceptualizing International Investment Law from the Global South*, Cambridge: Cambridge University Press, 2017, discussing alternative approaches to the regulation of international investment among states in the Global South.

[81] See S. Puig and G. Shaffer, 'Imperfect Alternatives: Institutional Choice and the Reform of Investment Law', *American Journal of International Law*, vol. 117(3), 2018, p. 361, p. 365:
In the last decade, countries have terminated BITs with ISDS clauses (such as Ecuador, Indonesia, and South Africa), withdrew from the ICSID Convention (notably, Bolivia, Ecuador, and Venezuela), threatened to leave it (including Argentina, El Salvador, and Nicaragua), or created new constraints on using ISDS (such as Norway and New Zealand).

– political, economic, military, or otherwise – to coerce other countries into improving their human rights record. This is because contrary to the extent of trade openness, a country and its citizens are hardly affected if the human rights of citizens from other countries are violated in other states.[82] Without powerful countries taking a strong interest in the effectiveness of international human rights regimes, there is little cost for those with a poor human rights record to ratify human rights treaties as a symbolic gesture of good will, while maintaining their poor record in reality.[83]

Moreover, unlike growth in gross domestic product, import and export data and foreign direct investment stocks and flows, numerical values are not entirely attributable to human rights practices. The effectiveness of human rights law is hardly measurable. Only some violations of human rights are reportable in statistics (e.g. prisons overcrowding or trials behind a reasonable time). For most violations, numbers are hardly telling, even in relation to the most fundamental rights. How to measure, for example, breaches of the rights to life and personal liberty arising out of extra-judicial killings and punishments – by definition, committed by state officials without the sanction of any judicial proceeding or legal process and as extra-legal fulfilment of their prescribed role? Statistics remain equally unsatisfactory with respect to the measurement of implementation of social and economic rights. Human rights indicators, such as those developed by the OHCHR,[84] do not fundamentally alter this picture.[85]

---

[82] E. Neumayer, *Do International Human Rights Treaties Improve Respect for Human Rights?*, New York: Oxford University Press, 2005, p. 926.

[83] J. L. Goldsmith and E. A. Posner, *The Limits of International Law*, New York: Oxford University Press, 2007.

[84] OHCHR, *Human Rights Indicators: A Guide to Measurement and Implementation* (2012). According to the foreword by Navi Pillay as the High Commissioner at the time, the *Guide* is premised on the recognition that 'In recent years, the critical need for such tools has become increasingly evident. On the eve of the Arab Spring, there were still reports about the remarkable economic and social progress and general improvements in governance and the rule of law that some countries in the region were achieving. At the same time, UN human rights mechanisms and voices from civil society were painting a different picture, and reporting on exclusion, the marginalization of communities, discrimination, absence of participation, censorship, political repression or lack of an independent judiciary and denial of basic economic and social rights.'

[85] On the use of statistics to measure human rights, see the interesting work by S. Engle Merry, *The Seduction of Quantifications*: *Measuring Human Rights, Gender Violence, and Sex Trafficking*, Chicago: University of Chicago Press, 2016, p. 1: 'Numerical assessments such as indicators appeal to the desire for simple, accessible knowledge and to a basic human tendency to see the world in terms of hierarchies of reputation and status. [. . .] Counting things requires making them comparable, which means they are inevitably stripped of their context, history, and meaning.' On the chal-

Even assuming that human rights violations can be measured, this is not necessarily telling of the impact of international human rights law, i.e. of the effects of human rights norms and institutions on human rights practices. Correlations can be established between improvement of human rights and certain data such as treaty ratification, acceptance of the jurisdiction of monitoring bodies and the number of international cases brought by private parties against the state concerned.[86] Attempts have also been made at singling out specific variables, specifically in relation to treaty ratification.[87] It is not possible, however, to completely isolate the effects of human rights norms and procedures. Although some scholars have provided the powerful explanation that human rights have contributed to change or have even transformed the sovereign state system, whether human rights treaties with their machineries have actually improved people's lives remains questionable: 'If they have, the effect has been small'.[88] Improvements have been in the details.

It is also difficult to deny that human rights improvements on the ground in various areas of the world in the last decade of the twentieth century were not the product of the human rights movement, but are rather attributable to economic growth, the collapse of communism and other offsetting factors.

---

lenges of measuring compliance and effectiveness, see O. A. Hathaway, 'Do Human Rights Treaties Make a Difference?', *Yale Law Journal*, vol. 111(8), 2002, p. 1935.

[86] See H. Smith-Cannoy, *Insincere Commitments: Human Rights Treaties, Abusive States, and Citizen Activism*, Washington, DC: Georgetown University Press, 2012, p. 1, noting that 'Between 1947 and 2007, more than one hundred new global human rights treaties emerged, covering a range of issues from prohibitions on torture and children in battle to apartheid in sports. And governments are signing on, making public commitments to protect the human rights of their citizens. Yet for all the progress on global human rights in the twentieth century, a series of battles remain.'

[87] See e.g. Neumayer, *Do International Human Rights Treaties Improve Respect for Human Rights?*, finding that rarely does treaty ratification have unconditional effects on human rights. A beneficial effect of ratification of human rights treaties is typically conditional on the extent of democracy and the strength of civil society groups as measured by participation in NGOs with international linkages. In the absence of democracy and a strong civil society, treaty ratification has no effect and is possibly even associated with more human rights violations. See also A. S. Chilton and E. A. Posner, 'Respect for Human Rights: Law and History', *Coase-Sandor Working Paper Series in Law and Economics* No. 770 (2016), providing evidence that for two treaties – the Convention on Elimination of Discrimination Against Women and the Convention Against Torture – recent improvements in human rights are attributable to long running trends that pre-date the emergence of the relevant treaty regimes. For a contesting view see: G. De Búrca, 'Human Rights Experimentalism', *American Journal of International Law*, vol. 111(2), 2017, p. 277, using 'experimentalist governance' as a theory of the causal effectiveness of human rights treaties.

[88] Posner, *The Twilight of Human Rights Law*, p. 27.

EFFORTS AT BRIDGING EXISTING DIVIDES FROM WITHIN THE HUMAN RIGHTS REGIME

With a view to filling the considerable gap between the recognition of human rights and their implementation on the ground, the UN has put great emphasis, in the first quarter of this century, on the universality, indivisibility, and interdependence of human rights.

According to the UN conceptual framework since the Vienna Declaration, '[a]ll human rights are universal, indivisible and interdependent and interrelated', and must be treated 'in a fair and equal manner, on the same footing, and with the same emphasis'.[89] The principle of universality means that human rights shall enjoy universal protection across all boundaries and civilizations, regardless of political, economic or cultural systems. Human rights are inalienable, i.e. they are inherent in all persons and cannot be alienated from an individual or group except with due process and in specific situations. They are interrelated, because improvement in the realization of any one human right is a function of the realization of the other human rights, and interdependent, as the level of enjoyment of any one right is dependent on the level of realization of the other rights. Human rights are finally indivisible: all civil, cultural, economic, political and social rights are equally important. Improving the enjoyment of any right cannot be at the expense of the realization of any other right.[90]

---

[89] Para. 5 of the Vienna Declaration and Programme of Action reads as follows: 'All human rights are universal, indivisible and interdependent and interrelated. The international community must treat human rights globally in a fair and equal manner, on the same footing, and with the same emphasis. While the significance of national and regional particularities and various historical, cultural and religious backgrounds must be borne in mind, it is the duty of states, regardless of their political, economic and cultural systems, to promote and protect all human rights and fundamental freedoms.' Prior to Vienna, the belief that human rights are 'indivisible' had been formally expressed in the Proclamation of Teheran 1968 (Final Act of the International Conference on Human Rights, Teheran, 22 April to 1 May 1968, UN Doc. A/CONF.32/41) and Alternative Approaches and Ways and Means within the United Nations System for Improving the Effective Enjoyment of Human Rights and Fundamental Freedoms 1977 (UNGA Res. 32/130 (XXXII), 16 December 1977), at para. 13 and preambular para. 6, respectively.

[90] Various UN organs and specialized agencies and the human rights commissions in a variety of states also advance the tenet. See e.g. United Nations Children's Fund, Human Rights Approach (2016), available at https://www.unicef.org/child-rights-convention/children-human-rights-explained. The UNGA resolution that established the Human Rights Council in 2006 underlines that 'all human rights are universal, indivisible, interrelated, interdependent and mutually reinforcing', UNGA Res 60/251, 3 April 2006, at preambular para. 3. This wording is found in basically all HRC resolu-

These concepts have been criticized on various fronts. The debate is intense, not at the level of legalization but at the level of implementation and enforcement.[91] A fundamental challenge to the universality of human rights, however, is China's 'cultural relativism'.

China's collectivist conception of human rights, including its emphasis on 'development first', won considerable support regionally, when forty-six Asian governments convened at the Bangkok Conference,[92] a regional prelude to the 1993 World Conference on Human Rights in Vienna. The right to development then found its way into the Vienna Declaration, which, significantly, endorsed that rights are 'universal' and 'inalienable', but in the 'context of a dynamic and evolving process of international norm-setting' in which 'national and regional particularities' are to be borne in mind.[93] In the twenty-first century, China still promotes the concept that human rights must be 'based on national conditions, with the right to development as the primary basic human right', a point emphasized in the Beijing Declaration in 2017.[94]

The indivisibility of human rights is also part of the normative backbone of the UN official doctrine of human rights. The idea is that improvement in the realization of any one right is a function of the realization of the others and that improving the enjoyment of any right cannot be at the expense of the realization of any other right. The UN, however, have never provided a firm definition of what indivisibility means, or the policy implications of asserting

---

tions. See also OHCHR, *Your Human Rights*, 2016, available at https://www.ohchr.org/en/issues/pages/whatarehumanrights.aspx.

[91] N. Deitelhoff and L. Zimmermann, 'Things We Lost in the Fire: How Different Types of Contestation Affect the Validity of International Norms', *PRIF Working Papers No. 18* (2013), available at https://www.files.ethz.ch/isn/175046/PRIF_WP_18.pdf.

[92] The regional conference's final document, the Bangkok Declaration, claims that human rights must be approached from a pluralistic perspective that respects differences in culture, region, religion and history, and makes several references to a nation's right to 'freely pursue' its development in economic and other spheres, citing the right to self-determination but also a right to development as such. Final Declaration of the Regional Meeting for Asia of the World Conference on Human Rights (Report of the Regional Meeting for Asia of the World Conference on Human Rights (Bangkok, 29 March – 2 April 1993), UN Doc. A/CONF.157/ASRM/8A/CONF.157/PC/59, 7 April 1993.

[93] Vienna Declaration and Programme of Action, at para. 5.

[94] Beijing Declaration, 8 December 2017, available at http://www.xinhuanet.com//english/2017-12/08/c_136811775.htm, preambular para. 5. The Beijing Declaration was adopted by the First South–South Human Rights Forum, attended by delegates from 70 developing countries from Asia and Africa. See K. Kinzelbach, 'Will China's Rise Lead to a New Normative Order? An Analysis of China's Statements on Human Rights at the United Nations (2000–2010)', *Netherlands Quarterly of Human Rights*, vol. 30(3), 2012, p. 299.

it as a principle. Nor is there any evidence that the UN's adoption and promotion of the idea was ever informed by empirical fact.[95] The indivisibility of human rights has also received little philosophical attention, especially when compared to the purported universality of human rights.[96]

The core difficulty that the thesis of indivisibility faces is that it is possible to fully implement or secure certain human rights (for example, rights not to be enslaved or tortured) without fully implementing or securing other human rights (for example, rights to education or food), and vice versa. Moreover, it has long been recognized that not only ESC and collective rights, but also classical liberal rights imply positive obligations. The realization of all rights and freedoms requires choices as to ways in which to implement them and to what extent, and resources.[97] Moreover, most (not absolute) rights can be balanced against public interests (public order, health, security, etc.). But they can equally be balanced against other rights.[98] Asymmetrical implementation of rights, therefore, is not only possible, but – to some extent, at least – a necessity. Beyond theoretical and political criticisms of principle, there are very few win-win situations in human rights and human rights are hardly a zero-sum up game. Very few people on earth would not wish for a world where all rights are equally protected, respected, and fulfilled for everyone. However, to ensure to the maximum extent the realization of all rights and freedoms by all at any given moment is an unattainable goal, as much as it would be worth pursuing.

---

[95] The empirical literature does not unanimously support the existence of indivisibility among human rights. Most of the studies find that the relationship between human rights is neither bidirectional nor simultaneous. Furthermore, the robustness of the few studies that do find support for simultaneous achievement is questionable. See S. Soiffer and D. Rowlands, 'Examining the Indivisibility of Human Rights: A Statistical Analysis', *Journal of Human Rights*, vol. 17(1) 2018, p. 89, p. 102, holding that 'empirical testing reveals that there is reason to believe that only some pairs of human rights are indivisible'.

[96] M. Goodhart, 'None So Poor That He Is Compelled to Sell Himself: Democracy, Subsistence, and Basic Income', in S. Hertel and L. Minkler (eds.), *Economic Rights: Conceptual, Measurement, and Policy Issues*, Cambridge: Cambridge University Press, 2007, p. 94, p. 104: 'Only a few scholars, however, have explored the analytic bases of this claim [concerning the indivisibility of human rights].' For an historical and political discussion of indivisibility, see D. Whelan, *Indivisible Human Rights: A History*, Philadelphia: University of Pennsylvania Press, 2010. On the philosophical thesis of the indivisibility of human rights, see A. Zyberman, 'The Indivisibility of Human Rights', *Law and Philosophy*, vol. 36(4), 2017, p. 389.

[97] In a human rights perspective, one can even say that one of the essential functions of the state is precisely to synthesize the multiple claims and aspirations to the realization of various rights and freedoms by multiple stakeholders. And in a democratic state, the right to participate in the political process leading to such choices is a prerequisite to the realization of all other rights and freedoms.

[98] '[T]he rights and freedoms of others', in the wording of Arts. 9–11 ECHR.

A more radical attempt at bridging the divide between human rights and international economic and development law has recently been put forward by China, as part of its broader effort to redefine its role on the world scene, challenging existing – and assuming – leadership in economic and non-economic fields.[99] The rise of China as an international actor on the international arena, however, seems to have incrementally progressed largely unnoticed in recent years. Attention so far has been mainly focused on single economic initiatives, such as the creation of the Asian Infrastructure Investment Bank, the New Development Bank, and, most notably, the so called Belt and Road Initiative, a multi-trillion dollar development strategy announced by the Chinese government in 2013, to address an 'infrastructure gap' across the Asia Pacific area and Central and Eastern Europe.[100] But China has also established an 'international commercial court' (*guoji shangshi fating*), marking the first time it has created a world legal institution.[101] Moreover, unlike some other BRICS states (Brazil, Russia, India, China and South Africa) that have shied away from investor protection and ISDS,[102] China has extended the jurisdiction

---

[99] Since the turn of the millennium, China has emerged as a major player in multilateral contexts – from its membership in the WTO, its avowal since 9/11 to counter international terrorism and its key role in seeking to defuse the threat of nuclear conflict on the Korean peninsula, to its increasing participation in UN peace-keeping operations. C. Cai, 'New Great Powers and International Law in the 21st Century', *European Journal of International Law*, vol. 24(3), 2013, p. 755. On China's rapid moves to the centre stage of world politics, see also R. Foot and A. Walter, *China, the United States, and Global Order*, Cambridge: Cambridge University Press, 2011; Y. Zhang, '"China Anxiety": Discourse and Intellectual Challenges', *Development and Change*, vol. 44(6), 2013, p. 1407; D. Shambaugh, *China Goes Global: The Partial Power*, Oxford: Oxford University Press, 2013; E. Goh (ed.), *Rising China's Influence in Developing Asia*, Oxford: Oxford University Press, 2016.

[100] The project not only cements China as a major source of outward international investment (some estimates list the Belt and Road Initiative (BRI) as one of the largest infrastructure and investment projects in history, covering more than 68 countries, including 65% of the world's population and 40% of the global GDP as of 2017). The BRI is broadly viewed also as a commercial and geo-political project to enhance China's international status and to export the products of its excess capacity.

[101] On 1 July 2018, the Supreme People's Court, pursuant to its power to set up 'tribunals' issued the 'Supreme People's Court Regulations on Certain Issues in Establishing an International Commercial Court'. The Supreme People's Court is establishing three such tribunals – in Shenzhen, Beijing and Xi'an. Opening ceremonies have already been held in Shenzhen and Xi'an, although it is unknown when the courts will start accepting cases. M. S. Erie, 'The China International Commercial Court: Prospects for Dispute Resolution for the "Belt and Road Initiative"', *ASIL Insights*, 31 August 2018, available at https://www.asil.org/insights/volume/22/issue/11/china-international-commercial-court-prospects-dispute-resolution-belt.

[102] See *supra* notes 62 and 81.

of existing domestic commercial arbitral institutions in the country to cover foreign investment disputes and created new Chinese institutions to deal with such disputes, as well as joint arbitration centres with states in regions where China invests heavily, such as Africa.[103] And China has been moving beyond trade and investment policies in the Asia Pacific Region, Central and Eastern Europe, and other areas of the world.[104]

One dimension that has received little attention so far is China's attempt to establish itself as an international human rights world champion, with the HRC as the natural arena for the display of such a move. Along with the former Soviet Union, China contributed to the rise of the second generation of rights and played an important role in the three-generation debate. After Tiananmen, however, human rights had become a structural weakness that China had to overcome through active diplomacy. As mentioned in the previous paragraph, under the Chinese conception, civil and political rights, deemed essentially individual rights, are, at China's present state of national development, subsidiary to a claimed '*people's* right to subsistence', termed 'the most important of all human rights, without which the other rights are out of the question'.[105] In the multilateral setting, China also asserts a right to develop in a manner linked to its own cultural framework and economic development, different from the liberal West. Both these positions have now found an embodiment in two recent HRC resolutions, both sponsored by China, and a number of other states.

On 7 July 2017, the HRC passed resolution 35/21 untitled 'The contribution of development to the enjoyment of all human rights',[106] by a recorded vote of 30 to 13, with 3 abstentions. All Westerns countries sitting in the Council

---

[103] H. Chen, 'China's Innovative ISDS Mechanisms and Their Implications', *AJIL Unbound*, vol. 112, 2018, p. 207, concluding that Chinese innovations of recent years in ISDS should be understood as reflecting three important goals of China's broader international strategy: to protect China's outbound investors, to help shape international investment treaty discourse, and to offer alternative Chinese-initiated international institutions so as to disrupt the monopoly currently enjoyed by Western-initiated international institutions.

[104] On 4 April 2018, for example, China filed a request for consultation with the US with a view to ascertaining whether US tariff increases on steel, aluminium, and other Chinese products are in conformity with WTO law. China claims the tariffs would be in excess of the US' and are inconsistent with Arts. I and II GATT and Art. 23 DSU. WTO, *United States – Tariffs Measures on Certain Goods from China*, Request for consultation by China, 4 April 2018, WT/DS543/1.

[105] Government White Paper, *Human Rights in China, Preface, Information Office of the State Council of the People's Republic of China*, November 1991, available at www.china.org.cn/e-white, at Section I, first unnumbered para.

[106] HRC, Resolution 35/21, UN Doc. A/HRC/RES/35/21, 22 June 2017.

voted against.[107] The resolution reaffirms that 'all human rights are universal, indivisible, interdependent and interrelated and that the international community must treat human rights globally in a fair and equal manner, on the same footing and with the same emphasis' and '[r]*ecognizes* that development and the realization of human rights and fundamental freedoms are interdependent and mutually reinforcing'. It also affirms that the Sustainable Development Goals (SDGs) 'are integrated and indivisible, global in nature and universally applicable, take into account different national realities, capacities and levels of development and respect national policies and priorities' and that 'the existence of extreme poverty inhibits the full and effective enjoyment of human rights'. On this basis, resolution 35/21 calls upon all states 'to realize people-centred development of the people, by the people and for the people' and 'to spare no effort to promote sustainable development, in particular while implementing the 2030 Agenda for Sustainable Development, as it is conducive to the overall enjoyment of human rights' (paragraphs 2–3).

The link between development and human rights, in particular first generation rights is not new,[108] nor is China's expressed support for economic, social and cultural rights and its often-claimed record in lifting some of its citizens out of poverty. The resolution does spell out a number of sensible things, but it also seeks to frame the right to development as a right for states, not for people and communities. Far from achieving its purpose of empowering vulnerable populations, when cast this way, the right to development can be used by states to justify major construction and development projects, which often trample the rights of the very populations the norm is intended to protect.[109] Moreover, the right to development has a collective (though not statist) component, but its exercise presupposes popular participation in the political process of development. Such a right of participation can only be meaningful if those who will reap the fruits also bear the burdens of development, and are able to exercise

---

[107] The voting was as follows: *In favour*: Bangladesh, Bolivia (Pluri-national State of), Botswana, Brazil, Burundi, China, Congo, Côte d'Ivoire, Cuba, Ecuador, Egypt, El Salvador, Ethiopia, Ghana, India, Indonesia, Iraq, Kenya, Kyrgyzstan, Mongolia, Nigeria, Philippines, Qatar, Rwanda, Saudi Arabia, South Africa, Togo, Tunisia, United Arab Emirates, Venezuela (Bolivarian Republic of); *Against*: Albania, Belgium, Croatia, Germany, Hungary, Japan, Latvia, Netherlands, Portugal, Slovenia, Switzerland, United Kingdom, United States of America; *Abstaining*: Georgia, Panama, Republic of Korea.

[108] See the Declaration on the Right to Development, *supra* note 26.

[109] M. Kothari, 'China's Trojan Horse Human Rights Resolution', *The Diplomat*, 22 March 2018, available at https://thediplomat.com/2018/03/chinas-trojan-horse-human-rights-resolution/.

their civil and political rights.[110] The right to development is a human right enjoyed by peoples but also by individuals.[111] And empirical evidence suggests that the open society attainable through many first generation rights does not impair, but indeed strengthens, national development.[112]

Resolution 37/23, adopted by the HRC on 23 March 2018,[113] by a recorded vote of 28 to 1, with all 17 Western states but the US abstaining rather voting against,[114] also seeks to promote a state-centric approach in the implementation of all human rights, including the right to development. Under the title 'Promoting mutually beneficial cooperation in the field of human rights', the resolution states that the work of the HRC shall be guided by the 'principles of universality, impartiality, objectivity and non-selectivity', but also by the principles of 'constructive international dialogue and cooperation'. The notion of 'mutually beneficial cooperation', however, remains vague and undefined – the resolution requests the Council's Advisory Committee to conduct a study and submit a report on the matter. The main emphasis is on 'technical

---

[110] Before it was replaced in 2006 by the HRC, the UN Human Rights Commission, whose membership reflected a wide cross-section of human, legal and political cultures, affirmed that democracy, development and human rights are interdependent and mutually reinforcing and that democracy is based on the freely expressed will of the people to determine their own political, economic, social and cultural systems and on their full participation in all aspects of their lives. Commission on Human Rights, Resolution 2003/36, UN Doc. E/CN.4-RES/2003/36, 23 April 2003, Interdependence between democracy and human rights.

[111] Declaration on the Right to Development, Art. 1. See D. I. Fisher, 'The Emerging Right to Development and its Relationship to First Generation Rights: An Analysis of the "Asian Values" View', *Scandinavian Studies in Law*, vol. 55, 2015, p. 321, p. 338: 'The "Asian values" claim to place the interest in national development before respect for first generation rights is not borne out by an examination of the right to development as it has come to expression in various international instruments.'

[112] I endorsed this approach in my report to the UNGA (72nd session), in my previous capacity as UN Special Rapporteur on the rights to freedom of peaceful assembly and of association: Report of the Special Rapporteur on the rights to freedom of peaceful assembly and of association, UN Doc. A/72/135, 14 July 2017, at 7–8: 'a major shift in the global human rights conversation requires the recognition that the interaction between development and human rights is twofold. Development contributes to human rights, and the enjoyment of those rights promotes development.'

[113] HRC, Resolution 37/23, UN Doc. A/HRC/37/23, 23 March 2018.

[114] The voting was as follows: *In favour*: Angola, Brazil, Burundi, Chile, China, Côte d'Ivoire, Cuba, Democratic Republic of the Congo, Ecuador, Egypt, Ethiopia, Iraq, Kenya, Kyrgyzstan, Mexico, Mongolia, Nepal, Nigeria, Pakistan, Panama, Philippines, Qatar, Saudi Arabia, Senegal, South Africa, Togo, United Arab Emirates, Venezuela (Bolivarian Republic of); *Against*: United States of America; *Abstaining*: Afghanistan, Australia, Belgium, Croatia, Georgia, Germany, Hungary, Japan, Peru, Republic of Korea, Rwanda, Slovakia, Slovenia, Spain, Switzerland, Ukraine, United Kingdom.

assistance and capacity building' and the UPR 'as a mechanism based on cooperation and constructive dialogue' (paragraphs 3 and 5). Again, this resolution privileges the sovereign state over peoples and communities, and interstate dialogue and cooperation over recognition, monitoring, and accountability for violations and justice for victims.[115]

Whatever their shortcomings and uncertain future,[116] these two recent HRC resolutions address existing gaps: eradication of extreme poverty is paramount to the enjoyment of rights and international cooperation is key to sustainable and inclusive development. It is paradoxical, however, and again perhaps an irony of history, that they were proposed by one of the states with the worst historical human rights record (regularly cited in Secretary-Generals' reports as engaging in persistently unpunished reprisals against human rights defenders at both the national and international levels). And they find no support – where not the open opposition – of the traditional human rights champions.[117]

---

[115] 'The "cooperation" which the resolution presents can become an escape route for governments who prefer an absence of scrutiny for their questionable practices, and go to great lengths at home and abroad to avoid it. For civil society and affected populations, however, the move away from scrutiny is a move to entrench impunity for human rights violations.' Kothari, 'China's Trojan Horse'.

[116] After just over a decade of existence, the HRC itself risked following its predecessor's faith because of the US resigning its membership, effective 19 June 2018; On 13 July 2018, however, Iceland was elected to serve as a member from 13 July 2018 to 31 December 2019 to replace the vacancy left by the US. See OHCHR, Current Membership of the Human Rights Council, available at https://www.ohchr.org/en/hrbodies/hrc/pages/currentmembers.aspx.

[117] See H. Joon Kim, 'The Prospects of Human Rights in US–China Relations: A Constructivist Understanding', *International Relations of the Asia-Pacific*, 2018, p. 3, considering it likely that relations between the US and China – the two most important actors in world politics today – will profoundly affect the twenty-first century international order and that international human rights norms will become increasingly important in the future US–China relations: 'although convergence is not completely impossible, the past dynamic of competition and confrontation will continue and human rights will still be a contentious issue in U.S.-China relations'. Admittedly, the cause of 'China anxiety' is not the material aspect of power that China has been projecting in the world but rather the challenge made by the political and economic success of China to the fundamental philosophical assumptions and political beliefs of the US and other Western countries, such as belief in democracy or a liberal world order. G. J. Ikenberry, 'The Rise of China and the Future of the West: Can the Liberal System Survive?', *Foreign Affairs*, vol. 87(1), 2008, p. 23; G. J. Ikenberry, *America's Challenge: The Rise of China and the Future of Liberal International Order* [online video], 2011, available at https://www.youtube.com/watch?v=Lv7TVg1Cfvs.

REUNITING HUMAN RIGHTS WITH TRADE, INVESTMENT AND DEVELOPMENT UNDER FTAS AND THE SDGS

Outside the framework of the international human rights regime, numerous attempts are ongoing to reunite trade, investment and development both with each other and with human rights.

Since the failure of the Doha Round, many countries have increasingly negotiated bilateral and regional trade deals in which they agree to eliminate tariffs for products made within the trading bloc.[118] In principle, this new generation of Free Trade Agreements (FTAs) falls under the exception of Article XXIV GATT. FTAs, however, have grown in number and scope to such an extent that they risk segregating the world into overlapping trading blocs with different rules that will substitute, rather than remain complementary to, the multilateral trading system.[119]

While primarily aimed to establish or further deepen preferential trade relations between the parties, several FTAs now include an investment chapter – comprehensive of both investment protection and dispute settlement provisions.[120] Increased recognition that Western power has become less extensive, while certain non-Western states are more active in the investment treaty system, has led to efforts to reform the regime,[121] with a view to rebalancing

---

[118] For example, the now defunct Trans-Pacific Partnership negotiated by the US with Japan, Vietnam, and nine other countries. America and the EU also negotiated but failed to conclude the Transatlantic Trade and Investment Partnership. China, which was not part of the Trans-Pacific Partnership, has signed many bilateral and regional agreements and proposed a 16-country trade deal that would include India and Japan. For an overview of current FTAs and other trade negotiations see European Commission, Overview of FTA and Other Trade Negotiations, updated July 2019, available at http://trade.ec.europa.eu/doclib/docs/2006/december/tradoc_118238.pdf.

[119] For a different view see e.g. S. Urata, 'Mega-FTAs and the WTO: Competing or Complementary?', *International Economic Journal*, vol. 30(2), 2016, p. 231, arguing that mega-FTAs and the WTO can be complementary, as mega-FTAs could facilitate negotiations with a smaller number of negotiating members, and further stressing the importance of extending mega-FTAs to a global level by merging with other mega-FTAs and by accepting new members.

[120] For an interesting discussion of whether and to what extent considerations regarding transparency in trade dispute settlement under the recent FTAs concluded by the EU may be transposed on ISDS, see C. Schewe, 'Clearing Up? Transparency in the Dispute Settlement of International Trade Agreements', *German Yearbook of International Law*, vol. 59, 2016, p. 391.

[121] For recent work on this topic see A. Roberts, 'Incremental, Systemic and Paradigmatic Reform of Investor-State Arbitration', *American Journal of International Law*, vol. 112(3), 2018, p. 412; Cai and Roberts (eds.), 'Symposium on the BRICS

foreign investment protection with the regulatory powers of the host state and making ISDS more predictable, consistent and transparent. Among the proposals that have emerged is also the possibility of international investment courts instead of ISDS.[122] Some FTAs also include a development and/or an environment chapter.

It is too early to assess this new generation of FTAs with respect to their stated aim of fostering trade and investment while at same time promoting human rights, particularly labour rights, the protection of the environment, and other third generation rights (such as the right to clean water and other essential goods, usually provided by state public services).[123] They look more promising, however, than recent and current efforts at bridging the divides from within the human rights regime itself. And whether they will be successful or not, they represent a clear sign that there exists a need to 'reunite' within a single normative framework these multiple areas of the law.

In the same perspective, it is worth recalling that in 2000, building upon a decade of major UN conferences and summits, world leaders adopted the UN Millennium Declaration,[124] committing their nations to a new global partnership to reduce extreme poverty and setting out eight time-bound targets that have become known as the Millennium Development Goals (MDGs). The MDGs range from halving extreme poverty to halting the spread of HIV/AIDS and providing universal primary education, all by the target date of 2015. Starting from 2016, UN General Assembly Resolution 70/1 'Transforming our

---

Approach to the Investment Treaty System'. See also Morosini and Badin (eds.), *Reconceptualizing International Investment Law from the Global South*, discussing alternative approaches to the regulation of international investment among states in the Global South.

[122] On the EU proposed Multilateral Investment Court currently under discussion in the framework of the UN Commission on International Trade Law, see United Nations Commission on International Trade Law, Working Group III: Investor-State Dispute Settlement Reform, available at https://uncitral.un.org/en/working_groups/3/investor-state. Other efforts at bridging some of the existing gaps include the ongoing UN work on a declaration for the rights of peasants and negotiations of a binding treaty on business and human rights, which would regulate the activities of transnational corporations and other business enterprises with respect to human rights.

[123] For an overview see S. A. Aaronson and J. P. Chauffour, *The Wedding of Trade and Human Rights: Marriage of Convenience or Permanent Match?*, WTO research and analysis, available at www.wto.org/english/res_e/publications_e/wtr11_forum_e/wtr11_15feb11_e.htm. For a thorough examination of the social and labour provisions contained in the chapters on sustainable development of trade agreements negotiated by the EU since 2008, see L. Richieri Hanania, 'The Social Dimension of Sustainable Development in EU Trade Agreements: Strengthening International Labour Standards', *German Yearbook of International Law*, vol. 59, 2016, p. 435.

[124] UNGA Res. 55/2, 18 September 2000.

World: The 2030 Agenda for Sustainable Development' (2030 Agenda), set a new framework, the so-called SDGs: a collection of seventeen global goals, broad and interdependent, that cover social and economic development issues including poverty, hunger, health, education, global warming, gender equality, water, sanitation, energy, urbanization, environment and social justice.

Through the MDGs first, and the SDGs later, the right to development has thus been linked to economic growth and poverty reduction, rather than political rights and personal freedoms. It is also linked to the right to security. Furthermore, on 20 July 2016, the UN issued an updated overview of the major international economic and policy challenges that must be addressed to achieve the aims of the 1974 Declaration on the Establishment of a New International Economic Order.[125] The report finds that some of the ideas raised at the time are still relevant and useful for implementing the 2030 Agenda for Sustainable Development. This is another important recognition that the furtherance of development away from international cooperation in economic matters is an unattainable goal.

CONCLUDING REMARKS

This chapter retraced the main phases that brought about the divide between human rights and international trade and investment, which could have been instead each other's most natural allies. The relationship between human rights and development is equally marked by separateness – development having had a much later emergence as a matter of international concern. History shows that the particular evolution of human rights as a separate branch of international law, with its own form (treaties), substance (rights and obligations), and procedure (monitoring mechanisms), was the result of several failures during the Cold War and the decolonization period: the failures of the unitary design of the UDHR and the Havana Charter and the failure of the NIEO. So was the internal division into generations of rights, based upon the preponderance of their respective dimension (individual, ESC, or collective). Subsequent failures have deepened, rather than cured the divides.

The story of human rights is also a story of a rising divide between theory and practice. It is submitted that the particular historical evolution of human rights as distinct from other domains of global governance is at the origin of its current 'effectiveness' crisis. For the past seventy years, the development

---

[125] UN Secretary-General Report, 'Updated overview of the major international economic and policy challenges for equitable and inclusive sustained economic growth and sustainable development, and of the role of the United Nations in addressing these issues in the light of the New International Economic Order', 20 July 2016, UN Doc. A/71/168.

of international legal rules has been the central collective strategy to promote respect for, and observance of, human rights. International human rights law grows every day, enriching itself with new treaties, declarations and resolutions. States and NGOs continue to feel a need for such international instruments covering certain areas of human rights. Whether or not the twilight or decline of human rights is a plausible scenario,[126] however, it is at least doubtful that existing human rights norms and institutions possess the power to positively affect future human rights practices.

This chapter also examined some of the recent and current attempts to bridge the divides both internal and external to the human rights regime. It critically assessed the doctrine of the universality and interdependence of human rights as well as China's new international human rights diplomacy.

The new generation of FTAs and the SDGs are other efforts at filling existing gaps and reconciling actors, actions and policies. They may or may not be effective with respect to their stated aim, but they are worth exploring. While there might be reasons to resist the 'merger and acquisition of human rights'[127] by trade law or other branches of international law, there is a more compelling need to overcome historical divides and integrate human rights in development strategies and in the economic sphere, with a view to ensuring human rights-coherent development and economic policies. History illuminates the divides. It is up to international law and politics to bridge the gaps.

---

[126] S. Hopgood, *The Endtimes of Human Rights*, Ithaca, NY: Cornell University Press, 2013, arguing that we are on the verge of the global human rights regime.

[127] The expression is borrowed from the famous 'Petersmann–Alston debate': P. Alston, 'Resisting the Merger and Acquisition of Human Rights by Trade Law: A Reply to Petersmann', *European Journal of International Law*, vol. 13(4), 2002, p. 815 and E. U. Petersmann, 'Taking Human Dignity, Poverty and Empowerment of Individuals More Seriously: Rejoinder to Alston', *European Journal of International Law*, vol. 13(4), 2002, p. 845.

4. EU human rights law and history: a tale of three narratives
Sionaidh Douglas-Scott

INTRODUCTION

The twenty-first century European Union (EU) proclaims its respect for human rights.[1] Indeed, in an era of concern for human rights, it would seem strange if the EU did not engage with them. However, it is also clear that the EU's concern for rights may be explained in terms of different historical sources.

First, one source for the growth of an EU human rights law relates to the Union's earliest days and configuration as the European Economic Community (EEC), a clear response to the horrors of the earlier twentieth century. Its objective from the outset was to stop yet another deadly, destructive war in Europe. The European history of human rights is truly 'written in blood'.[2] But the aspiration to perpetual peace in Europe did not merely entail economic integration as an end to conflict – it also required the enforcement of standards to prevent any reappearance of the horrors of war and dictatorship.

One the other hand, the Single Market project has always been at the heart of the EU and requires the removal of national obstacles to integration – even

---

[1] A brief note of clarification is necessary. The EU has a Charter of *Fundamental Rights*, Article 6(3) of the Treaty on European Union (TEU) makes reference to *fundamental* rights as general principles of law (and the European Court of Justice uses this term in its jurisprudence) whereas Article 2 TEU refers to 'respect for *human* rights' which is also the term used in most Bills of Rights and international treaties. It is suggested that the distinction is not highly significant, but that 'fundamental' rights in the context of EU law tend to be those which have legal protection in constitutions or treaties, whereas 'human' rights denote a broader category of rights generally viewed as embodying widely shared values and deserving respect regardless of whether they have legal protection or not. This chapter will generally employ the term 'human rights' as being more broadly recognized and understood.

[2] Per K. Günther, 'The Legacies of Injustice and Fear: A European Approach to Human Rights and their Effects on Political Culture', in P. Alston (ed.), *The EU and Human Rights*, Oxford: Oxford University Press, 1999, p. 127.

possibly those predicated upon human rights. Consequently, the EU's own focus on human rights was initially developed as a response to the thinly veiled threat of national courts invoking their own human rights standards to review EU law.

Yet both of the above accounts are too simplistic: the latter is too cynical in its implication that EU human rights law developed to safeguard the Single Market, and the former too generous – for if preserving peace required enforcement of specific standards, why were human rights not specifically mentioned in the original EEC treaty? Further, both accounts fail to take account of the messy, complex reality that has inspired the EU to embrace and give effect to human rights.

NOT TWO BUT THREE NARRATIVES

In any case, by looking more closely with aid of an historical[3] lens, we can see that these accounts need to be augmented by a third, which considers the evidence for EU human rights law in a more measured and nuanced way. So it is possible to detect (at least) three distinct narratives at work in the arena of EU human rights law, each surveying the development of that law over the period of the EEC/EU's existence. Briefly summarized, they are as follows.

First, we might look at the development of EU human rights law through a narrative of progress, of the evolution of the EU in an affirmative, moral direction, complementing its economic focus. Conversely, a second approach, the reverse of this progress narrative, critiques it, and instead identifies the EU as in fact instrumentalizing human rights as tools for economic integration. A third narrative, more subtle, complex and nuanced, attempts to situate EU human rights more effectively within their context and history, arguing greater insights can be found in this way.

This narrative approach to EU human rights law follows the turn to history in international law. There already exists a growing body of scholarship on the relationship between history and EU law, although it constitutes a smaller body than has been developed on the turn to theory in EU law. More particularly, there exists rather little yet on EU law and history available in English,[4] but undoubtedly it is a developing field, and will expand as the EU itself ages.

---

[3] Although 'historical' in a certain sense, not necessarily one academic historians might share.

[4] Such examples include e.g. M. Rasmussen, 'Rewriting the History of European Public Law: The New Contribution of Historians', *American University International Law Review*, vol. 28(5), 2013, p. 1187; Court of Justice of the EU, *50th Anniversary of the Judgment in Van Gend en Loos 1963–2013*, Conference proceedings, Luxembourg, *13 May 2013*, Luxembourg: Office des publications de l'Union Européenne, 2013; F.

This turn to history prompts a question. Why should we look back instead of forward? Does a concern with historical scholarship and the past signify a coming of age for EU law, as indeed the recognition of its important anniversaries such as of the signing of the Treaty of Rome, or of the *Van Gend en Loos* judgment, might suggest?

But perhaps this historical turn in EU law might also signify that all is not right? Indeed, it is hard to escape the reflection that, within the EU, all is indeed not right. Given the quick succession of recent critical points and emergencies – the financial crisis within the Eurozone, the migration crisis, and now the prospect of Brexit – one might ask, whither the EU? Yet the EU has of course survived serious problems before, such as the 'Empty Chair' crisis in the 1960s provoked by the French Gaullists, or the resignation of most of the EU Commission in the late 1990s on grounds of fraud and mismanagement, for example. Hence, we might possibly see a turn to history as therapy.[5] In this sense, a turn to history might help illuminate how the EU has, in the past, used law as a remedy and cure for problems – to help structure, support and channel power and accountability. Yet there is also a politics of this turn to history – because history is not neutral, there exist different historical approaches and interests at stake, as reflection on the three narratives examined below reveals.

THE EU'S NARRATIVE OF PROGRESS

I start by considering EU human rights law in the context of a narrative of progress, one that focuses on the EU's (or EEC as it then was) starting point as an organization set up in the aftermath of the Second World War to help preserve the peace, and increase prosperity by securing a Common or Single Market. The tendency, and perhaps the danger, of this approach is to present the history of European integration in chronological fashion, a chronicle of a growing momentum toward European integration (if also one of fits and starts), as a progress, or pilgrimage, toward the apotheosis of a united European polity.

The institutional architects of the EEC – Spaak, Monnet and, a little later, Walter Hallstein – designed it to be evolutionary, an entity in the process of continuous creation. Even if Europe seemed (and often still does seem) to be on a journey to an unknown destination, with the benefit of hindsight it

---

Nicola and B. Davies, *EU Law Stories: Contextual and Critical Histories of European Jurisprudence*, Cambridge: Cambridge University Press, 2017.

[5] See M. Koskenniemi, 'What Should International Legal History Become?' in S. Kadelbach, T. Kleinlein and D. Roth-Isigkeit (eds.), *System, Order, and International Law: The Early History of International Legal Thought from Machiavelli to Hegel*, Oxford: Oxford University Press, 2017, p. 382, for further expansion on using 'history as therapy'.

is all too easy to present European integration in eschatological terms, as an onward process. Just as the Italian art critic, Vasari, writing at the end of the High Renaissance, could look back at Italian art over the previous 300 years as a march toward the grand 'terza maniera' of Michelangelo, with Giotto and Masaccio as staging posts along the way, so one might imagine some fictional (but all too probable) 'European' some time later this century, looking back at 100 years of European integration, and identifying the European Coal and Steel Community (ECSC), the EEC, the Single European Act, the Maastricht Treaty, the Charter of Fundamental Rights, the establishment of the Euro, the Lisbon Treaty, and so on, as important staging posts (or as what Bruce Ackerman has deemed 'constitutional moments') in the path to European unity.

Such a perspective comports with an approach taken by much international law scholarship, whereby texts are interpreted to display a kind of historical teleology, i.e. this approach begins with ancient city states, continues with expansion through Roman law, *ius gentium*, dearth of arrangements in the Dark and Middle Ages, through the Peace of Westphalia as symbol of the modern state system (perhaps identified as the latent object of prior history) followed by colonial expansion, with Hague Peace conferences paving the way for the development of the League of Nations and the United Nations, eventually bringing us up to date with a contemporary disposition toward globalization (not yet acknowledged by all).

This approach might seem to have something in common with what historian Herbert Butterfield termed 'the Whig interpretation of history', namely, reading history as a progress, starting in some benighted time and somehow directed upon, or inevitably culminating in, the glorious present, which Butterfield described as 'to emphasise certain principles of progress in the past and to produce a story which is the ratification if not the glorification of the present'.[6]

But such an optimistic, teleological approach is not only the preserve of Whig historians. Kant's *Idea for a Universal History with a Cosmopolitan Purpose* aimed to show that, behind the apparently 'senseless course of human events' it was nevertheless possible to identify a 'purpose in nature'. For Kant, moral progress required that humanity's unsocial qualities be brought under control to eventually embrace a 'universal *cosmopolitical existence*, [. . .] within which all the original capacities of the human race may develop',[7]

---

[6] H. Butterfield, *The Whig Interpretation of History*, London: Bell and Sons, 1931. It is worth noting that Butterfield was critical of this 'Whig' approach and was also himself criticized for not producing sufficient evidence of its existence.

[7] I. Kant, 'Idea for a Universal History with a Cosmopolitan Purpose', in H. Reiss (ed.), *Kant: Political Writings*, Cambridge: Cambridge University Press, 1991, p. 46.

a process requiring that competition and conflict be regulated by law. Law too, played an important role in Hans Kelsen's blueprint for 'Peace through Law', peace guaranteed by compulsory adjudication of international disputes, with the formation of a World Court with the authority to resolve international conflicts.[8]

The European Court of Justice and human rights

Yet, even within such a narrative of progress, all is not plain sailing. The EU suffered periods of stagnation in the 1970s, and even as late as March 1982, the cover of *The Economist* showed a tombstone with the words, 'EEC born March 25th 1957, moribund March 25 1982, "capax imperii nisi imperasset"'.

However, one institution apparently not affected by stagnation was the European Court of Justice (ECJ). From early days in the EEC's history – its 'heroic years' – the Court handed down judgments of great significance, instituting the doctrines of direct effect and supremacy of EEC law, actions sometimes perceived as the first steps toward the creation of a European constitution out of the treaties. As well as introducing these foundational principles, the Court also propelled the pace of European integration in a substantive sense. At a time when the Commission was embroiled in a tedious and torpid harmonization process, the ECJ, in landmark judgments such as *Cassis de Dijon*, upheld free movement by requiring member states to engage in mutual recognition of each other's products and product laws, denying them access to the domestic market only if the product failed to satisfy certain mandatory requirements recognized under European law.[9] In this way, continued European integration during this period was as much a legal as a political phenomenon.

However, it was only in December 2000 that the EU proclaimed its own Charter of Fundamental Rights, and only with the coming into force of the Treaty of Lisbon on 1 December 2009, that this Charter eventually attained legally binding force. Therefore, for most of its history, the EU possessed no Charter of Rights. Yet this does not mean that human rights were ignored. For over forty years, human rights had a recognized status in the EU as 'general principles of law',[10] a status confirmed by successive versions of Article 6

---

[8] H. Kelsen, *Peace through Law*, Chapel Hill: University of North Carolina Press, 1944.

[9] ECJ, Judgment of 20 February 1979, Case 120/78, *Cassis de Dijon*, *European Court Reports* 1979, p. 649.

[10] Article 6(3) TEU states that: 'The Union shall respect fundamental rights, as guaranteed by the European Convention on Human Rights and as they result from the constitutional traditions common to member states as general principles of Community law.'

TEU.[11] And there is of course Article 2 TEU's assertion of the foundation of the EU on respect for human rights, which is backed up by a sanctions procedure, in Article 7 TEU, whereby a member state's rights may be suspended if it engages in *'a serious and persistent breach [. . .] of values mentioned in Article 2'*.[12]

Given the absence of any EU Charter of Rights until 2000, protection of human rights for the first forty years of European integration developed through the case law of the European Court of Justice, which undoubtedly played a very important role – just as it had in keeping up the progress of integration in other areas when the political institutions were bogged down or incapacitated. This resulted in a system in which *litigation* has played a very large role in the development, profile and enforcement of human rights.[13]

The same ECJ, which developed the doctrines of direct effect and supremacy of EU law, neither of which doctrines finds explicit basis in the Treaty, also developed a complex doctrine of protection of human rights. The late Judge Mancini, writing in 1989, summed up the position the ECJ had achieved in relation to human rights in the following way: 'Reading an unwritten Bill of Rights into [Union] law is indeed the most striking contribution the Court has made to the development of a constitution for Europe.' But he continued by qualifying it in this way: 'this statement was forced on the Court by the outside, by the German and, later, the Italian constitutional courts'.[14]

It is to this qualification that we now turn.

A CRITIQUE OF THE PROGRESS NARRATIVE

Human rights have been introduced into the EU legal order to protect supremacy and autonomy of EU law

The ECJ has undoubtedly played an important role in the development of a human rights jurisprudence and is well known for its role in 'integration

---

[11] Starting with the insertion of Article F(2) by the Treaty of Maastricht in 1992, which had near identical wording to Article 6(3).

[12] A provision causing controversy because of the failure of the EU to use it swiftly against rule of law breaches by Hungary and Poland.

[13] In some of its earliest case law, the Court of Justice stated that 'the vigilance of individuals concerned to protect their rights amounts to an effective supervision in addition to the supervision entrusted to [. . .] the Commission and member States [. . .]'. ECJ, Judgment of 5 February 1963, Case 16/62, *Van Gend en Loos*, European Court Reports 1963, p. 1.

[14] F. Mancini, 'The Making of a Constitution for Europe', *Common Market law Review*, vol. 26(4), 1989, p. 595.

through law'[15] in the EU. But it did so, one account suggests, not because of any great enthusiasm for the noble ideas of human rights, but rather because the ECJ feared that if it did not, some member state courts, particularly the constitutional courts of Germany and Italy, would refuse to accord supremacy to (then) EEC law if they found it violated human rights in their own constitutions. Wishing to avoid this outcome, the European Court identified a respect for human rights within the Community legal order itself. These human rights have taken the form of *general principles of law*.

In brief, this critique, which forms the second narrative considered here, asserts that the ECJ is more concerned with integration and the supremacy and autonomy of EU law than with human rights *per se*. Indeed, in a well-known article, Coppell and O'Neill suggested that the European Court instrumentalized rights as tools for European integration.[16] Although in early cases ('sins of youth')[17] the ECJ had rejected any applications based on alleged breach of human rights by EEC institutions, by the late 1960s and early 1970s it was forced to acknowledge such claims, and to offer protection to individuals who asserted that the EEC was infringing their human rights. In *Internationale Handelsgesellschaft*[18] (a case brought from Germany alleging a breach of the claimants' rights by a European regulation) the ECJ asserted the (then) EEC's respect for human rights and so also maintained the primacy of EEC law, by ensuring that any breach of human rights (which it did not in the event find) would be a breach of EEC and not national law. Indeed, the European Court's strategy was reasonably successful, despite initial caution by the Italian[19] and German constitutional courts, and in subsequent case law the European Court developed this jurisprudence. In *Nold* in 1974, it made its first reference to the European Convention on Human Rights (ECHR).[20] Other important decisions

---

[15] See on this e.g. M. Cappelletti, M. Seccombe and J. Weiler (eds.), *Integration through Law*, Berlin and New York: Walter de Gruyter, 1986.

[16] J. Coppell and A. O'Neill, 'The European Court of Justice: Taking Rights Seriously?', *Common Market Law Review*, vol. 29(4), 1992, p. 669, at p. 689. Coppell and O'Neill claimed in very few of the cases where the Court used the rhetoric of fundamental rights did the applicant actually succeed in their claim.

[17] The reference is taken from M. Hilf, 'The Protection of Fundamental Rights', in F. Jacobs (ed.), *European Law and the Individual*, Amsterdam: North Holland, 1976.

[18] ECJ, Judgment of 17 December 1970, Case 11/70, *Internationale Handelsgesellschaft*, *European Court Reports* 1970, p. 1125.

[19] Constitutional Court of Italy, Judgment No. 183 of 27 December 1973, *Frontini v. Ministero delle Finanze*, reprinted in English in *Common Market Law Reports*, vol. 2, 1974, p. 372.

[20] ECJ, Judgment of 14 May 1974, Case 4/73, *Nold*, *European Court Reports* 1974, p. 491. Although references to the ECHR had previously been made in pleadings and by Advocates General.

followed, and by the late 1980s, the German constitutional court seemed to think that the EU standard of protection was adequate, when it gave its *Wunsche Handelsgesellschaft* judgment (otherwise known as *Solange II*).[21]

The basic thrust of the critique is that EU human rights protection too strongly reflects the specific form of the EU, and its stress on the Single Market. More specific criticism from the left alleges that the EU overemphasizes market values, for example from Perry Anderson,[22] who argued that the EU developed to ensure preservation of the capitalist economic system in Europe.

The Court's willingness to equate market freedoms in the EU treaty, such as the free movement of goods and services, with human rights, has drawn fire and the counterclaim that the free movement of goods and services are in no way equivalent to human rights. This has become particularly pertinent where there are conflicts of rights, for example, in the conflict between the free movement of services and labour law rights. In both *Viking* and *Laval*,[23] it was claimed that the applicant companies' market freedoms were restricted by trade union collective action. Although the right to take such collective action was acknowledged by the Court as a 'human right', in both cases it was held to be outweighed by the human market freedom of services. The Court found that the right to strike had not been exercised proportionately. Yet such reasoning is antipathetic to human rights and has been strongly criticized,[24] especially in its application of a proportionality test to human rights themselves. Normally, as in the test applied by the European Court of Human Rights, it is the *restrictions* on human rights that must satisfy a proportionality test.

To some extent one could argue that the Court in *Viking* and *Laval* was caught in a bind. If national labour standards in the host state are too high (in the context of posted workers) this renders market penetration from a posting state, with lower labour standards, impossible – thus retarding market integration. On the other hand, with degrading labour standards in the host state, the risk of social dumping arises. Therefore, how the ECJ balances economic human rights with social human rights is critical and,

---

[21] ECJ, Order of 5 March 1986, Case 69/85, *Wunsche, European Court Reports* 1986, p. 947, also known in German as the *Mittlerweile* decision.

[22] P. Anderson, 'Depicting *Europe*', *London Review of Books*, 20 September 2007.

[23] ECJ, Judgments of 18 December 2007, Case C-341/05, *Laval, European Court Reports* 2007, vol. I, p. 11767; and Case C-438/05, *ITWF v. Viking Line, European Court Reports* 2007, vol. I, p. 10779.

[24] See e.g. C. Barnard, 'Social Dumping or Dumping Socialism', *Cambridge Law Journal*, vol. 67(2), 2008, p. 262; D. Nicol, 'Europe's Lochner Moment', *Public Law*, vol. 2, 2011, p. 308.

with respect, it is submitted that the Court failed to achieve that sensitivity in *Viking* owing to its particularly harsh proportionality test.[25]

For all that the competences of the EU have moved beyond its economic origins and the Single Market, the EU still maintains its focus on the economic, as cases such as *Viking* and *Laval* reveal. Indeed, this criticism takes on particular resonance in the context of the Eurozone crisis, which is an area in which EU human rights might have had great value. The provision of monetary assistance – 'bailouts' – to Eurozone countries in severe financial difficulties resulted in heavy interference by the EU in economic policies of recipient member states. However, in the process human rights and the rule of law have been sacrificed.

Has the EU Charter been of any use in protecting those rights? There have been several references to the ECJ (e.g. cases from Portugal, Romania, Cyprus and Greece) on whether reforms to national labour law (required by the EU) were compatible with the Charter.[26] The Court usually found these references inadmissible. Partly, this has been because the Court decided that relevant acts taken were not those of *EU* institutions. One issue of critical importance has been the question of whether EU institutions could disregard the Charter if acting *outside* the EU framework, for example in the context of the European Stability Mechanism (ESM) Treaty, which is an international treaty, not EU law.

Overall, then, the European Court has not acted as an effective counterbalance to the imposition of Eurozone measures on sensitive domestic fields of social policy. It might be thought that the European Court's disinclination to address such cases is understandable. The cases raise human conflicts between, on the one side, large bailouts, complex and fragile political compromises, and the success of the European monetary union project, and on the other side, national labour policy and law. However, the Court has not been so unwilling to hear arguments concerning the Charter in cases of other sorts, and it is hard

---

[25] However, a more nuanced approach was suggested by AG Trstenjak, Opinion of 14 April 2010, Case C-271/08, *Commission v. Germany (Occupational Pensions)*, *European Court Reports* 2010, p. 183; and the European Commission tried to mitigate (unsuccessfully) the effects of *Viking* and *Laval* in the (unadopted) 'Monti II' Regulation.

[26] See e.g. ECJ, Order of 14 December 2011, Case C-434/11, *Corpul National al Politistilor v. Ministerul Administratieis, i Internelor (MAI) and Others*, *European Court Reports* 2011, vol. I, p. 196; see also the Greek cases concerning the Council decision adopted within the framework of the excessive deficit procedure (Cases T-541/10 and T-215/11); see the further cases arising from the Cypriot banking crisis (Case T-327/13; opinion in Joined Cases C-8/15 P, C-9/15 P and C-10/15 P; opinion in Joined Cases C-105/15 P to C-109/15 P).

to see why the Charter should be seen as inoperable in cases arising out of EU measures on the financial and economic crisis.[27]

However, perhaps the culmination of the ECJ's approach to human rights lies in its *Opinion 2/13*, in which it rejected the draft accession agreement on EU accession to the ECHR.[28] Peers went so far as to characterize the Court's *Opinion 2/13* as 'a clear and present danger to human rights protection'.[29] Undoubtedly, the Court's *Opinion* is shot through with statements on the autonomy and special position of EU law, and most particularly with concern for its own prerogatives as ultimate determinant of the EU legal order, rather than any abiding concern with human rights. Thus, the old critique that the ECJ does not take rights seriously springs back to mind. As Leonard Besselink reminds us, rather we must take seriously the ECJ President's announcement at the FIDE Conference 2014: 'The Court is not a human rights court: it is the Supreme Court of the Union.'[30] Indeed, there is something ironic in *Opinion 2/13*, in that the ECJ appears to be opposing ECHR accession for fear this might result in a loss of its sovereignty – a position uncannily similar to that taken by UK Eurosceptics, who desire ECHR membership only on their own terms.

Human rights as political myth of the EU

Indeed, Smismans[31] has developed the arguments above to argue that the EU's approach to human rights has the function of an ancestral, political myth. His argument is as follows.

---

[27] See further on this, C. Barnard, 'The Silence of the Charter: Social Rights and the Court of Justice', in S. de Vries, U. Bernitz and S. Weatherill (eds.), *The EU Charter of Fundamental Rights as a Binding Instrument: Five Years Old and Growing*, Oxford: Hart Publishing, 2015; also C. Kilpatrick, 'Are the Bailouts Immune to EU Social Challenge Because They Are Not EU Law?', *European Constitutional Law Review*, vol. 10(3), 2014, pp. 393–421.

[28] ECJ, Opinion 2/13 of 18 December 2014, *European Court Reports* 2014, vol. I.

[29] S. Peers, 'The CJEU and the EU's Accession to the ECHR: A Clear and Present Danger to Human Rights Protection', *EU Law Analysis*, 18 December 2014, available at http://eulawanalysis.blogspot.com/2014/12/the-cjeu-and-eus-accession-to-echr.html.

[30] L. Besselink, 'Acceding to the ECHR Notwithstanding the Court of Justice Opinion 2/13', *Verfassungsblog*, 23 December 2014, available at http.//www.verfassungsblog.de/en/acceding-echr-notwithstanding-court-justice-opinion-213.

[31] S. Smismans, 'Fundamental Rights as a Political Myth of the EU: Can the Myth Survive?', in S. Douglas-Scott and N. Hatzis (eds.), *Research Handbook on EU Law and Human Rights*, Cheltenham, UK and Northampton, MA, USA: Edward Elgar Publishing, 2017, pp. 13-34.

Human rights have been presented as a ground, an existential basis, of the EU. For example, Article 2 TEU now states that the EU is founded on respect for human rights, strengthened by a reference in that Treaty's Preamble, to 'peace through European integration'. Article 49 TEU makes respecting EU values (including human rights) a condition for EU membership and Article 7 TEU provides that the violation of those values will be grounds for suspending membership. Furthermore, Advocate General Maduro in *Centro Europa 7* interpreted the provisions for human rights in Article 6 TEU as ensuring that 'the very existence of the European Union is predicated on respect for human rights' (a statement notably not adopted by the ECJ) and an 'existential requirement' which aimed to situate the EU beyond market constitutionalism.[32]

In response, Smismans asserts that claims for human rights as a ground for the EEC/EU are just exercises in myth making that have no real basis in fact. The original Treaty of Rome contained no reference to human rights, and the ECJ's early case law ignored human rights. Respect for human rights was not an explicit condition for EEC membership – as illustrated by the fact that there was originally no complaint from other member states to the desire of fascist Spain to join the EEC.

Instead, the EEC/EU developed such claims for the ancestral status of rights retrospectively, for example through the ECJ's 'Copernican revolution' in *Stauder*, and *Handelsgesellschaft*, whereby it found human rights to be 'enshrined in' general principles of law. However, the ECJ provided no specific definition of such human rights, perhaps evidence of their cloudy, myth-like status.

However, Smismans asserts that we should not dismiss this political myth – instead we should try to understand why it is employed. For myths are important, and that is why the EU uses them. A political myth is a story people may wish to believe, even if it includes factual errors. Myths have an important emotional and affective dimension, as Ernst Cassirer recognized, when he wrote that 'myth sprouts forth from deep human emotions'.[33] In these times of 'post truth', it is all too easy to acknowledge that people's belief is contingent on their feelings, emotions and desire to believe, as much as, if not more, than on facts. This motivational dimension,[34] capable of inspiring action, is something much needed in an EU often castigated for its technocratic, market-driven approach. And of course, myths, however factually

---

[32] AG Maduro, Opinion of 12 September 2007, Case C-380/05, *Centro Europa 7*, European Court Reports 2008, vol. I, p. 349, at para. 19.
[33] E. Cassirer, *The Myth of the State*, New Haven, CT: Yale University Press, 1946.
[34] See e.g. R. Barthes, *Mythologies*, London: Paladin Books, 1973.

erroneous, can provide legitimacy, which is why they have proved so useful for nation-states seeking service and compliance from their citizens.[35]

However, in spite of acknowledging the utility and value of ancestral myths, Smismans' argument is that the EU myth is now in crisis, due to expansion of EU competences to areas such as criminal law and anti-terrorism that challenge human rights, as well as from the Eurozone problems which have proved to be an existential crisis for the EU, undermining the belief that economic cooperation would lead to more welfare and peace.

Smismans' conclusion is that the EU can no longer 'myth free ride' on human rights, supposedly shared by its member states, in a present in which populism, nationalism and claims for more national sovereignty are made. (Brexit provides a further example of this.) The myth is simply not strong enough to outweigh these factors.

Andrew Williams[36] similarly alleges that the ECJ ignored rights in its early days, after which it constructed a powerful myth, articulating a value of respect for rights as *already written*. However, respecting human rights was not the primary aim, and indeed the foundations for human rights were unstable. The ECJ coped with uncertainty, and the lack of a clear ethical foundation, by focusing on principles (e.g. supremacy, direct effect, effectiveness) as a substitute. This provided integration, stability and order through law, rather than ethical values. However, in times of crisis, lacking in coherent values, the EU has little to fall back on and its legitimacy proves elusive.

A more general critical narrative

These specific critiques are mirrored more generally by revisionist accounts of human rights, such as those of Samuel Moyn.[37] Moyn's claim is that, although it is common to see the rise of human rights as inevitable, in fact there was no inevitability to their ascendancy and human rights emerged as what Moyn calls 'the last Utopia' because other visions (such as communism) imploded. Today, for many, the primary purpose of international law is to protect human rights, it is no longer the law of nations. But this is a very recent development and

---

[35] E.g. E. J. Hobsbawm, *Nations and Nationalism since 1780*, Cambridge: Cambridge University Press, 1992.
[36] See e.g. A. Williams, *The Ethos of Europe*, Cambridge: Cambridge University Press, 2010.
[37] S. Moyn, *The Last Utopia: Human Rights in History*, Cambridge, MA: Harvard University Press, 2012. Note, however, that Moyn's account has also been criticized as over-reductive, US-centric, and lacking in historical insight, focusing only on human rights in the late twentieth century. See also B. Simpson, *Human Rights and the End of Empire*, Oxford: Oxford University Press, 2004.

was not ineluctable. Indeed, for Moyn, the growth of human rights, through the ECHR for example, was 'a kind of footnote to reinvention of conservatism in power'.[38] Indeed, for Moyn, the founding and earlier days of the ECHR was more of a case of 'ideological signaling about the values on which Western European Identity depended than [. . .] legally enforceable guarantees'.[39]

Perhaps more pertinent is the general rejection of the progress narrative altogether, whatever its context. So for example, Walter Benjamin's *Theses on the Philosophy of History* argues that progress is chaotic, a mere accumulation of past events, not structured. Benjamin perceived progress as a pernicious force of nature, as 'one single catastrophe, which unceasingly piles rubble on top of rubble'.[40] Moreover, Benjamin's claim is that, because progress is unstructured and unstable, humanity is propelled indiscriminately into the future, lacking the ability to interpret and make sense of the past. Pushing this argument further, Adorno and Horkheimer in *Dialectic of Enlightenment*, contest Kant's positive view of Enlightenment.[41] Why would one extol the Enlightenment given its catastrophic effects, for example, the violent and barbaric path of Nazism and Auschwitz? They cite the tendency of rational progress to become irrational regress. And to turn back to the professional historian, Butterfield, again in *The Whig Interpretation of History*[42] is criticized for retrospectively creating of a line of progress from the past to the 'glorious' present, which it is asserted does not in fact exist. Such an approach contorts the past by viewing it through the lens of the present, when we should instead seek the ability to see events as they were perceived by those who lived through them.[43]

In any case, perhaps the most basic question is – what is progress?[44] Progress, like salvation, suggests some temporal improvement or amelioration, but the nature of this 'improvement' is questionable and usually not purely empirical.

---

[38] A point with which Conor Gearty agrees: see C. Gearty, *Can Human Rights Survive?* Hamlyn Lectures 2005, Cambridge: Cambridge University Press, 2006.

[39] Moyn, *The Last Utopia*, p. 79. Moyn, however, does acknowledge that the ECHR became very different in a later era once its original conservative Cold War origins had been forgotten. On the ECHR's conservative founding ethos, see M. Duranti, *The Conservative Human Rights Revolution: European Identity, Transnational Politics, and the Origins of the European Convention*, Oxford: Oxford University Press, 2017.

[40] W. Benjamin, 'Theses on the Philosophy of History,' in W. Benjamin (ed.), *Illuminations*, London: Fontana/Collins, 1973.

[41] T. Adorno and M. Horkheimer, *Dialectic of Enlightenment*, London: Verso, 1989.

[42] Butterfield, *The Whig Interpretation of History*.

[43] See further, Q. Skinner, 'The Practice of History and the Cult of the Fact', in Q. Skinner (ed.), *Visions of History*, Cambridge: Cambridge University Press, 2002, pp. 8-26.

[44] For more on this, see G. Galindo, 'Progressing in International Law' [Book Review], *Melbourne Journal of International Law*, vol. 11(2), 2010, p. 515.

Manley Hudson, in his work *Progress in International Organization*,[45] does not even define the term 'progress', perhaps seeing it as speaking for itself. But the concept of 'progress' is not self-explanatory. Elucidating 'progress' is subjective, an act of judgement, of ideology even. There is no agreed sense of what it might mean in either EU or international law. Is it 'progress' for the EU to have a common currency among its member states (given the problems of the Eurozone), or do the complicated law-making procedures the EU follows (which do not always result in speedy and efficient legislation) signal 'progress'? A lack of clarity over the concept of 'progress' casts doubt over the first progress narrative.

A NUANCED NARRATIVE OF THE EU AND HUMAN RIGHTS

This third narrative is in many ways linked to the second, but it is less critical, less ideological, and less negative.

History is not merely chronology

The opening chapters of textbooks on the EU tend to be chronological, evolutionary in nature. For example, in my own work, *Constitutional Law of the European Union*,[46] I attempted to set EU constitutional law in context, and part of that context is recent legal history, but very often pursued along teleological lines.

However, it might be asserted that we live in a world of historical contingency, rather than some ineluctable Hegelian progress of the *Weltgeist*, and European integration is not set in stone – so any attempt to do justice to European law must reflect that fact. To understand the wranglings of Maastricht, of Lisbon, as well as the EU's perceived lack of democracy, one has to understand its origins, and the purposes of its founders. If Jean Monnet had not been trained in the French *énarque* functionalist background, if Walter Hallstein had not battled with de Gaulle, if the Court of Justice had not picked up the momentum of integration at a certain point, the EU might look different today. Overall, it is important to try to provide a history of European legal integration which is not mere chronology, but one coupled with critical comment and a contextual approach, taking in legal and political theory and

---

[45] M. Hudson, *Progress in International Organization*, Stanford, CA: Stanford University Press, 1932.
[46] S. Douglas-Scott, *Constitutional Law of the European Union*, London: Longman, 2002.

philosophy, as well as political science approaches to that integration – but also to recognize that events have a contingent element and that things might have been different.

In the last five years or so, a new field of historical studies of European law has emerged, with an emphasis on using archival and/or documentary evidence to shed new light on the history of EU law.[47] Historians use such sources to interpret and explain European law in a broad political and societal context, but also try to use these sources to add more nuance to the legal, academic and institutional dimensions of the history of European law. Historians are relative latecomers to EU integration – in comparison with lawyers or political scientists. Historians also employ different methods of research, making use of archives – a crucial feature, as much of what we need to know about key events, including court decisions, took place behind closed doors. Historians can probe more closely the specific historical dynamics that shaped those events, the motivations of individuals, and their impact on important judgments. For example, constitutional reforms that took place in the Netherlands in 1953 and 1956 that introduced the concept of the supremacy of international law set the scene for the crucial *Van Gend en Loos* judgment. They thus provide new insights into how such pivotal cases emerged, into the activities and motivations of the Court's various parties and participators, which may then, in turn, help improve their doctrinal analysis by legal scholars.

Decisions such as *Handelsgesellschaft* were not merely the logical outcome of an EEC determined to protect human rights, but instead contingent on the actions of many players – for example, the litigants and imaginative work of the lawyers who asserted breaches of EU law,[48] the state court judges who made preliminary references to the ECJ,[49] and the courts who ultimately gave those rulings.

---

[47] See e.g. M. Rasmussen and B. Davies, 'From International Law to a European Rechtsgemeinschaft: Towards a New History of European Law, 1950–1979' in J. Laursen (ed.), *Institutions and Dynamics of the European Community 1973–83*, Baden Baden: Nomos, 2014, p. 97; M. Rasmussen, 'Rewriting the History of European Public Law: The New Contribution of Historians', *American University International Law Review*, vol. 28(5), 2013, p. 1187. See also F. Nicol and B. Davies (eds.), *EU Law Stories*, Cambridge: Cambridge University Press, 2017.

[48] For example, the Belgian lawyer Eliane Vogel Polsky, whose innovative work in the *Defrenne* case is detailed in S. Douglas-Scott, 'Subjects and Objects of EU Human Rights Law', in S. Bardutzky and E. Fahey (eds.), *Framing the Subjects and Objects of Contemporary EU Law*, Cheltenham, UK and Northampton, MA, USA: Edward Elgar Publishing, 2017.

[49] At first, the ECJ feared there would be no preliminary references and the story (probably apocryphal) is that champagne corks were popping on the first reference in Case 13/61, *Bosch v. van Rijn*, *European Court Reports* 1962, p. 45, referred in 1961.

An approach such as this notably reduces the autonomy allowed to law, instead positing a very human input.

International law and history: the rejection of a linear trajectory and an overly teleological approach

This turn to history in EU law reflects, more generally, the turn to history in international law, realized in a growing body of scholarship. It demonstrates an unwillingness to view international law as simply following a linear trajectory moving inexorably toward progress and a glorious present. This means a non-teleological history, looking not only at linear narratives, but at branch lines, side streets, discontinuities, missed trajectories, *culs-de-sac* and *impasses*.

For example, Martti Koskenniemi, in *The Gentle Civilizer of Nations*,[50] a well-known intellectual history of international law, invoked a 'turn to history', drawing attention to historical discontinuities developed in the work of Michel Foucault. In *The Archaeology of Knowledge*,[51] Foucault sought to demonstrate how the traditional history of ideas placed an emphasis on the continuities, creating a false sense of coherence in scientific discourse. Foucault suggested that a role for archaeology would be to unveil discontinuities and offer a less distorted view of the field of past events. Studies of past failures, such as the conditions imposed on Germany at the post-First World War Treaty of Versailles, can help elucidate subsequent events, while other historical investigations can make distant events closer.[52]

Roads not taken?

So what difference might it make to take this third approach, focusing on discontinuities, or even on missed trajectories in law? One example in the EU human rights field is provided by Gráinne de Búrca's 'The Road Not Taken: The EU as a Global Human Rights Actor'.[53] De Búrca remarks that while

---

[50] M. Koskenniemi, *The Gentle Civilizer of Nations*, Cambridge: Cambridge University Press, 2001. See also the growth of journals such as *The Journal of the History of International Law*, which evidences the growing interest in history of international law.

[51] M. Foucault, *The Archaeology of Knowledge*, 2nd ed., London: Routledge, 2002.

[52] See for example, C. Ginzburg, *The Cheese and the Worms: The Cosmos of a Sixteenth-Century Miller*, reprint ed., Baltimore: Johns Hopkins University Press, 1992 – sixteenth-century history seen through the eyes of a miller who was accused of heresy during the Inquisition.

[53] G. de Búrca, 'The Road Not Taken: The EU as a Global Human Rights Actor', *American Journal of International Law*, vol. 105(4), 2011, p. 649.

for many, the Lisbon Treaty marks the coming of age for the EU as a human rights actor (for whom the low point was the silence of the founding treaties on human rights in the 1950s) this narrative of progress may be questioned. Instead of placing the ECJ at the centre of the EU's human rights narrative, as a 'heroic and solitary actor', we should note that there has been no unidirectional progress but instead a dialectical tension between actors, officials and lawyers in the EEC/EU. For, if we look back to the European Political Cooperation (EPC) Treaty (never executed) in 1953, one may observe some very ambitious clauses, in some ways more ambitious than today's EU human rights provisions (e.g. the more robust incorporation of human rights into internal and external policy dimensions). Indeed, de Búrca remarks that none of the founding member states of the ECSC/EEC had any problem with a supranational community playing a prominent role in the human rights field. The fact that human rights were not included in the Treaty of Rome in 1957 was not due to any explicit decision to rule human rights out of the EEC, but rather to caution after the earlier failure of the European Defence Community and EPC treaties. This is a rejection of both the 'progress narrative' but also the view that sees the EU's later embrace of human rights as instrumental and cynical, given its earlier failure to incorporate them into the EEC Treaty. Instead, de Búrca concludes that it is misplaced to read too much into the silence of the EEC Treaty on human rights, given that member states in the early days of the EEC were merely seeking a pragmatic and workable path for this new community.

In the same vein, Martti Koskenniemi, in 'What Should International Legal History Become?',[54] appears to suggest that much is to be gained by a focus on historical events and issues not traditionally considered so important by international law. For example, he argues that international law should take note of the way that private interests, rather than states, have influenced its development – e.g. such issues as banking and credit systems that find little space in international law's history. The famous Dutch jurist Hugo Grotius regarded the Dutch East India Company as both a private enterprise and a representative of the United Provinces; and the British East India Company, a private chartered company, ruled and controlled much of the British Empire for many years up to its demise in the mid-nineteenth century, with a great impact on the laws of those colonies. To this we could add the importance of those Charters under which private companies ruled the thirteen British colonies in North America,[55] with far greater influence on North American law than the British state. Koskenniemi regrets that so little attention has been paid to the private

---

[54] M. Koskenniemi, 'What Should International Legal History Become?'
[55] See e.g. J. Muldoon, 'Colonial Charter: Possessory or Regulatory?', *Law and History Review*, vol. 36(2), 2018, p. 355.

law that so often provided the support for state action. International lawyers are undoubtedly interested in sovereignty, in the emergence of independent 'states', in war, and in treaty making, but too often ignore private relations, and so failed to notice so much of importance in earlier times – particularly the great shift in the seventeenth and eighteenth centuries that accounted for 'jealousy of trade', and the creation of the East India Companies and their growth in power and influence of laws.

How can we carry Koskenniemi's observations over to the field of EU law and human rights? De Búrca's article has already been noted, although its field largely relates to states, governments and traditional subjects of international law. However, looking to history, and also bearing in mind private interests and their importance in the EEC/EU, also provides a better interpretation of the field of EU human rights. We have already noted how a stress on free market rights can sit uneasily with human rights protection[56] – in most constitutions and international rights documents greater priority is given to civil and political rights. But in the EEC/EU, human rights grew out of private law, as did much of its 'Constitution'. It was traders in fruit, grain and other commodities[57] who first asserted human rights claims in EEC law to protect their trading rights. Nearly all of the EEC's human rights cases up until about 2000 involved manufacturers and traders, usually corporate claimants – of coal, wine, butter, milk, and so on. However, we may also locate the EEC/EU focus on economic rights in a historico-philosophical tradition. For Locke, property rights were the prototypical natural rights which became translated into a civil right under the law.[58] A formative influence on the EEC/EU Single Market was the ordoliberal economic theory of the market – but one in which market freedoms were seen as intrinsic to the notion of human dignity, as well as upholding the theory of contract and private property rights.[59] Thus, rather than uplifting the economic rights to the same status as a right to *human dignity*, it might be said that, under this vision, human dignity is achieved by the functioning of a free and equal market society. This certainly does not provide a full theory

---

[56] See the 'A critique of the progressive narrative' section above.
[57] As in Case 40/64, *Sgarlata v. Commission*, *European Court Reports* 1965, p. 215, and Case 11/70, *Internationale Handelsgesellschaft*, *European Court Reports* 1970, p. 1125.
[58] J. Locke, *Second Treatise* in P. Laslett (ed.), *Two Treatises on Government*, Cambridge: Cambridge University Press, 1963.
[59] See E. U. Petersmann, 'National Constitutions, Foreign Trade Policy and European Community Law', *European Journal of International Law*, vol. 3(1), pp. 1–35; see also D. Chalmers, 'The Single Market: From Prima Donna to Journeyman', in J. Shaw and G. More (eds.), *New Legal Dynamics of the European Union*, Oxford: Oxford University Press, 1996, pp. 55–72, who suggests that the European Court is now less influenced by ordoliberal theory than in its early days.

of human rights for the EU, nor one adequate to deal with the richness of its twenty-first century case law – indeed, many will find it ideologically unsympathetic and scanty – but it does temper and neutralize somewhat the second narrative explored earlier, by adding a more nuanced approach to the subject, and reminding us of the importance of private interests in history, and private law in the EU, and trading organizations more generally.

CONCLUSION

So what is to be gained then, from interpreting the history of EU human rights law in terms of these three narratives?

If we contrast them, then narratives one and two may seem overly simplistic. And, to a certain extent, narratives one and two do function as 'straw men', or heuristic devices, to highlight the issues, problems or benefits raised by certain legal events. The claim is that narrative three is more nuanced, less ideological, and can counterbalance brasher interpretations, and help shed new light. It can, in Foucauldian terms, allow the historian to discover a multiplicity of discourses operating within a field of knowledge. So, for example, a work like *EU Law Stories* claims to be able to assess much more accurately the historical dynamics that shaped an event, the precise motives of key actors, and, finally, the legal nature of the judgment.

However, we should not discard the merits and lessons of narratives one and two. They also serve their purposes. There is some sense in narrative one. In spite of the messiness and ad hoc nature of human rights law in the EU, it is, and has been, beneficial. (Of course, those of us in the UK are well-placed to appreciate the benefits of EU human rights law, given we may be in danger of losing them with Brexit.) We should not overemphasize the merits of a progress-driven narrative of human rights, but we do sometimes need to be able to tell a simple story, of how the EU's human rights law has benefited so many – including individuals, traders and workers. There is some truth in suspicions of human rights manipulation and instrumentalization by EU institutions. However, this is not the whole story. If the discourse of EU human rights were never more than rhetoric, merely a useful mechanism for those in power, human rights law would not have become hegemonic, nor would it have delivered actual results. Evidence of abuse of human rights for certain ends does not disqualify them as emancipatory devices. Human rights have succeeded as the contemporary expression of aspirations for justice in the EU because they can produce concrete benefits and improvements for those who assert them. The EU Charter of Human Rights can achieve this, containing in one document both civil and political rights and economic and social rights – thus stressing the indivisibility of human rights. The Charter also applies against the institutions and bodies of the EU itself, thus binding the

EU to standards which it has often imposed on others, and requiring the EU to make itself accountable. Narrative one has value because sometimes practical and pragmatic steps – litigating human rights – rely on a simple story, that the EU protects human rights, and has its own Charter of Rights, not a complex historical investigation.

The second narrative also has value, albeit that it opens our eyes to abuses, and engages in what a different group might describe as 'trashing'.[60] Yet it also recognizes the importance of myth, and that the EU needs its myths. EU governance is all too often experienced as devoid of ethically compelling nature, and law (EU law, as well as law more generally) as externally coercive and not internally binding. H. L. A. Hart described in his work something he termed an 'internal point of view', a normative and 'critical reflective attitude' toward one's legal system, ensuring engagement with it.[61] Yet few citizens experience law as internally binding nor feel any sort of fidelity toward it – there is a lack of reciprocity between citizen and law maker. So instead, governments tend to exert some control by a politics of fear and security, and justice is diminished to an emaciated 'administration of justice'. This provokes *anomie*, a crisis in which society provides little moral guidance to its citizens, engendering a sense of futility, emotional despair and emptiness. And at this point, human rights come into the picture. It is important to understand this facet of human rights – an almost irrational belief in its power – indeed, the enduring nature of human rights is inexplicable if we ignore this dimension. So this second narrative explains the function of a human rights law in the EU as a psychological, almost spiritual one – to fulfil an essential gap, a desire for ethical resolution and moral meaning. So the EU needs myths, its created traditions, identities, and emotional pull. And what better than a human rights myth?

And yet . . . the third narrative performs its task in revealing the oversimplification and reductive nature of the first two. EU human rights law needs these three narratives – they have their separate uses in different contexts. Kant, Benjamin, Koskenniemi – they all have their place.

---

[60] The term 'trashing' was widely used by the Critical Legal Studies movement. For a quintessential account see M. Kelman, 'Trashing', *Stanford Law Review*, vol. 36(1–2), 1984, p. 293.

[61] H. L. A. Hart, *The Concept of Law*, Oxford: Oxford University Press, 1961.

PART III

History, international humanitarian law and international criminal law

5. 'Treaty after trauma': 'protection for all' in the Fourth Geneva Convention

Gilad Ben-Nun

INTRODUCTION

Perhaps no other idea is so implicitly associated with the Fourth Geneva Convention for Civilians of 1949 ('GC-IV') as that of a set of minimum basic humanitarian protections, which apply to all human beings, whomever they may be, and under all circumstances. This idea, of extending protections to all, was conceived only after the Second World War, under the contextual settings of situations concerning non-international armed conflict ('NIAC') to which, until GC-IV's endorsement in 1949, no international legal instruments (with the exception of the rather vague 'Marten's Clause') applied.[1] The outlawry of torture, summary executions, taking of hostages, inhumane and degrading treatment and the like, which later received their embodiment in the Geneva Conventions' well-known Common Article 3, have long been hailed as one of GC-IV's greatest legal achievements. Given the paramount importance of this idea of 'protection for all', one is bound to posit some rather simple questions: How did this idea come about? Who were the intellectual and diplomatic 'midwives' who helped deliver it and who supported it through the GC-IV's long and torturous three-year drafting process? Seeing as much of this idea is indeed captured in what later came to be known as Common Article 3, what were the original intentions of its drafters, concerning who ought to come under its protective purview? And most importantly: did these drafters really mean

---

[1] Convention (IV) relative to the Protection of Civilian Persons in Time of War (Geneva, 12 August 1949) available at www.un.org/en/genocideprevention/documents/atrocity-crimes/Doc.33_GC-IV-EN.pdf; hereinafter ('GC-IV'). The rights of civilians and combatants under situations of International Armed Conflict ('IAC') between two sovereign states were already provided for, if not comprehensively, under the Regulations annexed to the Convention (IV) respecting the Laws and Customs of War on Land (The Hague, 18 October 1907, available at https://ihl-databases.icrc.org/ihl/INTRO/195).

protection for *all* under *all* circumstances, or were there already conditions of exception, under which even these basic protections need not apply?

Existing historical literature has credited the International Committee of the Red Cross (ICRC) with inserting this idea of a basic protection for all into GC-IV.[2] While there can be little doubt as to the ICRC's paramount role in this idea's development, this chapter concentrates on the vital supportive contributions of France, the Soviet bloc, and the World Jewish Congress, towards its making and securement.

The key materials underpinning this chapter consist of archival sources uncovered at the French Foreign Ministry Archives in Paris, at the ICRC archives in Geneva, at the Bulgarian National Archives (the former Soviet archives) in Sofia, and at the World Jewish Congress (WJC) archives in Cincinnati. These sources include the very first blueprint of the Civilian Convention text, elaborated at the Quai d'Orsay in preparation for the Geneva government experts' conference in April 1947.[3] Another relevant source is the conclusive fifty-page confidential report that Claude Pilloud, the director of the ICRC's legal division during the 1949 Conference of Plenipotentiaries, wrote to his superiors – the ICRC leadership – in September 1949, following the signing of GC-IV's Final Act. Lastly, this chapter is based on the reports of

---

[2] C. Rey-Schyrr, *From Yalta to Dien Bien Phu: History of the International Committee of the Red Cross 1945 to 1955*, Geneva: International Committee of the Red Cross, 2017, pp. 209–231; M. Lewis, *The Birth of the New Justice: The Internationalization of Crime and Punishment, 1919–1950*, Oxford: Oxford University Press, 2014, pp. 229–79; P. Pradelle, *La Conférence diplomatique et les nouvelles conventions de Genève du 12 août 1949*, Paris: Editions Internationals, 1951, pp. 267–84.

[3] While several subsequent sources have alluded to this draft, it has to date not been published. This study is the first one to fully examine this draft, which, together with the 1934 Tokyo draft, formed the basis for the later development of the Civilian Convention. That France was the country to draft this first full 'blueprint' of the Civilian Convention text and bring it to the Geneva government experts' conference in April 1947, and that this draft indeed provided the textual basis for the Civilian Convention is confirmed by several sources. Jurist Jean Pictet explicitly mentions this draft in the opening paragraphs of his commentary to the Civilian Convention: J. Pictet, *Commentary on the Geneva Convention Relative to the Protection of Civilian Persons in Time of War 12 August 1949*, vol. IV, Geneva: ICRC, 1958, p. 8. Pictet repeated his reference to this first French draft in Jean Pictet, 'La formation du droit internationale humanitaire', *International Review of the Red Cross*, vol. 751(1), 1985, pp. 3–23, at p. 12. Finally, the US delegate, Albert Clattenburg, also confirmed that the French draft served as the Civilian Convention's first blueprint. See his report to the employees of the US Department of State: A. E. Clattenburg Jr., 'International Red Cross Meeting', *Department of State Bulletin*, Washington, DC, 22 June 1947, pp. 1.205–1.207, at p. 1.206 (in the right-hand column). A copy of this report by Clattenburg can also be found at the Archives of the International Committee of the Red Cross in Geneva (AICRC) – CR-211/BIS 1.

the Civilian Convention's vice chairman (Committee III), who represented the Soviet bloc – the Bulgarian delegate Dr Nissim Mevorah.

The chapter's objectives are threefold. Firstly, it exposes the research community to these important and hitherto unpublished sources. Much of the existing literature has focused on GC-IV's last (and most crucial) drafting stage, which took place between April and August 1949 during its diplomatic Conference of Plenipotentiaries in Geneva. Much less study has been devoted to its drafting 'build-up', from 1946 up until the opening of the final diplomatic conference in 1949. This chapter comes to address this research lacuna.

Secondly, it exposes the hitherto unexplored decision of GC-IV's drafters to have its set of base protections specifically applicable to genocide, and conditions whereby governments target their own nationals. As shall be shown below, the ICRC was initially opposed to the idea that GC-IV would apply within a single country, when a government targeted its own population, as this might imply a breach of that country's untrampled sovereignty. The understanding that indeed GC-IV's protective provisions would also apply under these circumstances was achieved only during the very last day of the XVII Red Cross Conference in Stockholm in 1948 ('Stockholm Conference'). This was achieved in large part thanks to the efforts of the World Jewish Congress delegate Gerhart Riegner, and the French chairman of the legal commission's sub-committee III Georges Cahen-Salvador, who was entrusted with overseeing the drafting of the Civilian Convention text in Stockholm.

Thirdly, this chapter uncovers the extent of the Soviet bloc's involvement in GC-IV's three-year drafting process. Current historical scholarship has significantly underplayed the Soviet bloc's true role in promoting the idea of 'protection for all', as enshrined also into the textual ancestor of what later became Common Article 3. This chapter also comes to correct this gap existent in current historical accounts.

A word on concepts and categories. Seventy years since GC-IV's endorsement, the terminological and international legal frameworks within which it is set are clear and somewhat categorical. International lawyers routinely refer to the critical distinction between international armed conflict ('IAC'), and non-international armed conflict ('NIAC'), as if these were *idées fixes*, which have existed from time immemorial. In fact, this very clear and almost dichotomous distinction between IAC and NIAC, to which all international legal systems adhere to today, was only *born* during GC-IV's textual elaboration and the making of its Common Article 3, between 1946 and 1949. The very first ICRC text ever to carry the words 'conflict not of an international character', later to be transformed into 'non-international armed conflict' was the pre-Stockholm drafts for the newly proposed Geneva Conventions, sent by the ICRC to governments and National Red Cross and Red Crescent Societies in May 1948.

This point is crucial, when one speaks of the birth-moment of the NIAC category. The drafters who were coming up with the formulation of the NIAC concept certainly knew they were bringing a hitherto non-existent innovation into international humanitarian law (IHL). The 1934 Red Cross Tokyo draft of the Civilian Convention made no mention whatsoever of the words 'non-international'. In the beginning, back between 1946 and 1949, the drafters had absolutely no idea that this new term they were developing would evolve into an entire new legal realm concerning the laws of war applicable to NIAC, as opposed to IAC. In short: the categorical distinctions we recognize today, between NIAC and IAC only came into existence *after* the signing of GC-IV's Final Act in August 1949, that is – *post eventum*. Historians and legal scholars who apply in retrospect the NIAC and IAC categories to GC-IV's *travaux préparatoires*, pre-1949, commit the fundamental methodological error of anachronism in historical research.

FRANCE AND GC-IV'S FIRST BLUEPRINT: FROM THE QUAI D'ORSAY (1946) TO THE GOVERNMENT EXPERTS' CONFERENCE (APRIL 1947)

In July 1945, in response to the ICRC's memorandum of 15 February that year, and with the Second World War not yet over in the Pacific, the French Council of Ministers began considering the need to revise the Geneva Conventions of 1929 (GC-III).[4] That same month, the ministers decreed the establishment of an inter-ministerial committee, composed of civil servants, advisers and

---

[4] French Foreign Ministry Archives (hereinafter FFMA), La Courneuve Paris, File 768 – SUP / 160, Gouvernement Provisoire de la République Française: Ministère des Prisonniers de Guerre, Déportés et Réfugiés. Révision de la Convention de Genève, 9 July 1945, Ref. PL / AB (M. Lamarle – written in pencil over the printed stencil). See also in the same file: Decision of the French Council of ministers (10 July 1945) to create the inter-ministerial committee for the revision of the Geneva Conventions, signed 7 August 1945. On the ICRC memorandum sent by Max Huber to all heads of National Red Cross Societies declaring the beginning of the Geneva Conventions' revision process see Rey-Schyrr, *From Yalta to Dien Bien Phu*, pp. 212–14. It is worth noting here that within the French documents, there is absolutely no echo to the massacre of Sétif, which took place just two months earlier. This is not really surprising, as France saw the events in Algeria as totally an internal French affair, seeing Algeria as an integral part of France (three *départements* of the state as opposed to the Protectorates of Morocco and Tunisia), thus qualifying those events under domestic police actions which had virtually nothing to do with the International Red Cross Conventions. On this approach by France see R. Branche, 'The French Army and the Geneva Conventions During the Algerian War of Independence and After', in M. Evangelista and N. Tannenwald (eds.), *Do the Geneva Conventions Matter?*, Oxford: Oxford University Press, 2017, p. 161.

external legal counsel, whose task was to draw up France's official positions concerning these revisions, in preparation for the 1946 Preliminary Conference of Red Cross National Societies, which met in Geneva between 26 July and 3 August that year.[5] The French delegation included representatives from the ministry of war veterans, the French foreign ministry (colloquially known as the 'Quai d'Orsay'), the army's general staff, the surgeon general, and the ministries of welfare and education.[6] These governmental delegates were augmented by representatives of French associations of people affected during the Second World War under the German occupation of France. These included the representatives of two different national associations of deported and incarcerated members of the French *Résistance*, and a representative of the national federation of French forced-labour workers.

The inter-ministerial committee did not start its drafting efforts from scratch, as it had before it the draft Civilian Convention text elaborated during the Tokyo International Red Cross Conference of 1934 (the 'Tokyo draft').[7] The coordination of the committee was entrusted to Albert Lamarle – the director of the division of International Organizations at the Quai d'Orsay. A seasoned diplomat and veteran of the League of Nations with a rich experience in treaty making, Lamarle would become the ICRC's key ally throughout the Civilian Convention's three-year drafting process, alongside a formidable young female jurist – Ms Andrée Jacob, who served as the technical adviser to the French Ministry of Veteran Combatants. In his final confidential report to his superiors, after the signing of the Geneva Conventions' Final Act in August 1949, Claude Pilloud – the ICRC's legal-division chief – alluded to the close connections between the international organization and France, thanks to Lamarle's and Ms Jacob's long-standing support of its causes:

> The French Delegation was almost identical in its composition to its predecessors in 1947 and in 1948 in Stockholm . . . within Commission III [i.e. the commission mandated to elaborate the new Civilian Convention] this delegation provided great support ("*un très grand secours*") to the ICRC. Very frequently, this delegation

---

[5] ICRC, *Report on the Work of the Preliminary Conference of National Red Cross Societies for the Study of the Conventions and of Various Problems Relative to the Red Cross Geneva, July 26–August 3*, Geneva, January 1947, available at https://www.loc.gov/rr/frd/Military_Law/pdf/RC_report-1946.pdf.

[6] FFMA, File # 768 – SUP / 160, Dossiers: Création d'une commission interministérielle chargée d'étudier les modifications des Conventions de Genève, letter from French Red Cross President Sice to Foreign Minister Georges Bidault, 11 June 1946.

[7] The Tokyo draft is available at https://ihl-databases.icrc.org/ihl/INTRO/320?OpenDocument.

accepted to adopt as its own the amendments which we [i.e. the ICRC, Pilloud being the speaker] wanted to see presented.[8]

At the top of the French bureaucratic pyramid, to which Lamarle ultimately reported, stood the Vice President of the French Council of State (*Conseil d'État*) – the renowned international jurist (and later Nobel Peace Prize laureate) René Cassin. Given his contemporary involvement in the elaboration of the UN's Universal Declaration of Human Rights, in addition to his many other responsibilities at the *Conseil*, Cassin delegated his oversight role concerning the new Geneva Conventions to two of his most trusted subordinates: Pierre Mendes-France (then the French ambassador to the UN's Economic and Social Council, ECOSOC, and later France's prime minister) and Georges Cahen-Salvador. The latter, who served as the president of the Council's Economic Section, was an expert on issues concerning prisoners of war, being the former director of the office for French war prisoners after the First World War. In early 1947, the French Red Cross informed Lamarle that its delegate to the inter-ministerial committee would be Georges Cahen-Salvador, in parallel to his roles within the *Conseil d'État*.[9]

Notably, all three men – Cassin, Mendes-France and Cahen-Salvador – were French Jews, who had been exiled from France during the Nazi occupation. Yet while Cassin and Mendes-France accompanied the French leader Charles de Gaulle to London during his exile, Cahen-Salvador was the only one of the three to directly experience the horrors of the Nazi Holocaust on French soil. In 1940, Cahen-Salvador's family members were incarcerated in the Drancy Concentration Camp, north of Paris. On the night of 20 November 1943, upon Adolf Eichmann's dispatched deportation order, they boarded transport no. 62 from Drancy to Auschwitz.[10] Thanks probably to the help of former colleagues who served in the French Vichy Government, the train carrying Cahen-Salvador's family was stopped near Lerouville, where nineteen family members were taken off, and, after a journey of some 500 kilometres, made their way to the border of the Swiss Canton of Geneva. On 23 November 1943, the Cahen-Salvador family received political asylum in Geneva.[11]

---

[8] AICRC, File # CR-254 / 1 bis, Les Conventions de Genève du 12 août 1949, 0 – 32, Doc. 1 *bis*, 'Confidentiel: Conférence Diplomatique: Rapport Special Etabli par M.C. Pilloud, Genève, 16 Septembre 1949', p. 6 (author's translation).

[9] *Les Obsèques de President Georges Cahen Salvador* ('The obituaries for Georges Cahen Salvador') Bibliothèque nationale de France – François Mitterand, filing reference: 8-LN27-74932.

[10] S. Klarsfeld, *La Shoah en France. Volume 3: Le calendrier de la persécution des Juifs de France. Tome 3, septembre 1942–août 1944*, Paris: Fayard, 2001, p. 1705.

[11] A. Chatriot, 'Georges Cahen-Salvador, un réformateur social dans la haute administration Française (1875–1963)', *Revue d'Histoire de la Protection Sociale*,

In August 1948, at the outset of the Stockholm Conference, Georges Cahen-Salvador was unanimously voted as the chairman of sub-commission III of the legal commission and charged with elaborating the new Civilian Convention text. In April 1949, as the Geneva Conference of Plenipotentiaries opened its doors, Cahen-Salvador was unanimously elected once again as the President of Commission III – the same commission that oversaw the drafting of the newly proposed Civilian Convention. At the end of the Plenipotentiaries Conference, he would sign the Fourth Geneva Convention for the Protection of Civilians on France's behalf.

Towards the end of 1946, probably around October, the French inter-ministerial committee had already managed to elaborate a preliminary concept paper for the textual development of its version of the Civilian Convention.[12] While certainly influenced by the harsh French experiences under German occupation, the authors were well aware that they needed to strike a balance between the rights of the occupied and those of the occupying forces – if only because France itself was a military occupier in post-war Germany, in addition to its colonial control of French West Africa, North Africa, and Indo-China:

> There should be a general effort, on behalf of all committee members and especially by us – members of the federation of deported and incarcerated fighters of the *Résistance* who have been impacted by the unequal fight against the atrocious German occupation . . . to look at the other side ("*passer de l'autre coté de la barricade*"), and avoid seeing the problem as one of a "Resistant" on the one hand and an Occupying Power on the other. We must not forget that today, France is

---

vol. 1(7), 2014, pp. 125–6 nn.100–110. See also the official registry of persons who requested entry into the Canton of Geneva during the Second World War. Archive of the Canton of Geneva (*Archive d'état de Genève*), pp. 1–26, at p. 1, available at http://archive.wikiwix.com/cache/?url=http%3A%2F%2Fetat.geneve .ch%2Fdt%2FSilverpeasWebFileServer%2Fc.pdf%3FComponentId%3Dkmelia106 %26SourceFile%3D1249035575442.pdf%26MimeType%3Dapplication%2Fpdf %26Directory%3DAttachment%2FImages%2F.

[12] FFMA, File # 768-SUP / 160 bis, Rapport sur la nécessité d'élaborer un projet de convention internationale pour la protection de la population civile en temps de guerre, et sur les principes qui doivent présider à sa rédaction, Féderation Nationale des Déportes et Internes de la Résistance, no date. Given the rudimentary nature of this document, and the fact that the first full draft of the French Civilian Convention text already existed by February 1947 and given that most sessions of the inter-ministerial committee actually took shape after the summer break of July–August 1946, my best guess is that this concept paper was probably drawn up around October 1946. Its language is very reminiscent of the statements made by the federation's representatives Jacques Duhamel and Pierre Hemery within the transcripts ('*Process Verbaux*') of the inter-ministerial committee at this time.

an Occupying Power, and the Convention Project is an international, or rather – a humanitarian one.[13]

In a similar manner to the ICRC's work, the textual basis for the French draft Civilian Convention text was in fact the 1934 Tokyo draft. To this, Lamarle and Jacob now added the points that France considered crucial for inclusion, and which did not exist in the Tokyo draft, as set out prior to the unprecedented horrors of the Second World War. The solution for which Ms Jacob opted was simple and straightforward. Visually, the method of textual incorporation for these additional points was executed through the splitting of the document's pages across the middle with a dotted line. The parts of the pages above the dotted line comprised the Tokyo draft text of 1934's proposed Civilian Convention text. The part of the page beneath the dotted line comprised the additional text that the French inter-ministerial committee wished to add to the Tokyo draft.

As an additional stipulation to Article 1 of the Tokyo draft, France opted to incorporate the first three articles of the annexed regulations for war on land of the 1907 Hague Conventions (the so-called 'Hague regulations'), which described the conduct that armed occupying forces were to abide by vis-à-vis the civilian population of the invaded country. These included the stipulations for recognizing lawful combatants (command structure, emblem, open carriage of arms, etc.), the regulations governing an uprising of the civilian population ('*levé en masse*'), and the granting of prisoners of war (POW) status to lawful militia and resistance fighters within the zone of occupation.[14]

To contemporary readers, this might seem as a strange mix-up of IAC and NIAC, given that the French team referred to *all* resistance fighters, both ones within the territory being invaded (as in Nazi-occupied France during the Second World War) *and* those targeted by their own government (as happened to the French *Résistance* fighters targeted by 'their own' Vichy government). In short: the whole point which the French legal team wanted to stress was the rights of resistance fighters, combatants and civilians *wherever* they were geographically, and to provide them with a basic set of legal protections vis-à-vis the authorities targeting them.

---

[13] Ibid., p. 2 (inverted commas around the word Resistant in the original; author's translation).

[14] FFMA, File # 768-SUP / 160 bis, Davinroy, Duhamel, Hemery, Jacob, Mechbert, 'Commission Interministérielle Chargée de l'étude des Additions et Modifications à Apporter aux Conventions de Genève du 27 Juillet 1929: Sous-Commission pour l'Elaboration du projet de la Convention Relatif à la Protection des Civils en Temps de Guerre', Projet de Convention Internationale pour la Protection des Civils en Temps de Guerre (1947).

Back in 1946, The Hague regulations were the only legally existent international norms which said anything about the protection of civilians in times of war. Thus, the French legal team's idea was simple and straightforward: to take these existing rules and apply them 'across the board' to all civilians, in all cases, and under all circumstances, thus bringing them all under the Civilian Convention's protective purview. It is worth noting here that this idea, of the protection to be afforded to all resistance fighters and civilians, was also endorsed in full by the military representative within the inter-ministerial committee – Colonel Rousenne, who signed off on its final version as elaborated by Jacob and Lamarle.[15]

LAMARLE'S FAILED ATTEMPT TO CONVINCE THE GENEVA GOVERNMENT EXPERTS' CONFERENCE OF APRIL 1947

While the French draft Convention text underwent several changes, the wording of its three first Hague Regulations Articles, as annexed to the Tokyo draft, remained unchanged. And it was this draft, with the wording of these three new Articles prioritized, that Albert Lamarle brought with him to the government experts' conference on 14 April 1947.[16] In Geneva, the reaction of other governments was at best lukewarm. The Anglo-Saxon governments, headed by the UK and the US, were outright hostile towards them. The Commonwealth countries (Australia, South Africa, Canada and New Zealand) largely fell in line behind the UK positions.

At its outset, the government experts' conference's plenary elected a sub-commission mandated to deal with the issue of 'Partisans'; the very term being reminiscent of the realities of the Second World War. It was within this

---

[15] FFMA, new archiving filing numbers, File # 768 SUP / 160 bis. Révision des conventions de Genève. At the end of this file are deposited the private papers of Colonel Rousenne, bound by a paper written in red. The file contains an exchange of several handwritten notes between Lamarle and Rousenne, written in personal, non-formal and friendly language, indicating their long-time acquaintance. 'Interministerial commission for the revision of the Geneva Convention of 1929, Drafting Committee of the Text to be Approved by the Commission, drafted by Jacob, Chayet, Perrin'. This draft Convention text has 18 pages (not numbered) and is full of handwritten corrections in turquoise fountain-pen ink over the printed black-and-white text, written by Colonel Rousenne.

[16] For the ICRC record of this Conference, see ICRC, *Report on the Work of the Conference of Government Experts for the Study of the Conventions for the Protection of War Victims (Geneva, April 14–26, 1947)*, available at https://www.loc.gov/rr/frd/Military_Law/pdf/RC_report-1947.pdf.

working group that Lamarle's three new Articles first came up for discussion.[17] As the debates within this working group intensified, Lamarle so reacted to the full force of the Anglo-Saxon opposition to his views:

> In the sub-committee charged with studying the problem of the protection of "internal combatants" ("*combatants de l'intérieur*") the French delegation [i.e. Lamarle himself] stressed the risk of the conflict taking on a more violent and terrorizing character in the case where "partisans" were to feel less protected...as an "internal war" ("*guerre de l'intérieur*") could take on far more violent and vicious forms in future conflicts. The British delegate, who was totally opposed to this idea, said that it "might be timely within ten or twenty years" . . . to which the French Delegate [i.e. Lamarle] replied that it would be regrettable to wait for yet another conflict . . . so as to recognize the keen necessity for the codification of these new laws of war.[18]

The next day saw considerable successes for France's efforts on behalf of the new Civilian Convention. Article 21 of the French draft, which prohibited several practices by occupying forces which were not mentioned in the 1934 Tokyo draft, was adopted into the draft Civilian Convention text. Nevertheless: 'difficulties have appeared from the side of the British and American delegations concerning the status of "partisans"'.[19]

By the end of the government experts' conference, it became abundantly clear to the French that extending protections to all 'partisans' and 'internal combatants' was not going to be easily accepted by the Anglo-Saxons. The

---

[17] Ibid., pp. 107–10.

[18] FFMA, File # 768-SUP / 159, Télégramme à l'arrivée, Genève le 16 Avril 1947, reçu par avion le 17 Avril à 16 heures, 'Conférence préliminaire en vue de la révision et de l'extension des conventions de Genève de Juillet 1929, N. 34, de la part de M. LAMARLE'. Note that the term '*combatants de l'intérieur*' is also a Second World War term very specifically referred to with regard to both French Resistance fighters, and the resistance against the Nazis in Greece. Double inverted commas around the words 'might be timely within ten or twenty years', as in Lamarle quoting his own words to the UK delegate – in the original (author's translation).

[19] FFMA, File # 768-SUP / 159, Télégramme à l'arrivée, Genève, le 17 Avril 1947, reçu par avion le 19 Avril à 16 heures, 'Conférence préliminaire en vue de la révision et de l'extension des conventions de Genève de Juillet 1929, N. 40, de la part de M. Lamarle'. The wording of the French draft Convention's Article 21 read: 'The High Contracting Parties shall not take any measure, against a collective or against individual inhabitants of an occupied country, which is contrary to their integrity and human dignity. Any measure of discrimination dictated and motivated by national, racial, confessional, cultural or political grounds shall be rigorously excluded. The condemnation of any person whose individual responsibility has not been judicially proven is prohibited. Measures such as the taking of hostages and their summary execution, deportations, collective punishments ('*les amendes collectives*'), the destruction of villages and towns are all prohibited.' Double inverted commas on the word 'partisans' in the original (author's translation).

UK and the US were now occupiers in Germany and Japan. They were certainly not inclined to adopt regulations which would curtail their abilities to control these occupied areas. In several world regions, the UK was operating under conditions where sovereignty was highly ambiguous, as in formerly Dutch-controlled Indonesia, in Malaya, in Palestine, and in the unfolding Raj of India. In one of his last reports from the Geneva, Lamarle concluded:

> . . . The tendency which is prevailing here is to avoid . . . the issue of the Convention's scope of application, colonial rules, and civil wars . . . therein lies a delicate problem because of its legal aspects, and the discussions centred around the legality or illegality of these or those authorities.[20]

THE FRENCH PUSH TO BRING THE SOVIETS TO GC-IV'S DRAFTING TABLE

Lamarle's dispatches from the government experts' conference, and the British remark that the French ideas in favour of extending the protections afforded by the Geneva Conventions to civil wars and partisans 'might be appropriate in ten or twenty years', reverberated loudly through the corridors of the Quai d'Orsay in Paris. The Anglo-Saxon countries, which had not undergone Nazi occupation, did not identify with this cause as championed by France and supported by the Benelux and Scandinavian countries, who suffered similar experiences under the Nazi yoke. Yet there was another group of countries that could well side with this French position. These were the members of the Soviet bloc, with the Soviet Union at their helm. If France were to secure a voting majority for its ideas, these countries would have to be engaged – and the sooner the better.

The biggest hurdle to overcome in this regard concerned the visceral hostility that the Soviets harboured towards the ICRC.[21] From the Soviet perspective, the ICRC stood idly by as the Nazi regime obscenely and criminally mishandled everybody in its spheres, from Soviet war prisoners, to civilians, up to the deportation of Soviet nationals as slave labour back into German territories, so as to continue aiding the German war machine. During the 1946 Red Cross youth conference hosted by Count Folke Bernadotte and Prince

---

[20] FFMA, File # 768-SUP / 160, 'Lamarle à le ministère des affaires étrangères', projet de convention pour la protection des populations civils en temps de guerre, 22 April 1947, no. 453, receipt stamp – Foreign Ministry Secretariat – 24 April 1947, p. 3 (last para., before the fountain-pen signature). Author's translation.

[21] FFMA, File 768-SUP / 160, Albert Lamarle Telegram No. 44, Conférence préliminaire pour la révision des Conventions de Genève: Abstention de l'USSR, Geneva, 21 April 1947, received in Paris 23 April 1947.

Charles of Sweden, the French ambassador to Stockholm informed Prime Minister Bidault that:

> the delegates of the countries of Eastern Europe . . . had issued a violent political attack against their Western adversaries, concerning future international Red Cross plans. According to them the Red Cross, prior to its recent change of leadership, was directed by "supporters of fascism" and "murderers" ('*suppôts du fascisme – assassins*').[22]

Indeed, there was very little sense in redrafting the laws of war if the Soviet bloc – the 'other side' in the nascent Cold War conflict – was going to refrain from participation.

To make things worse, no Western country (France included), really understood what the Soviet world had experienced under the Nazi occupations of the Second World War, on the east–west axis between western Poland and the St Petersburg–Kursk line west of Moscow, and the north–south axis – from the Baltic Sea to the Balkans, Greece and Crete. The picture which has emerged from Snyder's and Levene's recent studies, on what they have termed as the 'Bloodlands' and 'European Rimlands', is truly horrifying.[23] Out of some 50 million casualties of the Second World War, roughly half perished solely within the Soviet sphere of influence.[24] Sadly, in the world prior to GC-IV, most of these victims did not enjoy any recourse to the legal protections offered by the three already existing Geneva Conventions.

The example of Belarus is a case in point. Of its 9 million inhabitants in May 1941, prior to the German invasion of the Soviet Union ('Operation Barbarossa'), 1.6 million civilians were directly killed by the Germans, primarily due to a deliberate policy of their starvation, instigated by the Germans thanks to the 'intentional refusal on the Wehrmacht's part to give *available* food to them'.[25] Another 700 000 Soviet war prisoners were executed by the Nazis, who grotesquely argued that their 'blood was free' since the Soviet Union did not sign up to the 1929 POW Geneva Convention. A further 500

---

[22] FFMA, New archiving filing numbers, File # 76 CPCOM / Box 76 (old Nantes diplomatic archives reference Y – Internationale 76 Y-23-4), Ambassador Jean Baelen to Prime Minister and Foreign Minister Georges Bidault, 'Congress de la Croix Rouge de la Jeunesse', 5 September 1946, received at the Quai d'Orsay in Paris, 11 September 1946, p. 2 (author's translation).

[23] T. Snyder, *Blood Lands: Europe Between Hitler and Stalin*, London: Penguin 2010; M. Levene, *The Crisis of Genocide, Vol. 2: Annihilation – The European Rimlands 1939–1953*, Oxford: Oxford University Press, 2013.

[24] For these casualty figures see R. G. Suny, *The Cambridge History of Russia, vol. III: The 20th Century*, Cambridge: Cambridge University Press, 2006, pp. 225–8.

[25] Snyder, *Blood Lands*, p. 251. Levene, *The Crisis of Genocide*, p. 240 (emphasis in the original).

000 Jewish Belarusians were exterminated as part of the Nazi 'Final Solution' to Europe's Jews, who being civilians, did not come under the ICRC's purview absent a Red Cross Civilian Convention in force. A further 320 000 Belarusians, counted as partisan 'enemy combatants' (most of whom were in fact unarmed civilians), were also killed. Finally, an estimated 2 million Belarusians were deported as slave labour back to Germany and western Poland, with an additional 1 million fleeing east to the Russian-controlled areas of the Soviet Union.

As Snyder has noted: 'By the end of the war, half of the population of Belarus had either been killed or moved. This cannot be said of any other country.'[26] In a world where humanitarian law had more exceptions than categories of people it covered, and yet where half of a country's population was decimated, one could at least concede to the Soviets that their suspicions of the ICRC's rigid and restrictive legal reading of its own conventions was well-merited. Given the objections of the UK and US to the extension of Red Cross protections to both resistance fighters and civilians at the recent government experts' meeting in Geneva, conscripting the help of the Soviet bloc was now seen as an absolute diplomatic necessity.[27]

From May 1947 onwards, a full diplomatic *démarche* was set in motion, as the French ambassadors in Washington, London, Brussels and Moscow all attempted to engage with the Soviets via the Soviet Red Cross.[28] In November 1947, Foreign Minister Bidaut reported to the French ambassador in London that:

> ... during a regional conference of Red Cross Societies in Belgrade, Dr. Depage [the Belgian Red Cross president] managed to meet with the representative of the Soviet Red Cross Alliances ... Mr. Petrovski ... who wished for more humanitarianism in a war to come, and who stressed the need to cooperate with the national Red Cross societies of the UK, the US, Sweden and the Lower Countries, which were currently showing hostile sentiments towards the U.S.S.R.[29]

---

[26] Snyder, *Blood Lands*, p. 251.

[27] See the official request tabled by the president of the Belgian Red Cross to France to take up this issue, in the hope of bringing the Soviets on board preferably before the following year's Stockholm Conference: FFMA, File 768-SUP / 159, Note: 'Prochaines Conférences en vue de la révision des Conventions de Genève', Paris, 24 May 1947, p. 4.

[28] FFMA, File # 768-SUP / 160, File: 'USSR: Abstentions', marked as a separate file in blue pencil within this archive carton. FFMA, File # 768-SUP / 160, Albert Lamarle Telegram No. 44, 'Conférence préliminaire pour la révision des Conventions de Genève: Abstention de l'USSR', Geneva, 21 April 1947, received in Paris 23 April 1947.

[29] FFMA, File # 768-SUP / 159, Le Ministère des Affaires Etrangères à M. l'Ambassadeur à Londres, 'Révision et extension des Conventions de Genève de 27 juillet 1929, No. 4070 UN', 10 November 1947 (author's translation).

Following this initial sign of Soviet good will, in late February 1948, the Soviet government officially informed the French ambassador in Moscow that it viewed favourably the review of the Geneva Conventions, in accordance with the commonly accepted practice of submitting the proposed texts first to a conference of Red Cross societies coming up in Stockholm, later to be worked over by an international conference of states parties.[30]

Much of this Soviet conciliatory sentiment towards renewed cooperation with the Red Cross movement is corroborated by sources at the Bulgarian national archives' files from the Soviet era.[31] From November 1947 until after the official opening of the Stockholm Conference in mid-August 1948, an extensive exchange of policy-related letters took place between the Bulgarian, Czechoslovakian, Yugoslav, Hungarian and Soviet Union National Red Cross Societies.[32] In preparation for the Stockholm Conference, the Bulgarian Foreign Ministry and National Red Cross representative jointly prepared an extensive memorandum, written in the vernacular and translated into French, which was sent to the Swedish Red Cross in Stockholm. It detailed in full the positions that the entire Soviet bloc would favourably advocate for at the XVII Red Cross Conference in Stockholm. Concerning the newly proposed Civilian Convention and its novel ideas of protecting 'internal combatants' the memorandum stated that:

> The modifications which we have proposed to bring into the Convention . . . for the protections of civilians in times of war, should assure better protections for the rights of the civilian populations and partisans, which under current prescriptions concerning "internal combatants" have proven to be insufficient by the developments of warfare which have outrun these existing provisions. It would seem important . . . to benefit from the experiences which these countries [i.e. the Soviet bloc] have acquired during the last war.[33]

---

[30] FFMA, File # 768-SUP / 160, File: USSR: 'Abstentions, Telegram No. 358, 22 February 1948 at 15:15 hours', received 22 February 1948 at 22:30 hours, official, receipt stamp 24 February 1948. This file at the French Foreign Ministry archives is a full folder of well over 50 documents and French inter-embassy communiqués solely concerned with getting the Soviets 'on board' in the drafting of GC-IV, between April 1947 and August 1948.

[31] Bulgarian National Archives – Sofia, Fund # 1481, ОП1, File 1040, 'Bulgarian Red Cross Correspondence: 1947–1952'.

[32] Ibid. See memorandum from the Czechoslovakian Government to the Bulgarian Government to coordinate positions vis-à-vis the Stockholm Conference (Doc. # 40, 7 February 1948), from several Eastern bloc governments, including the Hungarian government (Doc. # 62, 29 May 1948), the Yugoslav government (Doc. # 112), and the Soviet Union (Doc. # 105).

[33] Ibid., Memorandum of the Popular Republic of Bulgaria to the Red Cross Conference in Stockholm, 12 June 1948, Doc. # 70–71, last paragraph. The full memo-

The Bulgarian four-page preparatory memorandum for Stockholm concludes with the following simple statement: 'we repeat: the revision of the Geneva Conventions and their extension to civilians are the most important issue of the Conference in Stockholm'.[34] In February 1948, the Soviets were thus bent upon coming to Stockholm and contributing from their experiences for the betterment of the Geneva Conventions.

Five days before Stockholm's opening ceremony, the entire array of Soviet Red Cross delegations informed the Swedish Red Cross that they would not attend the Conference.[35] Citing their protest at the invitation of the National Red Cross Society of Franco's fascist Spain, the Soviets would send only a delegation of so-called 'observers' to the meeting of the Red Cross and Red Crescent societies, but would boycott the deliberations over the Geneva Conventions' revision. Given their ample preparation for Stockholm, this last-minute rebuttal is somewhat puzzling.

The answer to it, however, lies in understanding Soviet pains at the sight of the wholesale murder of communist resistance fighters around the globe, from Indo-China, through Malaya, through Indonesia, to the Greek civil war. What began as a rivalry between royalists and communists under the Nazi occupation of Greece, metamorphosed into an all-out proxy war between the royalists supported by the UK and the US, and the communists backed by Tito's Yugoslavia, Bulgaria and Albania. The development of the Greek civil war coincided almost to the month with GC-IV's three-year textual elaboration process, as the last royalist offensive ('Operation Torch'), which crushed the communists in the north-west and north-east of the country, ended the war in September 1949, one month after the signing of GC-IV's Final Act.[36]

From the Soviet bloc's perspective, while the ink had barely dried on the newly proposed Civilian Convention text and its Article 2 (paragraph 4) which extended protections to the exact type of resistance fighters as the Greek communists, these were being executed *en masse*, by British military personnel deployed in Greece, with active US support. By mid-1947, the British had lost some 2000 of their own troops in the fighting in Greece, which also served

---

randum can be found in Doc. # 87–90 in the same file. Translation from the French by the author.

[34] Ibid., Doc. # 90, p. 4. Translation of this final sentence from the Bulgarian text by Martin Petrov.

[35] Ibid., letter from Peter Poplatzeff, Extraordinary envoy and Plenipotentiary Minister of the Popular Republic of Bulgaria, to Henrik Beer, Secretary General of the Swedish Red Cross, 19 August 1948, Doc. 103.

[36] A. Gerolymatos, *The International Civil War: Greece, 1943–1949*, New Haven, CT: Yale University Press, 2016, pp. 99–178.

as the first theatre of operations where the US employed its well-known (and ruthless) anti-communist Truman Doctrine.[37]

To add insult to injury, the predecessors of the Greek royalist-fascist executioners – the Spanish fascists, who carried out much of the same carnage a decade earlier – were now being internationally rehabilitated, as in their invitation to join the Stockholm Conference. With the recent experiences of the Nazi conduct in the very same 'European Rimlands', all this was, understandably, a bit too much for the Soviet bloc to fathom. The president of the Soviet Red Cross thus wrote to Count Bernadotte that:

> The Soviet Red Cross and Red Crescent could not find it possible to attend this gathering for the following reasons. The second world war had demonstrated that fascist governments (Germany, Italy, Japan) do not observe the Geneva Conventions. As is well known, cruelties hitherto unknown in human history were committed in the POW camps and in camps for civilians by these countries. The ICRC, upon whom it is incumbent . . . to safeguard the rigorous observation of these conventions, knew of these cruelties, yet shut its eyes in their face, and did not take any measures to counter these violations of the Conventions by these countries.[38]

Thus far, Dr Cholodkoff was explicitly referring to the discrepancy between the legalistic positions taken by the ICRC, and the horrific realities of what happened within the Soviet zones occupied by the Germans. Yet Cholodkoff was not merely speaking of the infringements *of the past*, but also referred to the ones taking place *in the present*:

> And even after the war, the ICRC has not protested even one single time against the crimes of the monarchist-fascists in Greece, nor against the wholesale bloodletting in Indonesia and Vietnam.[39]

What exactly was there to misunderstand in the Soviets' boycott of Stockholm?

The very same communists who fought and died against the Nazis in Greece, and against the Japanese in Malaya, were now being murdered whole-

---

[37] A. Nachmani, 'Civil War and Foreign Intervention in Greece: 1946–49', *Journal of Contemporary History*, vol. 25(4), 1990, pp. 489–522 at p. 500.

[38] FFMA, File # 768-SUP / 159 ter, Albert Lamarle to Foreign Minister Bidault, Lettre du Président de la Croix Rouge Soviétique au Président de la Conférence de Stockholm, 31 août 1948 with the French translation of Letter of Cholodkoff to Bernadotte, 15 August 1948. This letter was translated from Russian into French by the French foreign ministry. The same letter by the Soviet Red Cross can be seen in the UK National Archives (London, Kew Gardens), file # FO 369/3969. K.9831. See also D. D. Junod, *The Imperilled Red Cross and the Palestine-Eretz-Yisrael Conflict 1945–1952*, London: Kegan Paul International Publishers and the Graduate Institute for International Studies in Geneva,1996, p. 249 nn. 708–10 (author's translations).

[39] Letter of Cholodkoff to Bernadotte, 15 August 1948, p. 2 (author's translations).

sale by the British armed forces who executed a 'no-quarters' policy against them, in the very same places – Greece and Malaya.[40] To add insult to injury, Franco's fascist Spain was now being rehabilitated back into the community of nations, as if those same atrocities which it committed during the Spanish civil war, a decade earlier never happened. To say that the Soviets had ample and justifiable reasons for boycotting Stockholm would be an understatement!

REVOLUTION IN STOCKHOLM: GERHART RIEGNER, GEORGES CAHEN-SALVADOR, AND THE EXTENSION OF COMMON ARTICLE 3 TO ALL CIVILIANS

It is thanks to recent scholarship that the Stockholm Conference's paramount importance, both for GC-IV's textual development, and more broadly for the evolvement of the entire Red Cross movement, can now be better appreciated.[41] At the centre of French interests in Stockholm lay the desire already advocated for in the governments' experts' conference – to extend to all resistance combatants some basic measures of humanitarian protections. That said, one should not infer from this that France took this to imply the extension of protections to *all civilians* everywhere.

That the civilian population of a country invaded by another power was entitled to protections under the already-existing Hague Conventions was clear. Granted, the Second World War did a lot to erode the legal stature of the Hague regulations. Yet these were still enshrined into the widely accepted body of the international laws of war. And Nazi legal theorists, such as Carl Schmitt and Werner Best, who expressly denied Hague's applicability and justified the targeting of civilians under their own alternative concept of *Machtrecht*, had barely escaped post-war prosecutions for their crimes.[42] In 1948, there was

---

[40] On the Malayan emergency and the British harsh measures against both combatants and civilians there during July–August of 1948 see the recent book by the well-known BBC correspondent: C. Hale, *Massacre in Malaya: Exposing Britain's My Lai*, Gloucestershire: The History Press, 2013, pp. 278–82. On the connection between the Malaya uprising, and the actions of the British in Dutch Indonesia, and the efforts of the ICRC to provide humanitarian assistance and intervene on behalf of incarcerated combatants, so as to try and have the British recognize their rights as POWs see C. Rey-Schyrr, *From Yalta to Dien Bien Phu*, pp. 293–333.
[41] G. Steinacher, *Humanitarians at War: The Red Cross in the Shadow of the Holocaust*, Oxford: Oxford University Press, 2017, pp. 211–37.
[42] It should be noted here that the concept of military occupation and its legal corollary – the law of occupation – stem first and foremost from the establishment of the concept of non-recognition of territorial acquisition by force under international law. The person who first elaborated non-recognition, almost a decade prior to its application in the Japanese occupation of Manchuria under the 'Stimson Doctrine',

hardly any question that an invaded country's civilian population merited full Red Cross humanitarian protections – legal and otherwise.

But what about civilians who were being targeted by their own government within the boundaries of a sovereign state? Could the Red Cross, under the stipulations of the upcoming new Civilian Convention, intervene on their behalf? To be sure, it was to this type of civilians which the Hague regulations certainly *did not* apply. In fact, at the time, no official law of armed conflict applied to them. Asked about this glaring lacuna by the World Jewish Congress delegate Gerhart Riegner in March 1947, Max Huber – the foremost of all humanitarians – openly stated:

> The ICRC would not be permitted by states concerned to intervene in favour of their own nationals in times of peace or war . . . The ICRC could only act in places where inter-state reciprocity was granted and the protection of nationals of the persecuting state was a typical example where this was not the case.[43]

---

was the Danish Jewish international Jurist Georg Cohn. In 1922 Cohn sent to all states, on behalf of the Danish government, the first full elaboration of the non-recognition principle, stressing that a territory conquered by force shall remain 'militarily occupied' in international legal eyes, rather than being annexed, as in the transfer of sovereignty over that forcefully conquered territory. It is exactly against this logic that Schmitt and Best retaliated with their *Machtrecht* theories, which opted to bestow international recognition over the Nazis' forceful conquests during the Second World War. Importantly here, the Danish delegate to GC-IV, both in Stockholm, and in 1949 in Geneva, was the very same George Cohn, who survived the Holocaust and Werner Best's personal persecution of him as the chief Nazi administrator of Denmark. It was Cohn who in GC-IV's drafting brought forth his wartime experiences and codified them in Articles 49 (6) concerning the illegality of the transfer of the occupier's population into the territory occupied, and Art. 68, concerning the limitation upon the execution of the death penalty in occupied lands under GC-IV. On Georg Cohn's role in the codification of GC-IV, and his fight against Schmitt's and Best's legal theories see G. Ben-Nun, *The Fourth Geneva Convention for Civilians: The History of International Humanitarian Law*, London: I. B. Tauris, 2019, pp. 115–94. On Carl Schmitt's concept of *Grossraum* and on his refusal to accept the notion of a territory militarily occupied, which later led Werner Best to development his SS typology for the different modalities of the Nazi occupation of Europe, see M. Mazower, *Hitler's Empire: Nazi Rule in Occupied Europe*, London: Allen Lane, 2008, pp. 236–8. On Schmitt's arrest by the Nuremberg prosecution team, his interrogations, his pending indictment on account of his elaboration of *Grossraum* theory of Nazi conquests, and his eventual release see J. J. Bendersky, *Carl Schmitt: Theorist for the Reich*, Princeton, NJ: Princeton University Press, 1983, pp. 265–73. On Werner Best's escape from prosecution for war crimes in Denmark, and later in Germany see U. Herbert, *Best: Biographische Studien über Radikalismus, Weltanschauung und Vernunft 1903–1989*, München: C. H. Beck, 1998, pp. 273–89.

[43] World Jewish Archives at the Hebrew Union College Cincinnati (hereinafter 'WJCA'), File # 10 Box D 106, International Red Cross Conferences 1946–8, original filing under WJC 265, note 1947, Gerhard Riegner to the directorate of the WJC: The

So much for the lessons from the Jewish Holocaust. Astonishingly though, the text which resulted from the 1947 governments' experts' conference, and which was sent out to all delegations ahead of the XVII Red Cross Conference in Stockholm, was nothing less than revolutionary. Article 2 of all the newly proposed Geneva Conventions stated:

> In all cases of armed conflict which are not of an international character, especially cases of civil war, colonial conflicts, or wars of religion, which may occur in the territory of one or more of the High Contracting Parties, the implementing of the principles of the present Convention shall be obligatory on each of the adversaries.[44]

France was present at the debate where Riegner was logically struck down by Max Huber, back in 1947. And when Lamarle brought his notes back from the government experts' conference to the Quai d'Orsay in Paris, these were read attentively by the three Jewish leaders of the French *Conseil d'État*: Cassin, Cahen-Salvador and Mendes-France. In turn, they instructed Lamarle not to give in to the UK and US positions, and to press on regardless, for the protection of both resistance fighters and civilians.

Four days prior to the opening of the Stockholm Conference, on 16 August 1948, Pierre Mendes-France sent a long report to the French Foreign Minister Robert Schuman. Following up on a meeting between Lamarle and Raphael Lemkin in Stockholm, the ambassador took the time to share with his foreign minister the dilemmas and cross-over of categories, between civilians and combatants, as these had come to the fore during the last war. Lemkin was a well-respected international lawyer, who had invented the term 'genocide', and whose mission in life as embodied in the elaboration and endorsement of the Genocide Convention was approaching its fruition. Explaining to Schuman the intricate connection between a civilian population and the resistance fighters it might be harbouring, Mendes-France wrote:

> Professor Lemkin, who is one of the initiators of the project for a Convention against Genocide, and who is following the debates of ECOSOC closely, shared with Monsieur Lamarle his views on . . . the protection of civilian populations in times of war . . . there is an interest in engaging in a discussion on this problem at the international Red Cross Conference in Stockholm. The principles at the base of the Genocide Convention affirm that a national group, ethnic or religious, who

---

Revision of the Conventions on Prisoners of War and Civilian Internees: eight-page Report on a Conference in Geneva, March 1947, p. 5, third para.

[44] 'Draft revised or new Conventions for the protection of war victims established by the International Committee of the Red Cross with the assistance of government experts, national Red Cross societies and other humanitarian associations for the XVII International Red Cross Conference', Geneva, May 1948, p. 153, available at https://www.loc.gov/rr/frd/Military_Law/pdf/RC_Draft-revised.pdf.

is threatened due to the prospects of its systematic destruction . . . would be in a situation of legitimate defence . . . The uprising of the Ghetto of WARSAW is, even before the principle is laid down (*"avant la lettre"*), a typical example of this legitimate right of defence.[45]

Lamarle was now instructed to fight in Stockholm for a minimal protective purview for *all people* – combatants and civilians alike. He already knew all too well that the Soviets, upon whose support he depended so as to counter the UK and the US positions, would not show up. Nevertheless, this time round, he would not stand alone in the contest against the UK and the US. Georges Cahen-Salvador would be there right besides him.

In Stockholm, the textual development of the Geneva Conventions was entrusted to the Red Cross Conference's legal commission, presided over by Judge Emil Sandström. A recognized international legal authority, a Swedish Supreme Court judge, and since 1946 a member of the Permanent Court of Arbitration, Sandström had just finalized his tenure as the chairman of the United Nations Special Committee for Palestine (UNSCOP), which recommended the partitioning of Palestine to the UN General Assembly. The legal commission's work was divided up between its different sub-commissions, each looking deeper into one specific Geneva Convention. The division of labour between the sub-commissions and the plenary was rather straightforward. Each sub-commission discussed its draft Convention and consolidated its text to be brought forward before the plenary for approval. Points of contestation would be worked over in the sub-commissions, and in the absence of agreement, would be shared with the legal commission's plenary for their final wording. At the helm of sub-commission III, mandated to oversee the textual development of the newly envisaged Civilian Convention, stood its now-unanimously elected chairman – Georges Cahen-Salvador.

Already during the first week at Stockholm, in sub-commission III's session of 21 August, the issue of whether the new Civilian Convention would apply to genocide and domestically self-targeted civilians came to a head. Following the adoption of a Norwegian proposal to include under its purview also civilians incarcerated during a civil war within their own country, chairman Cahen-Salvador gave the floor to the World Jewish Congress delegate Gerhart Riegner. Riegner proposed to equally insert paragraph 4 of Article 2 of the POW Convention into the Civilian Convention text, thus extending the protections for civilians to officially also cover nationals targeted by their own

---

[45] FFMA, File # 768-SUP / 159 t.e.r., AL/ CL.No. /21/CES, Pierre Mendes-France to Robert Schuman: 'Le crime de Génocide et la protection des populations civilise en temps de guerre', Délégation française après du Conseil Economique et Social des Nations Unies, Geneva, 16 August 1948, pp. 1–2 (author's translation).

government. This was exactly what Max Huber had refused to undertake back in 1947. Taking the floor directly after Riegner, Claude Pilloud, the director of the ICRC's legal division, starkly contravened against this motion:

> (Mr. Pilloud – ICRC): responded that the objective of the Convention **was not** to protect civilians from their own government ('*la Convention n'a pas pour object de protéger les civils contre leur propre Gouvernement*').[46]

With the question of the Civilian Convention's application remaining unresolved within sub-commission III, the issue was to resurface in the legal commission's plenary, this time under Judge Sandström's chairmanship.[47] This debate, on whether to include under the Civilian Convention's protective purview peoples targeted by their own government, was left to the very last day of the legal commission's deliberations – Friday 27 August 1948. As Judge Sandström opened the debate that morning, he bestowed the first *droit de parole* upon the WJC observer Riegner, who stated that he:

> would like to draw attention to internal conflicts *within* a country . . . for example the scenes which took place in 1938 in Germany where the State's armed forces literally annihilated ('*écrasé*') thousands of civilians, and burnt their houses and their places of worship . . . We [i.e. the WJC] believe this case should also be covered . . . We have undoubtedly been opposed on account of the argument that this Convention is not intended to protect people against their own proper government.[48]

Throughout the Stockholm Conference, the debates surrounding the application of the Civilian Convention to situations of non-international armed conflict revolved around the question as to which cases ought to be covered by this clause, as in the words 'civil wars, colonial conflicts, or wars of religion'. Riegner wished to add another category to the cases mentioned, so as to also include genocides. Yet when President Sandström turned to hear the ideas of Georges Cahen-Salvador – the chairman of the Civilian Convention's drafting committee – the debate took a striking turn.

Applying a methodologically opposed approach to that of Riegner, Cahen-Salvador opted to *reduce* Article 2's wording and restrict it to its bare minimum of general principle. Rather than trying to hopelessly cover the

---

[46] Stockholm XVII Red Cross Conference, Debates of the Sub-Commissions of the Legal Commission, afternoon session of Saturday 21 August 1948, p. 50 (emphasis added; author's translation), available at https://library.icrc.org/library/docs/DOC/11670.pdf.

[47] Stockholm XVII Red Cross Conference, Debates of the Legal Commission, morning session of Friday 27 August 1948, discussions of Article 2, pp. 36–7, available at https://library.icrc.org/library/docs/DOC/18382.pdf

[48] Ibid. (author's translation).

infinite array of possible cases which might one day arise, Cahen-Salvador stated:

> I fully understand the preoccupations of the previous speaker [i.e. Riegner] and completely identify myself with them ('*Je m'y associe pleinement*'). And yet, I believe that within an international convention such as ours, the more we try to precise, the more we weaken its dominating principle. I would therefore opt to restrict the wording to the bare general minimum **covering all cases**, and solely maintaining the words "international war or civil war" . . . In short, I believe we have an interest in leaving the text as brief and simple as possible.[49]

With President Sandström now firmly behind his line of argumentation Cahen-Salvador thus sealed the debate:

> The more our legal formulations are imperative, clear, precise, and non-detailed, the higher our chances to achieve our goals. It is impossible, within a legal text, to preview all the circumstances which could come about in the future . . . I worry, lest our text remains a dead letter, and hope it is rapidly and completely adopted by governments. The more we complicated it, the more we preclude the possibility of obtaining its unanimous endorsement. It is under this preoccupation that I demand to maintain the text as it is . . . and strike out . . . the words 'especially in cases of civil war, colonial conflicts, wars of religion'. Let us leave nothing but the general formula, which incorporates ('*qui englobe*') **all possible cases, including those we at the moment cannot envisage**.[50]

And so it came about that the final text concerning non-international armed conflict, adopted by the Stockholm conference, came to read:

> In all cases of armed conflict not of an international character which may occur in the territory of one or more of the High Contracting Parties, each of the Parties to the conflict shall be bound to implement the provisions of the present Convention.[51]

Cabling WJC headquarters in New York, Gerhart Riegner rejoiced at the fact that thanks to the sole maintenance of this general formula, *all* civilian

---

[49] Ibid., p.40 (emphasis added; author's translation).
[50] Ibid., p. 43 (emphasis added; author's translation).
[51] 'Revised and new Draft Conventions for the protection of war victims: texts approved and amended by the XVII international Red Cross Conference', Geneva, October 1948, p. 114. Note 2 on the same page laconically states that: 'The words "especially cases of civil war, colonial conflicts or wars of religion" have been deleted'. Available at https://library.icrc.org/library/docs/CDDH/CI_1948/CI_1948_PROJET_ENG_04.pdf.

victims, including those targeted by their own governments, would be covered by the newly proposed Civilian Convention.[52]

As the WJC got its textual victory in Stockholm, the French scored their own serious diplomatic victory as Lamarle secured the renewed engagement of the Soviets. Speaking 'off-record' to a Soviet 'observer' in Stockholm, Lamarle managed to convince him that the cause of protecting communist combatants, by bringing them under GC-IV's protective purview, was not at all lost, and that this idea was fully shared by France:

> A few hours ago, I had a conversation with the senior figure of the three "auditors" from the Soviet Red Cross who . . . completely understood and identified with the French motion in favour of a broad wording of Common Article 2, and who stressed that . . . the International Committee of the Red Cross ought, in the case of civil wars as currently in Greece, to proceed with enquires once atrocities have been committed . . . Had the Soviets participated in Stockholm and proposed such an ICRC enquiry capacity, they would have received serious objections . . . and would have been defeated by the overwhelming Western majority. I [i.e. Lamarle – being the speaker] stressed to my interlocutor that if the Soviets desired to raise this or that issue, that was all the more reason for them to participate in future Conferences, and that contrary to his belief, the result of any vote was most certainly not predetermined . . . The Soviet "auditor" expressed his desire to discuss with me further.[53]

THE FINAL ACT – THE SOVIETS SAVE THE DAY: GENEVA 1949

The remaining stages of how protection for all was enshrined into GC-IV's Final Act, especially within the making of Common Article 3, during the 1949 Geneva Conference of Plenipotentiaries, has been amply told. In brief, the idea to extend the Geneva Conventions' protection to all combatants and civilians

---

[52] Riegner's telegram read as follows: 'Legal committee of the seventeenth International Red Cross Conference presided by Judge Sandstroem Ex-UNSCOP Palestinian enquiry passed important change to Article TWO of proposed convention treatment of civilians time of war removing limitation of it being operative solely quote in civil wars colonial conflicts and wars of religion unquote, and calling for obligatory implementation of the convention quote in all cases of armed conflicts which are not of an international character unquote thus giving principle convention clause wider possibilities of application specially point of view of Jews and other minorities incapable of warlike resistance stop'. WJCA, File # 10 Box D 106, International Red Cross Conferences 1946–48, original filing under WJC 265, RCA D 136 telegram, 30 August 1948 Stockholm 165/ 161, signed by Baum.

[53] FFMA, File # 768-SUP / 159 bis, Telegram No. 391, 'Absence de l'USSR à la Conférence de la Croix Rouge, Par M. Lamarle', Stockholm 28 August 1948, received 30 August 1948, 12:00 hours. All inverted commas in the original (author's translation).

saw two failed attempts, within the textual battles over the wording of what was then still Common Article 2, with the UK and the US attempting to limit its scope, against the Soviet, Scandinavian and Benelux countries which opted for its wide expansion.[54]

Wishing to break the *impasse*, Cahen-Salvador and Lamarle orchestrated yet another feat of what Best termed as a 'genius of French intervention', as they put forward the idea of creating a new common article which would cover all internal wars and non-international armed conflicts, and which would include a rudimentary set of basic protections applicable to all people, no matter who or where they were.[55] These protections, which outlawed torture, summary killings, degrading treatment, the taking of hostages, and targeted reprisals were non-derogable. The new Common Article 3 also stipulated the administration of fundamental due legal processes, and equally important, secured the ICRC's official role to intervene on victims' behalf. It was this French proposal, as embraced by the majority of the delegates in Geneva, which metamorphosed into the Common Article 3 we know today.

As Anthony Cullen has convincingly demonstrated, no delegation was more forcefully committed to the idea of a basic protection for all civilians as the Soviet Union, spearheaded by its gifted diplomat (and, years later, two-term judge at the International Court of Justice) Platon Morosov.[56] In his confidential report to his ICRC superiors, Claude Pilloud alluded to the vital role played by the Soviets in securing the Civilian Convention's text:

> We know that the delegation of the U.S.S.R. held, in defence of the texts adopted by the Stockholm Conference, the most general humanitarian attitudes . . . This frequently resulted in an accord between this delegation and the ICRC, and I had the occasion of coordinating many times with . . . the Russian delegates, in order to reach the best result possible . . . this delegation's role in the Conference was one of the most helpful ones, and I dare not think what would have become of the "Civilian" Convention had it not been for the presence of the Russian delegation (*"j'ose à peine songer à ce que serait devnue la Convention 'Civils' sans la présence de la délégation russe"*).[57]

---

[54] G. Best, *War and Law since 1945*, Oxford: Oxford University Press, 1994, pp. 94–179; A. Cullen, *The Concept of Non-International Armed Conflict in International Humanitarian Law*, Cambridge: Cambridge University Press, 2010, pp. 25–49; G. Mantilla, 'The Origins and Evolution of the 1949 Geneva Conventions and the 1977 Additional Protocols', in Evangelista and Tannenwald (eds.), *Do the Geneva Conventions Matter?*, pp. 43–9, at nn. 17–30.

[55] Best, *War and Law since 1945*, pp. 168–78, particularly p. 174.

[56] A. Cullen, *The Concept of Non-International Armed Conflict*, pp. 45–6.

[57] C. Pilloud, *Final Report – Annex*, pp. 7–8.

Historical scholarship has, for the most part, viewed the Soviet bloc's participation in GC-IV's drafting at the 1949 Conference of Plenipotentiaries as part of a broader, Machiavellian Soviet 'peace offensive'.[58] The Soviets were absent, so runs this narrative, from all of GC-IV's proceedings prior to 1949, and decided to 'show up' in Geneva – unexpected and unplanned – at the very last moment. Geoffrey Best spoke of 'the Soviet bloc's well-contrived humanitarian offensive, which put the US and the UK on the defensive'.[59] David Forsythe limited himself to observing that 'Moscow's policy was to damage an ICRC that was closely linked to a hostile Swiss Confederation'.[60] Catherine Rey-Schyrr wrote that the invitations to both Stockholm and to the Conference of Plenipotentiaries were sent without any explicit mention of the ICRC 'for fear of giving the Soviet Union and the Eastern European countries an excuse not to attend'.[61] At the end of the day, so concludes this line of argument, the Soviets never really cared for the development of international humanitarian law under the new Geneva Conventions and were devoid of true humanitarian intentions. Their participation in GC-IV's drafting, along with their unequivocal support for the Stockholm draft's textual version of Common Article 3, were nothing more than a propaganda stunt, aimed at unmasking the cynicism of Western countries such as the UK, who fought to reduce the Geneva Conventions' protective standards, so as to legally enable their unabated pounding of communist combatants from Greece to Malaya, as the end of their colonial rule unfolded.

Contrasting against this theory of Soviet Machiavellian intentions, the sources from the French, ICRC, and Bulgarian archives quoted throughout this chapter tell a very different story. As Pilloud explained to his ICRC's leadership:

> ... many times, I found myself in need of rallying behind the views of the U.S.S.R. against those of the Anglo-Saxons. We know that under the current political conditions such a position by the ICRC [i.e. that it aligns itself with the Soviet bloc and not with the position of Western allies] is sometimes hard to understand.[62]

---

[58] Best, *War and Law since 1945*, pp. 107–14.
[59] Ibid., p. 111.
[60] D. Forsythe, *The Humanitarians: The International Committee of the Red Cross*, Cambridge: Cambridge University Press, 2005, p. 53. One should note that the footnote to this text refers to Best's *War and Law since 1945*, in the same pages as are quoted above.
[61] Rey-Schyrr, *From Yalta to Dien Bien Phu*, p. 225.
[62] Pilloud, *Final Report – Annex*, pp. N-O, point 4, 'Friends and Adversaries' (author's translation).

The historical record merits a considerable revision here. To begin with, the theory of 'Soviet surprises', both of not coming to Stockholm, and of just 'popping up' in Geneva in April 1949 seems unconvincing to say the least. In the case of Stockholm, the French diplomatic *démarche* of 1947–48, and the ample Soviet preparations over the Stockholm texts speak for themselves. Lamarle's 'corridor discussions' with the Soviets 'observers' in Stockholm further attest to the continued willingness of the Soviet to re-engage in GC-IV's drafting process. But perhaps the strongest signal in favour of diplomatic reconciliation was sent by the Soviets to the Western powers some six weeks *prior* to the opening of the Geneva Conference in March 1949. This was the lifting of the Berlin blockade.[63]

The Soviet attempt to starve the German capital and bring about its fall into Soviet control began in June 1948, two months prior to the Stockholm Conference, and ended well in time for the beginning of the Geneva Conference of Plenipotentiaries, which opened its doors on 12 April 1949. The Berlin blockade represented one of the most dangerous flashpoints for a possible military escalation between the two world superpowers anywhere on the planet at that time. It constituted a condition tantamount to the eruption of war on an almost daily basis. During this ten-month airlift, some 101 airmen lost their lives in plane crashes and accidents, with aircraft landing at the rate of one per minute, day and night, including through the bitter 1948–49 Berlin winter. In a subsequent paragraph of his final report, Claude Pilloud explained this context further:

> The Conference was also influenced by the current political situation. It should be remembered that the Conference opened . . . after an agreement and a relaxation of tensions ("*une détente*") thanks to the interventions on the question of the Berlin Blockade. It could well be that even the very presence of the U.S.S.R. delegation, whom many did not expect to happen, probably did come about thanks to this political relaxation of tensions at this very stage.[64]

If the Soviets had reached an agreement to ease East–West tensions six weeks *prior* to the opening of the Geneva Conference of Plenipotentiaries,

---

[63] On the Berlin blockade and its considerable impacts on the later developments of the Cold War see D. F. Harrington, *Berlin on the Brink: The Blockade, the Airlift, and the Early Cold War*, Lexington: University of Kentucky Press, 2012, pp. 404–82. For a comprehensive study of the Berlin blockade's long-lasting impacts also on European politics and the EU see V. Mauer, *Brückenbauer: Großbritannien, die Deutsche Frage und die Blockade Berlins 1948–1949*, Berlin and London: Veröffentlichungen des Deutschen Historischen Instituts London und de Gruyter Verlag Berlin, 2018.

[64] Pilloud, *Final Report – Annex*, p. T, at point 20: 'political influences over the Conference' (author's translation).

then their desire to join the process of the codification of the new humanitarian laws they so painfully left off just before Stockholm, should have come as no surprise at all; all the more so as no one suffered more than the Soviets from *the lack* of these very laws during the Second World War.

Once in Geneva, the Soviet spirit of diplomatic reconciliation continued. Concerning the preparedness of the Soviet delegation, Pilloud noted:

> ... all the principle Convention texts [i.e. the Stockholm drafts] were translated into Russian, and within several weeks already before the conference these delegates became very well prepared ... It is certain that their lack of knowledge of the official languages of the Conference, and their corresponding necessity to always speak via translation rendered their situation amongst the delegations more difficult.[65]

Moscow knew well enough that it was linguistically and probably also technically inferior to the Western Allied delegations in Geneva. In order to make up for its deficiencies, the Soviet bloc proposed, and everybody unanimously accepted, that the Civilian Convention's vice-chairmanship be entrusted to the Bulgarian delegate – Dr Nissim Mevorah. Pilloud alluded to Mevorah's diplomatic skills and his vital role in bridging gaps between East and West:

> The delegations of eastern Europe followed scrupulously the positions of the Soviet delegation. The most active delegate of these countries, and certainly the most intelligent, was Monsieur Mevorah, the leader of the Bulgarian delegation, who tried repeatedly on many occasions, and very tactfully, to find good solutions and compromises.[66]

In the annex to his final report, Pilloud clearly demarks Mevorah as a 'friend' of the ICRC, with whom special contacts and an ongoing relationship ought to be cultivated.[67] Who then was Nissim Mevorah and why was he designated by the Soviet bloc for GC-IV's vice-chairmanship?

Born 1881 in Sofia to a family of sixteenth-century exiled Sephardic Jews who received asylum in the Ottoman Empire, Nissim Mevorah studied law in Sofia, and then completed his doctorate in law at the University of Geneva in 1914.[68] While in Geneva, as he developed a strong affinity towards Marxism, Mevorah befriended Vladimir Ilyich Lenin, who fled there in 1905, following

---

[65] Pilloud, *Final Report – Annex*, p. 7 (author's translation).
[66] Pilloud, *Final Report – Annex*, p. 10 (author's translation).
[67] Pilloud, *Final Report – Annex*, p. O.
[68] N. Mevorah, *De la Formation des contrats, doctrine et jurisprudence françaises considérées au point de vue des théories modernes, thèse de doctorat*, Lausanne: E. Toso and Cie, 1914. A copy of this thesis can be consulted at the Bibliothèque nationale de France François Mitterrand, ref. 8 – THETA GEN DR-80.

the failed Communist Revolution in Tsarist Russia that year.[69] Returning to Bulgaria, in 1920, Mevorah became one of the three original founding fathers of the Bulgarian Communist Party.

Being married to a non-Jew, Mevorah and his family were spared the fate of the rest of Bulgarian Jewry, who during the Second World War were deported from their homes into work-camps, albeit graciously saved from the fate of the rest of European Jewry in part thanks to the efforts of the Bulgarian Orthodox Church in Sofia. Being a senior figure in the Bulgarian post-Second World War communist regime, and after a spate as a judge in the post-war trials of Bulgarian fascists, in 1947, Mevorah assumed his country's second highest diplomatic commissioning, as its ambassador to Washington, presenting his credentials to President Truman later that year.[70]

With this biography in mind, the reasons behind Stalin's decision to appoint Mevorah as the Soviet bloc's vice-chairman in Geneva become clearer. A gifted jurist with a mother-tongue command of French and English, a communist-bloc ambassador to the US well acquainted with Washington's corridors of power, and yet a long-standing sworn communist, Mevorah could provide the Soviet bloc with the diplomatic clout and class-act it needed in Geneva. Furthermore, Mevorah was also a Holocaust-surviving Jew, and knew all too well what it meant to be a civilian targeted by his own government, as had in fact happened to 13 000 Bulgarian-Macedonian Jews, who were all deported and murdered in Auschwitz.[71] In his final report to the Bulgarian Foreign Minister Vladimir Poptomov, at the end of the Geneva Plenipotentiaries' Conference, Mevorah laconically captured the 'protection for all' spirit which eventually prevailed in GC-IV's making, under his vice-chairmanship.

> Evaluation of the conventions: The conventions can be characterised in short as an attempt at humanising war. They are dominated by the principles of the Red Cross and are strengthened by the bitter experiences of the barbaric outbursts of the Germans during the past world war. They now encompass humane treatment of prisoners of war, the outlawing of taking of hostages, the outlawing of torture, the outlawing of genocide, the outlawing of forced labour; the protection of the Red Cross emblem in any territory and on any vehicle, a wide protection for the civilian

---

[69] B. Mevorah, 'Professor Nissim Mevorah's Bulgarian-Jewish Way of Life', *East-European Quarterly*, vol. 19(1), 1985, pp. 75–80, p. 76.

[70] Mevorah, 'Professor Nissim Mevorah's Bulgarian-Jewish Way of Life', p. 77.

[71] N. Mevorah, *The Jews of Bulgaria before and after the 9th September 1944*, Sofia, 1946, p. 10. A copy of this pamphlet written by Mevorah, explaining the tragic fate of 13 000 Macedonian Jews, all killed by the Nazis, and the events which transpired so that the Jews of Bulgaria could be saved, with his explicit mention of the Bulgarian Church's Exarch Stefan I's actions in favour of the Jews and against their deportation, is deposited at the Bibliothèque nationale de France François Mitterrand, ref. 16-J PIECE-102.

population, especially children, women, and the elderly; the rule of law in war and the prohibition of retroactive laws, the limitation upon the administration of the death penalty, the outlawing of collective punishment, the outlawing of reprisals, regular humanitarian protection, the contact with protecting countries and powers, the right to correspondence, to receiving aid and so forth.[72]

CONCLUSION

It is to the credit of four actors – the ICRC, France, the Soviet Union, and the World Jewish Congress – that the notion of 'protection for all' was inserted into GC-IV, between 1946 and 1949. At the outset, none of these four actors harboured the desire to extend a basic set of protections to *all* civilians and *all* combatants. Rather, each of them advocated for an extension of GC-IV's protective purview to a specific category of persons previously not protected, whose rights they now wished to be secured, following the traumas of the Second World War. For France, this was first and foremost the combatants fighting an evil occupier. For the Soviets, it was communist combatants fighting against what they saw as non-legitimate regimes, either in-country or cross-border, and who in their eyes were deserving of POW status. For the World Jewish Congress, it was civilians targeted by their own proper government. For the ICRC, it was all of the above, yet without the self-targeted civilians advocated for by the WJC.

As the drafting process progressed, the interests of all four actors began to converge. Yet the first seeds of 'protection for all' were in fact sowed by the ICRC, in its amazing preparatory draft sent out to governments and National Red Cross societies back in May 1948. This was where the paradigmatic thinking implicit in the notion of 'protection for all' initially came to the fore. Nevertheless, its first full elaboration took place during the last day of the 1948 Stockholm Conference, when the textual ancestor of Common Article 3 was finally agreed upon between Georges Cahen-Salvador and Gerhart Riegner, under Judge Sandström's tutelage. 'Protection for all' then took its full and final shape once all four actors, who initially contributed to its elaboration, came to sit around the same drafting table for the first time. This took place during the Geneva Plenipotentiaries' Conference of 1949.

A good portion of this chapter has been dedicated to understanding the Soviet position which eventually secured the adoption of 'protection for all'. One should not attribute solely, either pure humanitarianism, or naked

---

[72] Bulgarian National Archives – Sofia, Fund 1481, ОП1, 851, Diplomatic New Conventions, Nissim Mevorah Final Report to Bulgarian foreign minister Vladimir Poptomov, 10 August 1949 (Doc. 121, p. 10; translation from Bulgarian by Martin Petrov).

Machiavellianism to the Soviet bloc's humanitarian agenda-driving in 1949. This is true of all the great powers who at that time, and without exception, were executing their fair share of atrocities the world over. Be it the UK in Greece, the French in Algerian Sétif, the Soviet Union in its Gulags, the US and its CIA operatives who supported the United Fruit Company in Latin America, Belgium in the Congo or Holland in Indonesia, none of these Western powers could claim an irreproachable international conduct.

That said, no one in 'the West' suffered anything remotely close to what the Soviet world had recently endured under the Nazis. The answer as to why of all peoples, it was the Soviets who were the most humanitarian-inclined in Geneva does not lie in some pseudo-romantic image of humanitarianism which they indeed attempted to project. Rather, it lies in the amalgamation between the Soviet experiences under the Nazis, and the more immediate evolvements accompanying GC-IV's drafting stages from 1946 to 1949, along East–West battlegrounds, from Greece, through Malaya, to Indonesia, and China. If all-out war was now being fought by all against all – with states targeting civilians, occupiers fighting national liberators, and foreign-deployed militaries (including mercenaries) fighting domestic forces – if this was now all part of the permanent reality of wars within international affairs, then what was most needed was some sort of fundamental humanitarian coverage for all. This was what 'protection for all' was about for the Soviets. It was also what was missing from the ICRC's rigid legalistic reading of the Geneva Convention during the Second World War prior to GC-IV's endorsement. Voicing his disapproval of this rigid legalism, Georges Cahen-Salvador sardonically noted that:

> . . . modern war, far from sparing civilian populations of its consequences, has hit them the hardest. No international instrument could have spared civilians the atrocities of collective executions, racial persecutions, tortures and assassinations. Civilians could also not avoid aerial bombardments that indiscriminately harmed them and combatants alike; and yet – it was solely for civilians that one had reserved the painful privilege of gas chambers! ('*mais on leur avez reserve le douleureux privilege des chambres à gaz!*').[73]

Cahen-Salvador's above-stated sarcasm should not be understood as directed specifically against the ICRC, but rather in a more general sense of international law's failures, when applied without a view to the harsh realities of war as these unfolded. That warfare had developed to the point where it now

---

[73] Archive du Conseil d'État de France, Fonds Cahen Salvador, Ref. # 9952/4, Conférence de M. Cahen Salvador – Académie Diplomatique, 6 December 1951, pp. 1–4 (exclamation mark on p. 4 after the words 'gas chambers' in the original; author's translation).

saw civilians as primary targets is one thing. The absurdity of the whole affair lay in the fact that people who were not party to hostilities (civilians) paradoxically enjoyed fewer privileges than those of active combatants (POWs). As the person most associated with the Civilian Convention's drafting and its two-time chairman, it was this type of legal fragmentation that Cahen-Salvador opted to do away with.

Nowhere was this more apparent than in Cahen-Salvador's success in applying GC-IV to victims of genocide targeted by their own government. This point is absolutely crucial, since it proves beyond any doubt that he, Gerhart Riegner, Judge Sandström, and later Nissim Mevorah, all understood full well that once they had managed to apply GC-IV to people being targeted by their own government, they had succeeded to enshrine a measure of *non-limitedness* into GC-IV's application. This was the legal litmus test which proved that indeed, now, all peoples were covered by the Geneva Conventions. So long as GC-IV's applicability was dependent upon exogenous considerations, such as reciprocity *vis-à-vis* another country, or the adherence of the opposing party to its stipulations – its applicability could always be denied. Conditionality and reciprocity were exactly the grounds cited by Max Huber when he refused Riegner's request to include victims targeted by their own government under GC-IV's coverage in 1947. Victims targeted by their own government were at the 'end of the human scale', so to speak. If the Civilian Convention now applied to them – it applied to all. Once the stipulations of Common Article 3 were legislated, so as apply to all, and under all circumstances, no human being could be considered beyond the pale. This is exactly how Riegner understood it, as he triumphantly cabled WJC headquarters in New York quoting Sandström. This is how Nissim Mevorah understood it, as he wrote back in August 1949 to Foreign Minister Poptomov after the signing of GC-IV's Final Act. And this is how Georges Cahen-Salvador understood it in his above-quoted speech to the Paris Diplomatic Academy in 1951.

The last nail in the coffin of GC-IV's conditionality and reciprocity was hammered in at the 1949 Conference of Plenipotentiaries, when states decided to apply Common Article 3's stipulations '*even if insurgents failed to apply them*'.[74] Torture, summary executions, or the taking of hostages were now firmly illegal, irrelevant of who the sides to the conflict were, or if an enemy non-state actor was committing these very atrocities, or when a government was doing these atrocious acts to its own people. They were now illegal under international law – pure and simple.

No one took 'protection for all' to heart more than the ICRC itself. Forty-seven years after Huber's words to Riegner, as the organization found

---

[74] Best, *War and Law since 1945*, p. 178 (emphasis in the original).

itself yet again in the midst of a genocide – this time in Rwanda – it applied 'protection for all' unconditionally. As the UN abandoned Rwanda and General Romeo Dallaire to their fate in the most morally repulsive manner, the ICRC, under the leadership of its country delegate Philippe Gaillard, significantly scaled up its Rwandan rescue operations. Thanks to its unwavering stance from Geneva headquarters, and Gaillard's outright heroism, the ICRC managed to save well over 65 000 lives in Rwanda. Ironically, it was exactly this category of people, whom Max Huber and Claude Pilloud insisted could not be protected by the Civilian Convention four decades earlier, that the ICRC now accorded GC-IV's humanitarian provisions. As Gaillard himself later noted, his decision to remain in Rwanda was intimately related to the ICRC's historical record during previous genocides where it was not active.[75] History had gone full circle.

---

[75] G. Barker, *Ghosts of Rwanda*, PBS Frontline documentary, Canada: Frontline, 2004, minutes 1:05:00–1:07:00 (available at www.youtube.com/watch?v=VJAuyIRfYIMandt=116s): 'The International Committee of the Red Cross, which is 140-year-old organization, was not active during the Armenian genocide, it shut up during the Holocaust – everybody knew what was happening with the Jews; in such circumstances if you don't at least speak out clearly – you are participating in the genocide. If you shut up when you see what you see – morally, ethically, you cannot shut up; it's your responsibility to talk, to speak'.

6. History and core international crimes: friends or foes?
Olympia Bekou*

INTRODUCTION

The year 2018 marked the twentieth anniversary of the adoption of the Rome Statute of the International Criminal Court (ICC).[1] The year also marked notable historic events including the centenary anniversary of the end of the First World War, the seventy-fifth anniversary of the Warsaw Ghetto Uprising, and the sixty-fifth anniversary of the armistice agreement of the Korean War. Whereas such historical events may not have received adequate legal attention in national and international trials, the influence of history on the development of the core international crimes as they are enshrined within the Rome Statute today should not be underestimated. For, history not only leaves its hallmark on contemporary provisions, through criminalisation of conduct, but also influences the way modern histories are read.

Negotiations during the Rome Diplomatic Conference were conducted against a backdrop of historic events: the then recently committed genocide in Rwanda, and the atrocities perpetrated in the former Yugoslavia. From the outset, it is evident that history plays an important role in shaping the law. This chapter focuses on history and the definitions of core international crimes as enshrined in the Rome Statute. It attempts to trace the effect some historical events may have had on some of the crimes provisions therein. Needless to say, this approach is, by definition, exceedingly selective. It is neither possible to trace the many historical events that shaped each and every crime, nor is it desirable. Instead, the aim of this chapter is to make a general point on the

---

* I would like to thank Ms Emma Sheffield for her research assistance. All errors or omissions remain mine alone.

[1] Whilst the Rome Statute of the International Criminal Court (17 July 1998, UN Doc. A/CONF.183/9, hereinafter 'Rome Statute'), Art. 5 provides jurisdiction over the crime of genocide, crimes against humanity, war crimes, and the crime of aggression, the chapter concentrates on the first three categories.

intersection between history and international criminal law, through a historical lens of some of the punishable acts in the Statute. In addition, there is a further caveat that ought to be explained: as the author is not a historian, the examination of the issues raised in this chapter is entirely legal, with references to historical facts from a lawyer's perspective. This may frustrate historians, not least because of the lack of historical method. Inevitably, there is a risk of the potential retrospective reading of history to explain legal choices, which the author is conscious of.

HISTORY AND THE CORE INTERNATIONAL CRIMES

Comparative to the relatively long history of war crimes under international criminal law, crimes against humanity and the crime of genocide are recent additions. Despite the presence of mass atrocity crimes throughout history, efforts to prohibit what is now known as crimes against humanity and genocide did not occur until after the First and Second World Wars.[2] Both of these categories of crimes are legacies of historic events. Whilst the concepts of crimes against humanity and genocide have become separate crimes under international criminal law, the terms were coined to describe similar mass atrocity events.[3] Their origins can be traced to two historic events: the Ottoman government's persecution and systematic extermination of their Armenian population between 1915 and 1918, and Nazi crimes committed against European Jewish populations, namely, the Holocaust.[4] The chapter will therefore begin by considering the influence of these events on the early development of the concept of crimes against humanity, focusing on legal developments which occurred in the wake of Nazi crimes.

It will then move to consider the content of crimes against humanity within the Rome Statute. Within that, the choice was made to focus on the crime of apartheid, to highlight the significant influence that a single historic event can have on the development of international crimes, as the explicit inclusion of the crime of apartheid within the Rome Statute under Article 7(1)(j), indeed the term 'apartheid', can be linked directly to the South African system of racial discrimination which operated between 1948 and 1994.[5] This strong historic

---

[2] S. Paylan and A. Klonowiecka-Milart, 'Examining the Origins of Crimes against Humanity and Genocide', in M. Bergsmo, C. Wui Ling, S. Tianying and Y. Ping (eds.), *Historical Origins of International Criminal Law*, vol. 3, Brussels: Torkel Opsahl Academic E-Publisher, 2015, pp. 558–9.

[3] Ibid., pp. 557–8.

[4] Ibid.

[5] Rome Statute, Art. 7(1)(j); C. Lingaas, 'The Crime against Humanity of Apartheid in a Post-Apartheid World', *Oslo Law Review*, vol. 2(2), 2015, pp. 86–115, p. 114.

influence, whilst providing the impetus for the crime against humanity of apartheid, has also proved problematic. The drafters of the Rome Statute consciously used wording which moved beyond South Africa; however, the South African apartheid system shaped the definition of the crime as one specifically of racial discrimination. Thus, the historical origins and resulting terminology determine its application, and arguably require an element of reinterpretation if it is to apply to situations of concern today. This problem will be considered in relation to the Democratic People's Republic of Korea (DPRK), and the Occupied Palestinian Territories (OPT).

Building on this theme, the chapter will then consider the influence of crimes committed in the former Yugoslavia. The crime against humanity of forced pregnancy under Rome Statute Article 7(1)(g) has been chosen for inclusion in that respect.[6] Forced pregnancy was controversial in Rome, with some delegations fearing it would be problematic in relation to their domestic laws on abortion.[7] Forced pregnancy was included, however, with concessional acknowledgement that the crime as enshrined in the Rome Statute 'shall not in any way be interpreted as affecting national laws relating to pregnancy'.[8] Whilst protection from forced pregnancy as a core international crime owes a debt to history, and outrage at crimes committed against women in Rwanda and the former Yugoslavia, both situations included crimes based on ethnic identity. Therefore, this historical association and the link between forced pregnancy and ethnicity through Article 7(2)(f) fuelled arguments that the provision may be more about protection from ethnic crimes, than about the protection of women.[9] It is the interpretation and application of forced pregnancy in the *Ongwen* case, without an ethnic dimension and in the context of the Lord's Resistance Army (LRA), which may break the crime from such historical associations.

The chapter will then trace the influence of history on the development of the crime of crimes: that of genocide. Beginning with Lemkin's work focusing

---

[6] Rome Statute, Art. 7(1)(g).

[7] A. M. Drake, 'Aimed at Protecting Ethnic Groups or Women – A Look at Forced Pregnancy Under the Rome Statute', *William and Mary Journal of Race, Gender, and Social Justice*, vol. 18(3), 2012, pp. 595–623, p. 607; R. Grey, 'The ICC's First "Forced Pregnancy" Case in Historical Perspective', Journal of International Criminal Justice, vol. 15(5), 2017, pp. 905–30, p. 919.

[8] Rome Statute, Art. 7(2)(f); Drake, 'Aimed at Protecting Ethnic Groups or Women', p. 608.

[9] Rome Statute, Art. 7(2)(f), states '"Forced pregnancy" means the unlawful confinement of a woman forcibly made pregnant, with the intent of affecting the ethnic composition of any population or carrying out other grave violations of international law. This definition shall not in any way be interpreted as affecting national laws relating to pregnancy'; Drake, 'Aimed at Protecting Ethnic Groups or Women', p. 596.

on occupied Europe, the evolution of the crime of genocide is the result of historic events that have shaped it as a crime against 'groups'.[10] There are several arising questions: first, which groups should be protected by the provision? Both the Genocide Convention and the Rome Statute protect national, ethnical, racial and religious groups. They do not protect social or political groups, for instance.[11] Therefore, the concept of a group and how we are to determine to which groups people belong has become central for the crime of genocide.

Continual and differing interpretation of this concept can be seen through the *Bashir* case before the ICC. Further, the failure to protect social and political groups has sparked debate about other prominent historical events such as crimes committed in Cambodia by the Khmer Rouge.[12] The final aspect considered is the phrasing of the term genocide, as interpreted in light of pre-ICC crimes committed at Srebrenica.[13]

In the final part of the chapter, the development of war crimes will be considered, concentrating first on environmental damage. Destruction of the environment as an act of war has been seen throughout history, from ancient times to 'total warfare' during the American Civil War and 'scorched-earth' policies during the Second World War.[14] However, prior to the Rome Statute it was not possible to prosecute the intentional use of chemical weapons under international criminal law, unless such use harmed human beings.[15] The Rome Statute enshrines environmental protection independently of human injury under Article 8(2)(b)(iv).[16] This arguably follows the influence of two historic events: the Vietnam and Gulf Wars respectively.

Having said that, it is possible that the approach to chemical, biological and nuclear weapons seen within the Rome Statute is an illustration of the limitation of historical influence. If we refer to customary international law for guidance, we can see that the prohibition on the use of poison as a method

---

[10] R. Lemkin, *Axis Rule in Occupied Europe*, Washington, DC: Carnegie Endowment for International Peace, 1944, p. 79.

[11] Rome Statute, Art. 6, provides protection to national, ethnical, racial or religious groups.

[12] M. Klamberg (ed.), *Commentary on the Law of the International Criminal Court*, Brussels: Torkel Opsahl Academic E-Publisher, 2017, p. 24.

[13] W. Schabas, *The International Criminal Court: A Commentary on the Rome Statute*, 2nd ed., Oxford: Oxford University Press, 2016, p. 134.

[14] J. Lawrence and K. Heller, 'The First Ecocentric Environmental War Crime: The Limits of Art. 8(2)(*b*)(iv) of the Rome Statute', *Georgetown International Environmental Law Review*, vol. 20(1), 2007, pp. 61–95, p. 63.

[15] Ibid., p. 61.

[16] Rome Statute, Art. 8(2)(b)(iv) and Lawrence and Heller, 'The First Ecocentric Environmental War Crime', p. 61.

of warfare is one of the oldest prohibitions in international law.[17] Despite that and despite all these heinous historical things like the atomic bomb, the use of Agent Orange in Vietnam, chemical use on northern Kurds in Iraq 1987–88, etc. there were huge difficulties in the drafting of legal instruments; states' interests will always triumph over historical influence and outrage. Syria is obviously the case in point here, to which we shall return.

This chapter argues that history has played a role in shaping the definitions of core crimes, but that does not mean that definitions are static. Crystallisation in the Statute is not the end of history. A continued reinterpretation of the definitions is often required to 'fit' modern histories.

ORIGINS OF THE CORE INTERNATIONAL CRIMES: CRIMES AGAINST HUMANITY

The influence of historical events on the development of contemporary core international crimes can perhaps be epitomised by one prominent early use of the term 'crimes against humanity'. Within the context of the First World War, a series of atrocities were committed by the Ottoman government against the Armenian population within the Ottoman Empire.[18] In response, the Allied governments of France, Britain and Russia made a joint Declaration on 24 May 1915, calling the massacres 'these new crimes of Turkey *against humanity and civilization*'.[19] The Declaration also stated that the Allied governments would 'hold personally responsible [. . .] all members of the Ottoman government and those of their agents who are implicated in such massacres'.[20] It is therefore a significant early suggestion that movement away from the sanctity of state sovereignty and head of state immunity may be necessary where mass atrocities have been committed.[21] However, the Declaration had little practical legal

---

[17] A. Zimmerman and M. Sener, 'Chemical Weapons and the International Criminal Court', *American Journal of International Law*, vol. 108(3), 2014, pp. 436–48.

[18] Paylan and Klonowiecka-Milart, 'Examining the Origins of Crimes against Humanity and Genocide', p. 559.

[19] Dispatch sent 29 May 1915 by US Secretary of State, William Jennings Bryan, to the US Embassy in Constantinople, Turkey to be forwarded to the Turkish government, Doc. No. RG 59, 867.4016/67, *US National Archives*; Paylan and Klonowiecka-Milart, 'Examining the Origins of Crimes against Humanity and Genocide', p. 559.

[20] Dispatch sent 29 May 1915 by US Secretary of State, William Jennings Bryan; Paylan and Klonowiecka-Milart, 'Examining the Origins of Crimes against Humanity and Genocide', p. 559.

[21] Paylan and Klonowiecka-Milart, 'Examining the Origins of Crimes against Humanity and Genocide', p. 560.

impact at the time and the atrocities are commonly referred to as the Armenian genocide.[22]

Whilst recognising these early beginnings, discussion of the relationship between history and crimes against humanity must be conducted cognizant of the influence of the Second World War. This time period contains multiple historic events which have subsequently shaped international criminal law, most notably the Holocaust. At the time it was feared that many acts perpetrated by the Nazis would not be punished under war crimes alone, particularly the pre-war persecution of German Jewish people, and political opponents.[23] This is because these crimes had been committed by a state, against its own citizens, on its own territory.[24] In accordance with traditional conceptions of sovereignty it was considered by some to be 'legally unsound' to prosecute members of the Nazi party for crimes committed against Germans, in Germany.[25] However, the especially heinous nature of the Holocaust and other atrocities which were not connected to military action spurred progressive change.[26]

In the aftermath of the Second World War, the United Nations War Crimes Commission discussed Nazi crimes in relation to the concept of crimes against humanity.[27] They found that these crimes *are* punishable, whether perpetrated in wartime or peacetime, and that states may prosecute such crimes in relation to 'any civilian population', i.e. including where a state has committed crimes against its own people.[28] The link between historic events and the development of international criminal law is therefore clear: whilst the concept of crimes against humanity had existed prior to the 1940s, it was finally codified in the wake of Nazi crimes with explicit recognition within Article 6(c) of the Nuremberg Charter.[29] It is important to note that initial progress was cautious; Article 6(c) provided for acts committed 'in execution of or in connection

---

[22] Ibid., pp. 562 and 564.

[23] Similarly, the pre-war persecution of Chinese nationals in Manchuria by Japanese troops could also be covered by the newly codified concept, K. von Lingen, 'Defining Crimes Against Humanity: The Contribution of the United Nations War Crimes Commission to International Criminal Law, 1944–1947', in M. Bergsmo, C. Wui Ling and Y. Ping (eds.), *Historical Origins of International Criminal Law*, vol. 1, Brussels: Torkel Opsahl Academic E-Publisher, 2014, p. 477.

[24] Von Lingen, 'Defining Crimes Against Humanity', p. 478.

[25] Ibid., p. 487.

[26] Ibid., p. 488.

[27] Ibid., p. 479.

[28] Ibid.

[29] Charter of the International Military Tribunal Annex to the London Agreement for the Prosecution and Punishment of the Major War Criminals of the European Axis, 1945 ('IMT Charter'), Art. 6(c); Von Lingen, 'Defining Crimes Against Humanity', pp. 477 and 493.

with any crime within the jurisdiction of the Tribunal'.[30] Accordingly, crimes against humanity were bound to crimes against peace and the traditional concept of war crimes as provided for within Article 6 of the Nuremberg Charter.[31] This binding to other crimes was deemed necessary to avoid criticism of retroactive law, and to make the concept of crimes against humanity judiciable.[32]

One consequence of this approach was the forming of a nexus between crimes against humanity and armed conflict.[33] This restriction has subsequently prevented the application of crimes against humanity to situations including crimes committed in relation to decolonisation, the Cold War, crimes of apartheid, and crimes by military dictatorships.[34] In light of these events, and others, the wording of crimes against humanity within Article 7(1) of the Rome Statute deliberately does *not* include a nexus to armed conflict: it states that for the purpose of the Rome Statute 'crime against humanity' means any of the listed acts 'committed as part of a widespread or systematic attack directed against any civilian population, with knowledge of the attack'.[35] Indeed, the features of crimes against humanity found in the Rome Statute follow the core features as they were originally discussed by the United Nations War Crimes Commission.[36] Again the influence of historic events on the development of the core international crimes is clear: in recognition of their continued perpetration not in connection to armed conflict, the restrictive armed conflict nexus has been broken.[37]

---

[30] IMT Charter, Art. 6(c) (n 29); Von Lingen, 'Defining Crimes Against Humanity', pp. 478 and 496.
[31] IMT Charter, Art. 6; Von Lingen, 'Defining Crimes Against Humanity', pp. 478 and 496.
[32] Von Lingen, 'Defining Crimes Against Humanity', p. 478.
[33] Ibid.
[34] Ibid., pp. 478 and 502.
[35] Rome Statute, Art. 7(1), states in full: 'For the purpose of this Statute, "crime against humanity" means any of the following acts when committed as part of a widespread or systematic attack directed against any civilian population, with knowledge of the attack'; Von, 'Defining Crimes Against Humanity', p. 503; Paylan and Klonowiecka-Milart, 'Examining the Origins of Crimes against Humanity and Genocide', p. 578.
[36] Von Lingen, 'Defining Crimes Against Humanity', p. 479.
[37] Paylan and Klonowiecka-Milart, 'Examining the Origins of Crimes against Humanity and Genocide', p. 577.

CRIMES AGAINST HUMANITY: APARTHEID

Having discussed the influence of history on initial development of the concept of crimes against humanity, let us now consider the relationship between historical events and the content of the term. For this discussion the crime of apartheid as a crime against humanity as provided for in Article 7(1)(j) and Article 7(2)(h) of the Rome Statute, has been (selectively) chosen.[38] Specifically, this section explores the influence of a single historic event, the South African apartheid system, which required the separation of racial groups and was implemented via a substantial legal regime,[39] on the definition of apartheid as a crime against humanity. The very term 'apartheid' is a result of this history, being coined in 1944 by D. F. Malan, the then Prime Minister of South Africa.[40] The South African policy of apartheid gained traction with the election into power of the National Party in 1948, and the subsequent stream of discriminatory legislation beginning with the Prohibition of Mixed Marriages Act 1949.[41] The apartheid system continued until 1994, and the election of Nelson Mandela of the African National Congress. During that time many human rights violations and atrocity crimes were committed, as recorded by the subsequent Truth and Reconciliation Commission.[42] The international community was united in its condemnation and efforts to abolish apartheid in South Africa.[43]

Against this context, the International Law Commission's commentaries on the 1994 Draft Statute for an International Criminal Court includes discussion

---

[38] Rome Statute, Art. 7(1)(j): The crime of apartheid; and Art. 7(2)(h): the 'crime of apartheid' means 'inhumane acts of a character similar to those referred to in paragraph 1, committed in the context of an institutionalized regime of systematic oppression and domination by one racial group over any other racial group or groups and committed with the intention of maintaining that regime'.

[39] See e.g. the Prohibition of Mixed Marriages Act, Act No. 55 of 1949, the Preservation of Coloured Areas Act, Act No. 31 of 1961, and the Terrorism Act, Act No. 83 of 1967.

[40] Lingaas, 'The Crime against Humanity of Apartheid in a Post-Apartheid World', p. 88.

[41] Prohibition of Mixed Marriages Act, Act No. 55 of 1949; other early apartheid era legislation includes the Immorality Amendment Act, Act No. 21 of 1950, amended in 1957 (Act 23), and the Population Registration Act, Act No. 30 of 1950. One of the last pieces of legislation enacted was the Bantu Homelands Citizens Act, Act No. 26 of 1970.

[42] Archbishop Desmond Tutu et al., *Truth and Reconciliation Commission of South Africa Report: Volume One*, Truth and Reconciliation Commission, 1998, p. 24, available at http://www.justice.gov.za/trc/report/finalreport/Volume%201.pdf.

[43] Lingaas, 'The Crime against Humanity of Apartheid in a Post-Apartheid World', p. 114.

around why apartheid had not yet been explicitly included as a crime against humanity.[44] At that time, a member of the Commission noted the inclusion of apartheid in the list of crimes pursuant to treaties under what was then Article 20(e), due to the International Convention on the Suppression and Punishment of the Crime of Apartheid.[45] Indeed, the Apartheid Convention is itself a direct legacy of the influence of South African history on the development of international law: the Commission recognised the outdated nature of its explicit reference to 'similar policies and practices of racial segregation and discrimination as practised in southern Africa'.[46] On the issue of explicitly including the crime of apartheid within the Draft Statute, members of the Commission noted the wide ratification of the Apartheid Convention and widespread condemnation by states of the South African system.[47] However, it was determined that the definition of the crime of apartheid was overly broad and that the status of apartheid as a crime under international law 'remained a disputed issue'.[48] One central question was whether apartheid was a purely South African phenomenon. The Commission determined that the international circumstances of the time, including newly implemented 'majority rule in South Africa', meant it was sufficient to include apartheid under the then Article 20(e) via the Apartheid Convention.[49]

During the Rome Diplomatic Conference the crime of apartheid was much debated.[50] The decision to include it came late, and was a result of com-

---

[44] The Draft provided only for the following acts as crimes against humanity: murder, extermination, enslavement, deportation, imprisonment, torture, rape, persecutions on political, racial and religious grounds, and other inhumane acts. International Law Commission Report to the General Assembly on the Work of its Forty-Sixth Session, 1996, Part 2, Draft Code of Crimes Against the Peace and Security of Mankind, *Yearbook of the International Law Commission*, 1994, vol. II, Part Two, at para. 16 (UN Doc. A/CN.4/SER.A/1994/Add.1).

[45] The International Convention on the Suppression and Punishment of the Crime of Apartheid, 30 November 1973 (hereafter the 'Apartheid Convention'); and Draft Code of Crimes Against the Peace and Security of Mankind.

[46] Apartheid Convention, Art. 2; Draft Code of Crimes Against the Peace and Security of Mankind.

[47] Although it is notable that the Apartheid Convention has mostly been ratified by non-Western states, see *United Nations Treaty Collection* [online], available at https://treaties.un.org/Pages/ViewDetails.aspx?src=IND&mtdsg_no=IV-7&chapter=4&lang=en; Draft Code of Crimes Against the Peace and Security of Mankind.

[48] Draft Code of Crimes Against the Peace and Security of Mankind; Lingaas, 'The Crime against Humanity of Apartheid in a Post-Apartheid World', pp. 87–8.

[49] Draft Code of Crimes Against the Peace and Security of Mankind.

[50] H. von Hebel and D. Robinson, 'Crimes Within the Jurisdiction of the Court', in R. S. Lee (ed.), *The International Criminal Court: The Making of the Rome Statute*, The Hague: Kluwer Law International, 1999, p. 92.

promise after its inclusion was suggested by the collective Southern African Development Community.[51] Whilst there was some resistance, the majority of states were in favour of recognising the crime of apartheid and noted that if it was not explicitly listed, it would be implicitly included under Article 7(1)(k) referring to 'other inhumane acts'.[52] This concept in itself was problematic as argument arose that a specific apartheid provision was superfluous: a widespread and systemic apartheid policy would be covered by Article 7(1)(h) which provides for persecution on racial grounds.[53] Its inclusion remains criticised as legally unsound by some scholars owing to this simultaneous presence of the crime of persecution.[54] Ultimately, the state representatives agreed that apartheid is of a significant gravity to merit its own provision, and it is explicitly included as a crime against humanity under Rome Statute Article 7(1)(j).[55] Therefore, whilst apartheid had previously been described as a crime against humanity, the International Criminal Court became the first major international court to include apartheid in its Statute.[56]

Arguments against the explicit inclusion of the crime of apartheid within the Rome Statute highlight the role of historic events in the development of international criminal law, and the potential pitfalls. It has been argued that referring to apartheid may be an example of using the law as a symbolic proclamation, an 'affirmation, exclamation, or denunciation' of conduct, rather than for purely prosecutorial purposes.[57] Essentially, the South African regime had been so widely condemned it may have been too controversial to omit direct reference to the crime of apartheid, despite the essential acts being covered elsewhere.[58] This need to include or otherwise acknowledge the crime of apartheid based on a single historic event arguably led to the enshrining of an imperfect provision within the Rome Statute.

Moving beyond the *chapeau* requirements of all crimes against humanity in Article 7(1), Article 7(1)(j) provides for the crime of apartheid in conjunction

---

[51] Lingaas, 'The Crime against Humanity of Apartheid in a Post-Apartheid World', pp. 91–2.

[52] Ibid., p. 92.

[53] Ibid.

[54] Klamberg (ed.), *Commentary on the Law of the International Criminal Court*, p. 59.

[55] Rome Statute, Art. 7(1)(j), 'The crime of apartheid'.

[56] Apartheid Convention, Art. 1; Lingaas, 'The Crime against Humanity of Apartheid in a Post-Apartheid World', pp. 90–1.

[57] R. Clark, 'Crimes Against Humanity and the Rome Statute of the International Criminal Court', in M. Politi and G. Nesi (eds.), *The Rome Statute*, Farnham: Ashgate Publishing, 2001, p. 88.

[58] Lingaas, 'The Crime against Humanity of Apartheid in a Post-Apartheid World', p. 93.

with Article 7(2)(h).[59] Accordingly, the crime of apartheid is defined as 'inhumane acts of a character similar to those referred to in paragraph 1, committed in the context of an institutionalised regime of systematic oppression and domination by one racial group over any other racial group or groups and committed with the intention of maintaining that regime'.[60] It has been argued that the attempted definition in Article 7(2)(h) is 'incoherent, ambiguous and inoperable'.[61]

Problems arise almost immediately as the term 'inhumane acts of a similar character' is not defined and may be applied to any of the acts which are contained within Article 7(1).[62] The International Criminal Court's Elements of Crimes provide some guidance in a footnote to Article 7(1)(j) stating that 'character' is a reference to the 'nature and gravity' of the acts, 'meaning that an act similar in quality or seriousness to other crimes against humanity could also constitute an inhumane act for the purpose of this offence'.[63] However, by requiring that the inhumane acts are 'of a character similar to those referred to in paragraph 1' there is a danger that inhumane acts of apartheid may be so similar to the other crimes that they may be subsumed under them.[64] Notably, this may occur with Article 7(1)(k) which describes other inhumane acts as those that 'intentionally cause great suffering or serious injury to body or to mental or physical health'.[65] Acts may also be covered by the crime of persecution in Article 7(1)(h), if they 'contain a discriminative intent based on the identity of a group' such as a racial group.[66] Either or neither may apply as the ambiguous wording of 'similar to those referred to in paragraph 1' does not provide a clear point of reference.[67]

Further complications may arise in relation to inhumane acts under Article 7(1)(k) as it provides a reduced burden of proof for the prosecutor. For the crime of apartheid the prosecutor must prove both the existence of the inhumane act *and* the 'context of an institutionalised regime of systematic oppression and domination by one racial group over any other racial group or

---

[59] Rome Statute, Art. 7(1), states: 'For the purpose of this Statute, "crime against humanity" means any of the following acts when committed as part of a widespread or systematic attack directed against any civilian population, with knowledge of the attack'; see also Art. 7(1)(j), Art. 7(2)(h).
[60] As found in Rome Statute, Art. 7(2)(h).
[61] Lingaas, 'The Crime against Humanity of Apartheid in a Post-Apartheid World', p. 93.
[62] Ibid., p. 95.
[63] Ibid.
[64] Ibid., p. 96.
[65] Ibid.
[66] Ibid.
[67] Ibid., p. 97.

groups' committed 'with the intention of maintaining that regime'.[68] The same conduct prosecuted under inhumane acts simply needs to meet the *chapeau* requirements, and provide proof of the inhumane act. An issue of avoidance may therefore arise, or preference for pursuing prosecution under Article 7(1)(k) which could qualify as a crime of apartheid under Article 7(1)(j). Similarly, the requirement that the oppression and domination be 'systematic' may be difficult for the prosecution to prove and arguably goes further than the *chapeau* requirements.[69] Rather than requiring a 'systematic or widespread attack', Article 7(2)(h) seems to introduce 'a mandatory requirement of systematicity'.[70] This may contradict the *chapeau* requirements as the concept of the attack needing to be both widespread *and* systematic has been determined by academics as no longer required: Lingaas argues Article 7(2)(h) seemingly reintroduces this requirement 'thereby countermanding the development of international criminal law'.[71]

Controversy has also arisen around the inclusion of the term 'institutionalised regime' within the definition of the crime of apartheid provided by Article 7(2)(h), specifically in relation to difficulties which arise when considering applying the crime of apartheid as it is enshrined within the Rome Statute to contemporary situations.[72] Some academics have suggested that 'regime' should be understood in the sense of a method or system rather than as a strict reference to a governmental system.[73] For example, the term could apply to a system of apartheid instituted by an armed group with territorial control, which under a broad definition may qualify as a regime.[74] However, others argue, the crime of apartheid requires a regime institutionalised by a recognised state government. It is noted that defining the term 'regime' too broadly would be legally problematic and could make the term 'too ambiguous and unidentifiable'.[75] This problem will likely be resolved through interpretation in line with the approach taken to other provisions: Rome Statute Article 7(2)(a) holds that the widespread and systematic attack directed against the civilian population should be 'pursuant to or in furtherance of a State or organisational policy to commit such an attack'.[76] In practice, 'organisational' has been

---

[68] Ibid.
[69] Ibid., p. 98.
[70] Ibid.
[71] Ibid.
[72] Ibid.
[73] Ibid.
[74] Ibid.
[75] Ibid.
[76] Rome Statute, Art. 7(2)(*a*); Paylan and Klonowiecka-Milart, 'Examining the Origins of Crimes against Humanity and Genocide', p. 580.

interpreted quite broadly; considering the situation in Kenya, the ICC Pre-Trial Chamber found that the drafters had not intended to exclude non-state actors and placed the focus on the capacity of an organisation to commit crimes against humanity.[77]

The ambiguity problem which affects the crime of apartheid under the Rome Statute stems from the states being careful to move beyond the historic origin of the crime. In contrast to the language of the Apartheid Convention, which refers explicitly to South Africa, the Rome Statute in Article 7(1)(j) and Article 7(2)(h) does not refer to South Africa at all.[78] Accordingly, 'the Southern African situation can no longer be used as a *conditio sine qua non* to determine the existence of the crime of apartheid in other cases'.[79] Lingaas notes that the threshold requirements for a contemporary situation of apartheid rest on the existence of 'systematic discrimination and oppression', and not from a comparison to the approach taken in South Africa.[80] However, with the term 'apartheid' having been coined in the South African context, the crime will likely always retain a link to its roots, even if only in the name.[81]

Alongside the ambiguity problem there is also the problem of limited application which simultaneously arises from the history of the crime. There exists a 'symbolic power' of apartheid terminology and a historic connection with racial discrimination which shaped the terms used to describe the crime.[82] Defining the crime of apartheid in light of the South African practice means it is described as: an institutionalised regime of systematic oppression and domination of *one racial group over any other racial group*.[83] This specific reference to racial groups and no other groups limits the applicability of the provision and makes proving the existence of a racial group an essential task for the prosecutor.[84] The definition of the term 'racial group' is made paramount as the classification of victims as part of a racial group now 'constitutes a legal threshold, which must be proven in order for the crime of apartheid to occur'.[85] This language and the subsequent definition are significant as the international crime of apartheid may not be prosecuted in situations where

---

[77] ICC Pre-Trial Chamber II, Decision pursuant to Art. 15 of the Rome Statute on the Authorization of an Investigation into the Situation in the Republic of Kenya, 31 March 2010, *Situation in the Republic of Kenya*, ICC-01/09, at paras. 89–93.

[78] Lingaas, 'The Crime against Humanity of Apartheid in a Post-Apartheid World', p. 102.

[79] Ibid.

[80] Ibid., pp. 97–8.

[81] Ibid., p. 111.

[82] Ibid.

[83] Ibid., p. 99.

[84] Ibid.

[85] Ibid., pp. 99–100.

it may apply. The potential application of the crime of apartheid will now be considered in relation to two contemporary situations, first the situation of the Democratic People's Republic of Korea (DPRK), and then that of the Occupied Palestinian Territories (OPT).[86]

In 2014, Michael Kirby, Chairman of the Commission of Inquiry made a public statement to the Human Rights Council in which he asserted that the DPRK should abolish 'immediately and completely' the *Songbun* social classification system, which he labels 'an apartheid of social class'.[87] The statement accompanied the release of a comprehensive report; however, the full report whilst detailing *Songbun*, does not refer to it as an apartheid system.[88] Kirby's statement opens with direct comparisons between the DPRK regime and historic events including Nazi crimes, the South African apartheid system, and the Khmer Rouge,[89] and concludes: 'Contending with the scourges of Nazism, apartheid, the Khmer Rouge and other affronts required courage by great nations and ordinary human beings alike. It is now your duty to address the scourge of human rights violations and crimes against humanity in the Democratic People's Republic of Korea'.[90] Former UN Commissioner for Human Rights, Navi Pillay, also stated that *Songbun* is 'a new example of apartheid'.[91] However, the *actus reus* of the crime of apartheid requires the involvement of two or more racial groups. It is 'highly unlikely' that the North Korean social groups prescribed by *Songbun* could be considered to be racial groups.[92] Article 7(1)(j) may apply should the court take a very broad approach and interpret the provision as including any group which differs from the perpetrator's group; however, this also seems unlikely.[93]

---

[86] Ibid., p. 93.

[87] M. Kirby, 'Statement by Michael Kirby Chair of the Commission of Inquiry on Human Rights in the Democratic People's Republic of Korea to the 25th session of the Human Rights Council, Geneva, 17 March 2014', United Nations Human Rights Office of the High Commissioner [online], available at http://www.ohchr.org/EN/NewsEvents/Pages/DisplayNews.aspx?NewsID=14385.

[88] Report of the Commission of inquiry on human rights in the Democratic People's Republic of Korea, 7 February 2014, UN Doc. A/HRC/25/63, at paras. 32–6.

[89] Kirby, 'Statement by Michael Kirby Chair of the Commission of Inquiry on Human Rights in the Democratic People's Republic of Korea to the 25th session of the Human Rights Council'.

[90] Ibid.

[91] E. Shim, 'Ex-UN official: North Korean caste system is the new apartheid (22 October 2015)', *United Press International* [online], available at https://www.upi.com/Top_News/World-News/2015/10/22/Ex-UN-official-North-Korean-caste-system-is-the-new-apartheid/1571445526152.

[92] Lingaas, 'The Crime against Humanity of Apartheid in a Post-Apartheid World', p. 110.

[93] Ibid., p. 111.

Similarly, consideration of the possible application of 'apartheid' to the Occupied Palestinian Territories from a legal standpoint begins with the Special Rapporteur, Richard Falk. The final Report of the Special Rapporteur on human rights violations in the OPT, presented to the UN Human Rights Council in 2014, considered 'the policies and practices of Israel in occupied Palestine in light of the prohibition on segregation and apartheid'.[94] In the absence of an ICJ advisory opinion on the issue, the Special Rapporteur states he assumes 'part of the task of analysing whether allegations of apartheid in occupied Palestine are well founded' and 'discusses Israeli policies and practices through the lens of the international prohibition of ethnic discrimination, segregation and apartheid'.[95] Falk identifies the issue of domination of one racial group over another racial group as a central element of the crime of apartheid to be problematic as 'some may argue that neither Israeli Jews nor Palestinians constitute racial groups *per se*'.[96] However, Falk takes a broad approach and draws on Article 1 of the International Convention on the Elimination of All Forms of Racial Discrimination to argue that racial discrimination may be based on 'any distinction, exclusion, restriction or preference based on race, colour, descent, or national or ethnic origin'.[97]

The report considers the actions of Israel in light of the Apartheid Convention and the relevant provisions in the Rome Statute, concluding that the prolonged occupation has employed 'practices and policies which appear to constitute apartheid and segregation'.[98] What becomes of this remains to be seen; there is some potential to apply the crime against humanity of apartheid to the situation after the Government of Palestine subsequently issued a declaration under Article 12(3) of the Rome Statute, accepting the ICC's jurisdiction.[99] The preliminary investigation of the ICC into the situation in Palestine remains ongoing, albeit for a different temporal jurisdiction to that of Falk's report, focusing on alleged crimes since 13 June 2014.[100] If an investigation were to be opened, and the OPT chose to investigate the possible application of the crime

---

[94] Report of the Special Rapporteur on the situation of human rights in the Palestinian territories occupied since 1967, Richard Falk, 13 January 2014, UN Doc. A/HRC/25/67, summary.
[95] Ibid., at para. 51.
[96] Ibid., at para. 53.
[97] Ibid., at para. 53.
[98] Ibid., at paras. 77–8.
[99] On 1 January 2015, the Government of Palestine lodged a declaration under article 12(3) of the Rome Statute accepting the jurisdiction of the ICC over alleged crimes committed 'in the occupied Palestinian territory, including East Jerusalem, since June 13, 2014': ICC, 'Preliminary Investigation: Palestine', *ICC* [online], available at https://www.icc-cpi.int/palestine.
[100] ICC, 'Preliminary Investigation: Palestine', *ICC*.

of apartheid it may be essential to determine whether or not Palestinians and Israelis are considered to be two distinct racial groups.[101]

Arguably, the crime of apartheid under the Rome Statute will not truly move beyond its image as a condemnation and legacy of South African crimes, and cement its purposeful role in international criminal law, until it is applied to a contemporary situation. Whilst reflecting the impact of a single historic event on a legal definition, it also encapsulates the constraints thereof.

CRIMES AGAINST HUMANITY: FORCED PREGNANCY

Alongside apartheid, the crime of forced pregnancy can also be applied to a contemporary situation to break its historical associations. Its inclusion as a crime against humanity under Article 7(1)(g) of the Rome Statute made the ICC the first international criminal tribunal to criminalise the act of forced pregnancy.[102] The move followed the work of the ad hoc Tribunals and noted atrocity crimes committed against women in Rwanda and the former Yugoslavia.[103] Whilst not one single historic event, mass atrocity crimes committed in Rwanda and the former Yugoslavia during the early 1990s can be considered as a catalyst for change, and another illustration of the link between history and the development of the core international crimes.[104] Notably, in the aftermath of the conflict in Bosnia between 1992 and 1995, it was alleged that Serb men had, as part of a systematic plan, impregnated Croat and Muslim women to force them to bear Serb children.[105] Problematically at that time the act of forced pregnancy had not yet been explicitly criminalised: in *Bosnia and Herzegovina v. Serbia and Montenegro*, the Bosnians alleged that rape was used as a means of affecting the demographic balance.[106] The ICJ subsequently found that Serb leaders did not have a policy of forced impregnation.[107]

---

[101] See also O. Holmes, 'Palestine files complaint against Israel under anti-racism treaty', *The Guardian*, 23 April 2018, available at https://www.theguardian.com/world/2018/apr/23/palestinians-file-complaint-against-israel-under-anti-racism-treaty.

[102] Rome Statute, Art. 7(1)(*g*); notably, forced pregnancy is also a war crime under Rome Statute Art. 8(2)(*b*)(xxii); Drake, 'Aimed at Protecting Ethnic Groups or Women', p. 595.

[103] Drake, 'Aimed at Protecting Ethnic Groups or Women', p. 595.

[104] Ibid.

[105] Ibid., pp. 595 and 596.

[106] ICJ, Judgment of 26 February 2007, *Case concerning the Application of the Convention on the Prevention and Punishment of the Crime of Genocide* (*Bosnia and Herzegovina v. Serbia and Montenegro*), *ICJ Reports* 2007, at para. 362; Drake, 'Aimed at Protecting Ethnic Groups or Women', pp. 595 and 602.

[107] ICJ, Judgment of 26 February 2007, at paras. 363–7.

Following these crimes, and similar ones committed in the Rwandan and former Yugoslavian contexts, forced pregnancy began to be singled out as a human rights violation which required a robust response.[108] Accordingly, forced pregnancy was one of a series of acts included within the Rome Statute with the intention to provide greater protection from sexual and gender-based crimes.[109] However, the process was complex as some states argued against including forced pregnancy for fear it would conflict with their own domestic legislation regarding abortion.[110] Indeed, direct reference was made to crimes committed during the conflict in Bosnia when it was argued that the crime should be termed as 'forcible impregnation' rather than forced pregnancy: states arguing for the crime of forced pregnancy rejected this suggestion contending that forced impregnation referred only to forcibly making a woman pregnant and not to keeping the woman pregnant, therefore it would have been inadequate in the context of Bosnia-Herzegovina.[111] Ultimately forced pregnancy was included with the acknowledgement that the crime as defined in the Rome Statute 'shall not in any way be interpreted as affecting national laws relating to pregnancy'.[112] Therefore the impetus provided by history again expanded the content of crimes against humanity within the Rome Statute.

---

[108] For example, in the Fourth World Conference on Women, Beijing, China, 4–15 September 1995, Report of the Fourth World Conference on Women, 17 October 1995, UN Doc. A/CONF.177/20 (hereinafter 'Beijing Declaration'); Drake, 'Aimed at Protecting Ethnic Groups or Women', pp. 595 and 605.

[109] Notable others include gender-neutral provisions around rape, sexual slavery, trafficking, forced prostitution, enforced sterilisation and 'any other form of sexual violence' as seen in Rome Statute Articles 7(1)(*g*), 7(2)(*c*), and 8(2)(*b*)(xxii); Drake, 'Aimed at Protecting Ethnic Groups or Women', p. 595.

[110] See e.g. UN Diplomatic Conference of Plenipotentiaries on the Establishment of an International Criminal Court, Committee of the Whole, 1998, Summary Records of the 3rd Meeting, Agenda Item 11, p. 32 (UN Doc. A/CONF.183/C.1/SR.3). Mr Madani of Saudi Arabia 'opposed the reference to "enforced pregnancy" . . . since his country was opposed to abortion'. Ms Shahen of the Libyan delegation stated that '[u]nder Libyan legislation, abortion, too, was a crime' (Summary Records of the 4th Meeting, p. 63). Mr Al Awadi of the United Arab Emirates 'shared the Libyan delegation's reservations about the inclusion of enforced pregnancy' (ibid., p. 66). Mr Madani of Saudi Arabia reaffirmed 'his delegation's view that references to enforced pregnancy should be deleted because the law in his country did not allow abortions, except for health reasons established by a doctor and in the event of danger to the mother' (Summary Records of the 5th Meeting, p. 21); Drake, 'Aimed at Protecting Ethnic Groups or Women', pp. 595 and 607; Grey, 'The ICC's First "Forced Pregnancy" Case in Historical Perspective', p. 919.

[111] Grey, 'The ICC's First "Forced Pregnancy" Case in Historical Perspective', p. 920.

[112] Drake, 'Aimed at Protecting Ethnic Groups or Women', pp. 595 and 608.

In the early days of the Rome Statute, the inclusion of forced pregnancy was seen as a positive forward move for international criminal law; however, it was highlighted that the act requires a high level of intent which makes it challenging to prosecute.[113] The Elements of Crimes specify what must be proven for a defendant to be prosecuted successfully for forced pregnancy under the Rome Statute.[114] For the forced pregnancy as a crime against humanity there are three elements: '1. The perpetrator confined one or more women forcibly made pregnant, with the intent of affecting the ethnic composition of any population or carrying out other grave violations of international law. 2. The conduct was committed as part of a widespread or systematic attack directed against a civilian population. 3. The perpetrator knew that the conduct was part of or intended the conduct to be part of a widespread or systematic attack directed against a civilian population.'[115] Given its historic associations with crimes committed based on ethnic identities, the higher intent threshold fuelled some debate. Writing in 2012, Drake argued that this may mean that the provision was designed more to prevent ethnic crimes than to prevent violence against women.[116]

The *Ongwen* case which commenced in 2016 represents the first time that charges of forced pregnancy were both considered before the ICC and considered outside of the contexts of genocide or ethnic cleansing.[117] The *Ongwen* case is also the first case to consider the reproductive autonomy of individual women and girls.[118] In light of reported 'forced sterilisation, forced abortion, forced miscarriage and forced (continuation of) pregnancy' in ongoing conflicts, including with 'the so-called "Islamic State"',[119] the ICC's application of the forced pregnancy provision may prove essential. Following the arrest and surrender of Dominic Ongwen to the ICC in 2015, Prosecutor Bensouda expanded the charges to include forced pregnancy as a war crime and as a crime against humanity.[120] The victims are stated to be women and girls who had been abducted by the LRA and forced into being Ongwen's sexual and

---

[113] Ibid., pp. 595 and 596.
[114] Ibid., pp. 595 and 598.
[115] ICC, Elements of Crimes, The Hague: International Criminal Court, 2011, p. 9; Drake, 'Aimed at Protecting Ethnic Groups or Women', pp. 595 and 598.
[116] Drake, 'Aimed at Protecting Ethnic Groups or Women', pp. 595 and 596.
[117] Grey, 'The ICC's First "Forced Pregnancy" Case in Historical Perspective', pp. 908–9.
[118] Ibid., p. 909.
[119] Ibid., p. 907.
[120] Ibid., p. 924.

domestic slaves.[121] They were then forcibly impregnated by rape and confined within the LRA.[122]

The prosecution argued that the special intent of the crime relates to the act of confining the woman, rather than to making her pregnant.[123] Further, it has been highlighted that the purpose of the confinement needs not be to keep the victim pregnant; it is enough for the perpetrator to intend to 'affect the ethnic composition of a population' *or* 'carry out other violations of international law'.[124] Therefore the case has reaffirmed the language of the provision and drawn attention to the equality of both possible intents against a backdrop of focus on previously ethnically motivated actions. Despite the inclusion of an ethnic aspect to the crime, forced pregnancy can also be prosecuted where other violations of international law are intended. This application of the crime can be seen as a positive step forward for a provision included within the Rome Statute following historic atrocities, which can now go on to provide protection for populations in vulnerable situations today.

The discussion of the crimes thus far has singled out two punishable acts contained in the definition of crimes against humanity found in the Statute where history has shaped the relevant provision, and where perhaps modern events do not quite fit the agreed definitions. It has been argued that reinterpretation may therefore be required. The next section will turn to the examination of genocide.

ORIGINS OF THE CORE INTERNATIONAL CRIMES: GENOCIDE

The introduction of the term 'genocide' into international criminal law stems from the work of Raphael Lemkin who coined the term from the Greek *genos* (race) and the Latin *cide* (killing) in line with homicide, infanticide and so on.[125] He first used the term in reference to the 'destruction of a nation or of an ethnic group'.[126] The influence of history is clear as Lemkin's work explicitly focuses on the atrocities committed by the Nazis in occupied Europe, noting that 'Hitler envisaged genocide as a means of changing the biological interrela-

---

[121] Ibid.
[122] Ibid.
[123] Ibid., p. 925.
[124] ICC Pre-Trial Chamber II, 22 January 2016, Transcript, Ongwen (ICC-02/04-01/15-T-21-Red2-ENG), 50, lines 25 to 49, line 2; at 49, lines 14–15; at 49, lines 22 to 50, line 1; Grey, 'The ICC's First "Forced Pregnancy" Case in Historical Perspective', p. 925.
[125] Lemkin, *Axis Rule in Occupied Europe*, p. 79.
[126] Ibid.

tions in Europe in favour of Germany'.[127] Genocide was mentioned in the text of the indictment at Nuremberg but was viewed as conduct 'which fulfilled the parameters of war crimes and crimes against humanity', and did not form an independent charge against the defendants.[128] The final text of the International Military Tribunal (IMT) Charter in Article 6 provides jurisdiction over crimes against peace, war crimes, and crimes against humanity: persecution and physical extermination of national, ethnic, racial and religious groups are provided for as crimes against humanity.[129] This omission of 'genocide' from the IMT's work has since been criticised, which led the General Assembly of the United Nations to adopt the Convention on the Prevention and Punishment of the Crime of Genocide on 9 December 1948.[130]

The definition of genocide as found in the Genocide Convention has remained unchanged and the wording of Article 2 of the Genocide Convention has been incorporated into Article 6 of the Rome Statute.[131] During discussion on the prospect of genocide as a crime before a future international court, some delegations proposed expanding the text of the Genocide Convention to include protection of social and political groups.[132] This approach was debated as an opportunity amid the creation of an international court to develop international criminal law, rather than merely reproducing the Genocide Convention.[133] However, concerns arose that amending the definition of genocide might lead to inconsistencies.[134] During discussions in the early 1990s, there were also cases pending before the ICJ in relation to Article 9 of the Genocide Convention: the ICJ had already issued two interlocutory decisions, and would provide a ruling on admissibility in 1996.[135] Ultimately, the Preparatory

---

[127] Ibid., p. 81.
[128] Klamberg (ed.), *Commentary on the Law of the International Criminal Court*, p. 19.
[129] Paylan and Klonowiecka-Milart, 'Examining the Origins of Crimes against Humanity and Genocide', pp. 571–2.
[130] Convention on the Prevention and Punishment of the Crime of Genocide, approved and proposed for signature and ratification or accession by UNGA Res. 260 A (III), 9 December 1948 (entry into force 12 January 1951, in accordance with Art. XIII; hereinafter 'Genocide Convention'); Paylan and Klonowiecka-Milart, 'Examining the Origins of Crimes against Humanity and Genocide', p. 573.
[131] Genocide Convention, Art. 2; Rome Statute, Art. 6; O. Bekou et al., *Implementing the Rome Statute*, Centre for International Law Research and Policy, 2017, p. 23, available at http://www.legal-tools.org/doc/e05157.
[132] Schabas, *The International Criminal Court*, p. 126.
[133] Ibid.
[134] Ibid.
[135] ICJ, provisional measures, Order of 8 April 1993, Case concerning the Application of the Convention on the Prevention and Punishment of the Crime of Genocide (*Bosnia and Herzegovina v. Serbia and Montenegro*), *ICJ Reports* 1993; provisional measures,

Committee's Working Group on the Definition of Crimes met in February 1997, and considered the proposed modifications before returning to the text of the 1948 Genocide Convention.[136] At the Rome Diplomatic Conference, it was proposed and widely accepted that the definition of genocide be taken 'literally' from Article 2 of the Genocide Convention.[137] Substantive changes to the substance of the definition of the crime of genocide were not discussed.[138]

The crime of genocide has been consistently determined as a crime against groups. The 1946 United Nations General Assembly Resolution described genocide as 'a denial of the right of existence of entire human groups'.[139] In the ICC, Pre-Trial Chamber I confirmed that 'the definition of the crime of genocide aims at protecting the existence of a specific group or people'.[140] However, under Article 6 the only groups protected are national, ethnical, racial and religious groups. During early drafting of the crime of genocide, proposals to expand the protected groups beyond these four were rejected.[141] Linguistic groups were not included as 'it was felt this was redundant'; however, political, economic and social groups were intentionally excluded as the drafters 'did not believe they should be protected by the Convention'.[142] Whilst there had long been calls in academic literature to expand the definition to include social and political groups, during the Rome Diplomatic Conference only Cuba argued as such.[143] The Preparatory Committee had noted the suggestion to examine how social and political groups might be addressed within the context of crimes against humanity rather than genocide.[144] Schabas argues that this limited approach suggests that the crime of genocide exists with the

---

Order of 13 September 1993, Case concerning the Application of the Convention on the Prevention and Punishment of the Crime of Genocide (*Bosnia and Herzegovina v. Serbia and Montenegro*), *ICJ Reports* 1993; Judgment of 11 July 1996, Case concerning the Application of the Convention on the Prevention and Punishment of the Crime of Genocide (*Bosnia and Herzegovina v. Yugoslavia*), *ICJ Reports* 1996; Schabas, *The International Criminal Court*, p. 126.

[136] Preparatory Committee, Decisions taken its sessions held from 11 to 21 February 1997, 12 March 1997, UN Doc. A/AC.249/1997/L.5, Annex 1.

[137] Schabas, *The International Criminal Court*, p. 127.

[138] Ibid.

[139] UNGA Res. 96(1), 11 December 1946, The Crime of Genocide.

[140] ICC, Decision on the Prosecution's Application for a Warrant of Arrest against Omar Hassan Ahmad Al Bashir, *Prosecutor v. Omar Hassan Ahmad Al Bashir* ('Omar Al Bashir'), 4 March 2009, ICC-02/05-01/09, at para. 115.

[141] Schabas, *The International Criminal Court*, p. 136.

[142] UN Doc. A/C.6/SR.128; Schabas, *The International Criminal Court*, p. 136.

[143] Schabas, *The International Criminal Court*, pp. 127 and 136.

[144] Preparatory Committee, Decisions taken at its sessions held from 11 to 21 February 1997, 12 March 1997, UN Doc. A/AC.249/1997/L.5, note 2.

purpose to protect groups characterised 'by race or ethnicity or some cognate notion' rather than a more general concept of a group.[145]

The definition of the included groups, and determination of what constitutes a protected group under the existing provision, continued to be debated. In the *Bashir* case, the ICC Pre-Trial Chamber found that the targeted group is determined by 'particular positive characteristics (national, ethnic, racial or religious), and not a lack thereof'.[146] Accordingly, the Pre-Trial Chamber considered the question of whether the Fur, Masalit and Zaghawa people can be considered distinct ethnic groups.[147] It found reasonable grounds to believe this is the case as despite shared characteristics, each of the groups 'has its own language, its own tribal customs and its own traditional links to its lands'.[148] However, it is clear that the issue remains open to interpretation as Judge Ušacka held the differing view that they were in fact not three targeted groups, but rather a single targeted group composed of 'African tribes'.[149] Indeed, should *Bashir* come before the ICC in the future, the interpretation and application of Article 6(a)–(c) in relation to defining the groups against which crimes were allegedly committed in Darfur may prove progressive and instructive.

There is one historical event which perhaps epitomises the difficulties arising from having the current four specified protected groups: the crimes committed by the Khmer Rouge, specifically, whether these crimes can be considered to be genocide.[150] Whilst the term 'genocide' is often colloquially applied to the situation, the crimes committed by the Khmer Rouge against Khmer people makes the legal application of the term debatable. This single historic event encapsulates difficulties which may arise from excluding political or social groups from the list of protected groups, and raises the important question of whether it is possible for genocide to be committed against the perpetrator's own group.[151] Within the Extraordinary Chambers in the Courts of Cambodia, former leaders of the Khmer Rouge have been indicted for genocide committed against the Cham and the Vietnamese, but crimes committed

---

[145] Schabas, *The International Criminal Court*, p. 136.

[146] ICC, Decision on the Prosecution's Application for a Warrant of Arrest against Omar Hassan Ahmad Al Bashir, at para. 135.

[147] Ibid., at paras. 136–7.

[148] Ibid., at para. 137.

[149] Separate and Partly Dissenting Opinion of Judge Anita Ušacka, at para. 25. ICC, Decision on the Prosecution's Application for a Warrant of Arrest against Omar Hassan Ahmad Al Bashir.

[150] Klamberg (ed.), *Commentary on the Law of the International Criminal Court*, p. 24.

[151] Ibid.

against the Khmer people have not been as crimes of genocide.[152] This would suggest that the domestic Cambodian approach is in line with the wider international consensus on the crime of genocide as not protecting political groups.

Beyond Cambodia, at the domestic level states have taken differing approaches to the groups which should be protected. Whilst most follow the international standard as enshrined in the Rome Statute, Bolivia has omitted racial groups, whilst El Salvador has omitted ethnic groups.[153] In contrast, Colombia and Costa Rica have extended protection to political groups.[154] Social groups are protected by Lithuania, Switzerland, Peru and Estonia.[155] Whilst Poland extends protection to 'groups with a different perspective on life',[156] France and Burkina Faso both protect a group 'determined by any other arbitrary criterion'.[157] Arguably the Canadian approach is the broadest, providing for 'an identifiable group of persons'.[158] If the definition of genocide were to be reopened, the case for protection of political groups would be vociferously made. However, there doesn't appear to be much appetite for this.

Moreover, as the definition of terms is key to the application of the provision, establishing what is meant by language such as 'destruction' of a group is essential. For the International Law Commission in 1996, the term 'destruction' was narrow and referred specifically to 'material destruction of a group either by physical or by biological means'.[159] However, in practice the interpretations have varied: in 2000, the German Constitutional Court took a broader approach, finding that 'destructive intent extended "beyond physical and biological extermination"'.[160] In 2004, the dissenting opinion of Judge Shahabuddeen found that intention could also include destruction of the group 'as a "social unit"'.[161] Similarly, in practice there have been differing

---

[152] Ibid.
[153] Bekou et al., *Implementing the Rome Statute*, p. 26.
[154] Ibid.
[155] Ibid., p. 27.
[156] Ibid., p. 28.
[157] Ibid.
[158] Ibid.
[159] Draft Code of Crimes Against the Peace and Security of Mankind, p. 46, para. 12; Klamberg (ed.), *Commentary on the Law of the International Criminal Court*, p. 20.
[160] Germany, Constitutional Court (*Bundesverfassungsgericht*), order of 12 December 2000, Case 2 BvR 1290/99, para. (III)(4)(a)(aa)); Klamberg (ed.), *Commentary on the Law of the International Criminal Court*, p. 20.
[161] Partial Dissenting Opinion of Judge Shahabuddeen, para. 51. ICTY Appeals Chamber, Judgment of 19 April 2004, *Prosecutor v. Radislav Krstić*, Case No. IT98-33-A; Klamberg (ed.), *Commentary on the Law of the International Criminal Court*, p. 20.

interpretations of the phrase 'in whole or part'.[162] One approach has been to consider the limitations on perpetration of the crime of genocide arising from geographical conditions.[163] For example, the International Law Commission recognised that the intended destruction of a group 'from every corner of the globe' was not necessary for the crime of genocide in relation to the killing of Palestinian civilians in refugee camps during the 1980s.[164]

The International Criminal Tribunal for the former Yugoslavia (ICTY) may have provided instrumental guidance on this due to another historic event: atrocity crimes perpetrated at Srebrenica. The ICTY had determined that a perpetrator must intend to destroy a 'substantial' part of the group.[165] In *Krstić*, it clarified that there are a number of considerations in determining if the targeted part of the group is substantial enough to meet the requirement of genocide noting: 'the intent to destroy a group, even if only in part, means seeking to destroy a distinct part of the group as opposed to an accumulation of isolated individuals within it'.[166] Considerations include the numerical size of the targeted group, evaluating the number of persons targeted both 'in absolute terms' and in relation to the size of the targeted group, and non-numerical concerns such as the importance of a target portion of a group to that group as a whole.[167] For the purpose of *Krstić* the Trial Chamber determined that the Bosnian Muslim population of Srebrenica, estimated at 40 000 individuals, was to be considered substantial.[168] Whilst they were not a numerically significant group in relation to the entire Bosnian Muslim population, the population was patriarchal and Srebrenica was geographically significant; the targeting of men at this location was therefore detrimental to the survival of the Bosnian Muslim community.[169]

The punishable acts provided for in the Rome Statute can also be seen to vary in the way the Statute is implemented by states: some have attached con-

---

[162] UNGA, 3rd session, 6th Committee, 73rd meeting, p. 92, p. 97; Klamberg (ed.), *Commentary on the Law of the International Criminal Court*, p. 21.

[163] Klamberg (ed.), *Commentary on the Law of the International Criminal Court*, p. 22.

[164] Draft Code of Crimes Against the Peace and Security of Mankind, p. 45, Art. 17, para. 8; Klamberg (ed.), *Commentary on the Law of the International Criminal Court*, p. 22.

[165] Schabas, *The International Criminal Court*, p. 134.

[166] ICTY Trial Chamber, Judgment of 2 August 2001, *Prosecutor v. Radislav Krstić*, Case No. IT-98-33-T, p. 204, at para. 582, and p. 208, at para. 591.

[167] Ibid., p. 208, at para. 590.

[168] Ibid., pp. 208–9, at para. 592.

[169] Ibid., pp. 209–11, at para. 593.

ditions to the acts, whilst others have expanded the list of punishable acts.[170] Examples include Lithuania, which has interpreted 'causing serious bodily or mental harm to members of the group' as referring to 'torturing, causing bodily harm to them, hindering their mental development'.[171] Mexico also provides for a specific interpretation regarding prevention of births, referring specifically to the infliction of 'massive sterilization intended to hamper the reproduction of the group'.[172] These restrictive provisions may hinder efforts to assert and determine that genocide has been committed.[173] Additionally, states which take this approach and are parties to the Rome Statute, may find their national legislation falling short of the Statute provisions and are therefore unable to meet the threshold for effective national prosecutions of the crime of genocide.[174]

States have also in some cases expanded the punishable acts of genocide by incorporating additional acts within their national legislation, in addition to those found in the Rome Statute.[175] Arguably these 'tweaks' to the provisions often reflect the histories of the states in question. Some states such as Armenia, Bolivia, Ethiopia, Italy, Lithuania and Spain expanded the list to include displacement or deportation.[176] Similarly, the Russian Criminal Code provides for 'forcible resettlement'.[177] The list of punishable acts has also been expanded in other ways, for example, Colombia provides for forced pregnancy.[178] Finland has included illness and interpreted 'conditions of life' as 'in any other way impairs the survival of the group'.[179] 'Italy refers to the imposition of distinctive signs, whereas Spain includes sexual attack, transfer of adults from one group to another, causing loss or uselessness of parts and body functions'.[180] Broadening the list of punishable acts 'is not against the spirit of the provision'; however, it may dilute the essence of the crime of genocide.[181] The broadening of the definition may therefore raise questions over the effectiveness of national genocide prosecutions.[182]

---

[170] Bekou et al., *Implementing the Rome Statute*, p. 29.
[171] Ibid., p. 30.
[172] Ibid.
[173] Ibid.
[174] Ibid.
[175] Ibid.
[176] Ibid.
[177] Ibid., p. 31.
[178] Ibid.
[179] Ibid.
[180] Ibid.
[181] Ibid.
[182] Ibid.

As with crimes against humanity, the weight of history is evident in the genocide provision. From the group element, to the destruction, to the punishable acts, history affects the drafting of the provision, but modern histories often rely on reinterpretation to make the provisions 'fit' with current events. Therefore, despite a firm crystallisation of the definition at the international level and subsequent historical events that significantly challenge the accepted definition, innovation comes from the domestic level, where national definitions of genocide push firmly established boundaries.

WAR CRIMES: ENVIRONMENTAL PROTECTION

The final category of crimes to be looked at in this chapter is that of war crimes – the oldest among the core international crimes. Of the war crimes contained in the Rome Statute, the focus of this section will be on a relatively overlooked provision, that of environmental protection. Destruction of the environment as an act of war is an act as old as the concept of war – examples include the ground being salted at Carthage by the Romans, policies of 'total warfare' during the American Civil War, and 'scorched-earth' policies during the Second World War.[183] Contemporary examples include the scorched-earth tactics used in Kosovo by Serbian forces in the 1990s, designed to expel Kosovar Albanians from their homes.[184] During the Vietnam War the American use of the chemical herbicide known as 'Agent Orange' devastated Vietnamese forests.[185] Similarly, during the Gulf War, Iraqi troops burned Kuwaiti oil wells and diverted pipelines into the Persian Gulf 'releasing massive lakes of oil into the desert'.[186] However, prior to the Rome Statute it was not possible to prosecute the intentional use of chemical weapons to cause 'egregious and unnecessary' environmental damage as a war crime under international criminal law, unless such use also harmed human beings.[187]

The Rome Statute enshrines environmental protection independently of human injury under Article 8(2)(b)(iv), which provides for the war crime of: 'Intentionally launching an attack in the knowledge that such attack will cause incidental loss of life or injury to civilians or damage to civilian objects *or widespread, long-term and severe damage to the natural environment* which would be clearly excessive in relation to the concrete and direct overall mil-

---

[183] Lawrence and Heller, 'The First Ecocentric Environmental War Crime', p. 63.
[184] Ibid., p. 64.
[185] Ibid., p. 63.
[186] Ibid., p. 64.
[187] Ibid., p. 61.

itary advantage anticipated'.[188] This terminology is significant as the use of 'or' indicates that an attack which causes long-term and severe damage to the natural environment could be considered a war crime even if no harm has been caused to human beings.[189] This development is progressive for international criminal law and arguably reflects the influence of two historic events: the Vietnam War, and the burning of Kuwaiti oil.

It was the environmental destruction perpetrated during the Vietnam War which first focused international attention on the issue of lacking environmental protection, and spurred a number of international agreements designed to prohibit environmental damage during armed conflict.[190] The first resulting instrument was the Environmental Modification Convention of 1976, which prohibits environmental modification with widespread, long lasting, or severe effects.[191] The second was the 1977 Additional Protocol I to the Geneva Conventions.[192] However, the primary goal of these instruments is to prohibit states parties from harming each other using environmental modification, rather than the explicit protection of the environment for the sake of the environment.[193] Additionally, there was a lack of enforcement as the agreements imposed state responsibility or otherwise placed the emphasis on states to criminalise such acts themselves, 'something States have proven exceedingly reluctant to do'.[194] This leads us to the second spurring incident: whilst the UN Security Council held Iraq liable for environmental damage which it had caused during the illegal occupation of Kuwait, and established the United

---

[188] Rome Statute, Art. 8(2)(b)(iv) (emphasis added); Lawrence and Heller, 'The First Ecocentric Environmental War Crime', p. 61.

[189] Lawrence and Heller, 'The First Ecocentric Environmental War Crime', p. 62.

[190] The Convention (IV) respecting the Laws of Customs and War on Land (The Hague, 18 October 1907), Art. 23, Art. 55; Convention (IV) relative to the Protection of Civilian Persons in Time of War (Geneva, 12 August 1949), Art. 53. The Hague Convention IV protects the environment to ensure populations have the natural resources they need to survive, or protect property, and the Geneva Conventions are similarly limited.

[191] Convention on the Prohibition of Military or Any Other Hostile Use of Environmental Modification Techniques, 10 December 1976, *UST*, vol. 31, p. 333, *UNTS*, vol. 1108, p. 152, Art. I; Lawrence and Heller, 'The First Ecocentric Environmental War Crime', p. 66.

[192] Protocol Additional to the Geneva Conventions of 12 August 1949, and Relating to the Protection of Victims of International Armed Conflicts (Protocol I), 8 June 1977, UNTS, vol. 1125, p. 3 (entered into force 7 December 1978), Art. 35(3); Lawrence and Heller, 'The First Ecocentric Environmental War Crime', p. 66.

[193] Lawrence and Heller, 'The First Ecocentric Environmental War Crime', p. 67.

[194] Ibid., p. 61.

Nations Compensation Commission, this has been of limited success and is the exception rather than the rule.[195]

Against this context, the inclusion of Article 8(2)(b)(iv) could offer the environment unprecedented protection.[196] By this provision, the drafters included individual criminal responsibility for crimes of environmental destruction.[197] Further, by including the 'or' within the text, the provision does not link environmental destruction to human destruction or property.[198] Finally, when such conduct falls under its jurisdiction, the ICC has the power to independently investigate and prosecute it, unlike previous reliance on state responsibility.[199] However, there are problems with the provision. One notable limitation on environmental protection under the Rome Statute is that Article 8(2)(b)(iv) does not apply to internal armed conflicts.[200] This is particularly problematic given the number of non-international armed conflicts occurring.

Problems also arise with the terminology of Article 8(2)(b)(iv), beginning with the vague *actus reus*.[201] Whilst it prohibits 'widespread, long-term and severe damage to the natural environment', the terms are not defined. It is therefore difficult to predict what damage the ICC will consider devastating enough to convict.[202] Additionally, the proportionality requirement may hinder the application of the provision, as it prohibits intentionally launching an attack 'in the knowledge that such attack will cause [. . .] which would be clearly excessive in relation to the concrete and direct overall military advantage anticipated'.[203] There is therefore a heavy weighting on finding an attack disproportionate, with use of the term 'clearly' further raising the threshold.[204] The *mens rea* is also noted as subjective, with difficulty arising around proving that the accused knew their attack would be disproportionate.[205]

---

[195] Ibid., p. 68.
[196] Ibid., p. 70.
[197] Ibid., p. 71.
[198] Ibid.
[199] Ibid.
[200] Ibid., p. 79.
[201] Ibid., p. 71.
[202] Ibid., p. 76.
[203] Rome Statute, Art. 8(2)(b)(iv); Lawrence and Heller, 'The First Ecocentric Environmental War Crime', p. 76.
[204] Lawrence and Heller, 'The First Ecocentric Environmental War Crime', p. 76.
[205] Under the current wording the attacker must: (1) know in advance that the attack would cause 'widespread, long-term and severe' environmental damage; (2) foresee little military advantage; and (3) know that the damage would be 'clearly excessive' in relation to the 'concrete and direct overall military advantage anticipated'; Lawrence and Heller, 'The First Ecocentric Environmental War Crime', p. 78.

In spite of these criticisms, the progressive protection of the environment afforded under the Rome Statute has arguably learned from historic instances of destruction. Protecting the environment independently of human beings underlines the seriousness of its destruction under international criminal law.

CONTINUING HISTORY: WAR CRIMES, CHEMICAL WEAPONS AND SYRIA

By contrast to environmental protection, the approach to chemical, biological and nuclear weapons under the Rome Statute is an illustration of the limitations of historical influence.

If we refer to customary international law for guidance we can see that the prohibition on the use of poison as a method of warfare is one of the oldest prohibitions in international law.[206] Instruments such as the 1907 Regulations Concerning the Laws and Customs of War on Land prohibit the use of 'poison or poisoned weapons'.[207] Again, the influence of the First World War can be seen as the use of chemical weapons prompted the prohibition within the Versailles Peace Treaty on the 'use of asphyxiating, poisonous or other gases and all analogous liquids, materials or devices'.[208]

The Rome Statute does not address chemical weapons by name, and originally addressed them as war crimes only in relation to international armed conflicts, under Article 8(2)(b):[209]

>   (xvii) Employing poison or poisoned weapons;
>   (xviii) Employing asphyxiating, poisonous or other gases, and all analogous liquids, materials or devices;
>   (xix) Employing bullets which expand or flatten easily in the human body, such as bullets with a hard envelope which does not entirely cover the core or is pierced with incisions;
>   (xx) Employing weapons, projectiles and material and methods of warfare which are of a nature to cause superfluous injury or unnecessary suffering or which are inherently indiscriminate in violation of the international law of armed conflict, provided that such weapons, projectiles and material and methods of warfare are the subject of a comprehensive prohibition and are included in an annex to this

---

[206] Zimmerman and Sener, 'Chemical Weapons and the International Criminal Court', p. 436.

[207] Hague Convention (IV) Respecting the Laws and Customs of War on Land, 18 October 1907, Stat., vol. 36, p. 2277, Bevans, vol. 1, p. 631 (available at http://www.icrc.org/applic/ihl/ihl.nsf); Zimmerman and Sener, 'Chemical Weapons and the International Criminal Court', p. 437.

[208] Zimmerman and Sener, 'Chemical Weapons and the International Criminal Court', p. 437.

[209] Rome Statute, Art. 8(2)(b).

Statute, by an amendment in accordance with the relevant provisions set forth in articles 121 and 123.[210]

Significant issues arose during the Rome Diplomatic Conference as states could not reach agreement on nuclear weapons, with the P5 being most adamant that they should not be prohibited.[211] The Draft Statute proposed by the Preparatory Committee included options on breaches in relation to international armed conflicts for the use of biological, chemical and nuclear weapons.[212] Clark notes the chaos of a conference with 160 participating states, and recalls 'whispers emanating from an unknown source that, if nuclear weapons were not to be included, then the poor person's weapons of mass destruction, chemical and biological weapons, should not be either'.[213] Indeed, they are not included by name, with provision instead for poison, asphyxiating gases and expanding bullets followed by the concluding clause (xx).[214] In 2010, the first amendment to the Rome Statute was adopted in Kampala expanding the war crimes in Article 8(2)(b)(xvii), (xviii), and (xix) to armed conflicts of a non-international character through new sub-paragraphs to Article 8(2)(e), (xiii), (xiv), and (xv).[215] However, states must accept the amendment in order to be bound by it; those which do not accept the amendment will not be bound.[216]

Whilst the focus at Kampala was primarily on the crime of aggression, the need to unify approaches and ensure the ability to address the use of such weapons, and others, in a non-international armed conflict has been foregrounded by a currently unfolding (historic) event: the Syrian Civil War.[217] Whilst the situation in Syria raises additional complexities for the ICC as the Syrian Arab Republic is not a party to the Rome Statute, the acts which have been committed and which continue to be committed merit consideration. There are many examples of war crimes, crimes against humanity, and

---

[210] Rome Statute, Art. 8(2)(b)(xvii), Art. 8(2)(b)(xviii), Art. 8(2)(b)(xix), Art. 8(2)(b)(xx).
[211] Clark, 'Crimes Against Humanity and the Rome Statute of the International Criminal Court', pp. 367–8.
[212] Ibid., p. 370.
[213] Ibid., p. 376.
[214] Ibid.
[215] A. Alamuddin and P. Webb, 'Expanding Jurisdiction over War Crimes under Art. 8 of the ICC Statute', *Journal of International Criminal Justice*, vol. 8(5), 2010, p. 1220.
[216] Ibid.
[217] Ibid., p. 1221.

potentially crimes of genocide being committed in Syria.[218] However, among these the use of chemical weapons has been prolific and poses significant challenges for the international community. The UN investigating mission yielded 'credible evidence' of the use of the chemical weapon 'sarin' in incidents including Khan al-Assal (19 March 2013); Saraqueb (29 April 2013); Sheikh Maqsood (13 April 2013); Bahhariyeh (22 August 2013); Jobah (24 August 2013); Ashrafiah Sahnaya (25 August 2013); and Ghouta (21 August 2013).[219] These alleged uses of chemical weapons have raised questions around whether or not the Rome Statute prohibits chemical weapons, despite the intentional omission of their mention by name, and the influence of the Kampala amendment.[220]

During the negotiations at Kampala the question again arose of whether the chemical and biological weapons are prohibited by the terms 'asphyxiating, poisonous or other gases, and all analogous liquids, materials or devices' as found in Article 8.[221] There exists a spectrum of opinions as some commentators have argued that chemical weapons are covered, but not biological weapons, whilst others have argued neither are covered.[222] The argument that neither are covered stems from Article 8(2)(b)(xx), which provides that other weapons not mentioned which cause superfluous injury or unnecessary suffering etc. must be 'subject of a comprehensive prohibition' and 'included in an annex to this Statute'.[223] Alamuddin and Webb argue that since there is no specific provision, and since no specific annex was added in Kampala, the Rome Statute does not include chemical and biological weapons.[224] Given the difficult drafting history, failure to add a specific annex, and the inclusion of Article 22(2) which provides that the definition of a crime shall be 'strictly construed', the position that the Rome Statute does not include chemical

---

[218] B. Van Schaack, 'Mapping War Crimes in Syria', *International Law Studies*, vol. 92, 2016, p. 282, pp. 283–4.

[219] P. Cho, 'What If the International Criminal Court Could Prosecute President Al-Assad for the Chemical Weapon Attacks in Ghouta?', *St. Mary's Law Journal*, vol. 49, 2017–18, p. 165, p. 169.

[220] Zimmerman and Sener, 'Chemical Weapons and the International Criminal Court', p. 436.

[221] Alamuddin and Webb, 'Expanding Jurisdiction over War Crimes under Art. 8 of the ICC Statute', p. 1227.

[222] Ibid.

[223] Rome Statute, Art. 8(2)(b)(xx); Alamuddin and Webb, 'Expanding Jurisdiction over War Crimes under Art. 8 of the ICC Statute', p. 1228.

[224] Alamuddin and Webb, 'Expanding Jurisdiction over War Crimes under Art. 8 of the ICC Statute', p. 1228.

weapons may seem to be supported.[225] However, it can be argued that in practice most uses of chemical weapons fall within the Article 8 prohibitions on poisons and asphyxiating, poisonous or other gases, and all analogous liquids, materials or devices.[226]

If the use of the chemical weapon 'sarin' by the Syrian government can be considered to be covered under the Statute, it is the decision at Kampala to extend the relevant provisions to non-international armed conflict which becomes vital.[227] Considering the alleged use of chemical weapons by the government of Syria in 2013, and other alleged crimes, there arise important jurisdictional questions.

The above example is illustrative of the fact that legal definitions need to be kept under review in order to address 'continuing histories'. Although history as such is likely to affect the criminalisation or crystallisation of punishable conduct, it is ongoing or current events that shape future histories and determine the success and/or failure of agreed legal concepts.

CONCLUDING REMARKS

After examining select issues arising out of provisions on crimes against humanity, genocide and war crimes, it is clear that history plays an important role. As we have seen, historical facts have the power to enter into law and crystallise in legal provisions – in this instance, the Rome Statute of the International Criminal Court.

Arguably, crystallisation in the definitions of legal instruments is not the end of history; history is not static. As new histories develop, at the time of writing amidst the migrant or Rohingya crises, the situation in Syria, the rise of ISIS, etc., to name a few, the agreed provisions are put to the test, and the need to break free from the original histories emerges. This is usually done through reinterpretation of the provisions at hand.

If anything, history, through crystallisation helps with deterrence, a core aim of international criminal justice as a whole. As historical facts get stripped of their historical contexts and provide the basis for adjudication, future generations of international criminal lawyers are able to apply such provisions, free from the shackles of history, to contemporary situations, whilst current international criminals may be deterred to break these laws.

---

[225] Zimmerman and Sener, 'Chemical Weapons and the International Criminal Court', p. 439.
[226] Ibid.
[227] Ibid., p. 442.

This, however, does not mean that legal provisions are free of any limitations or constraints. Inevitably, the weight of history may keep such provisions grounded to their original contexts or might lead to insufficient coverage. Legal interpretation, judicial activism and innovative implementation may go some way in re-contextualising or reframing otherwise rigid provisions. All in all, the bridge between history, crystallisation and reinterpretation is what makes any legal instrument, including the Rome Statute, a living instrument, able to serve its purpose, including reinstating the rule of law in the aftermath of contemporary mass atrocities.

7. The legacy of the ICTY in Croatia, Bosnia and Serbia

Katarina Ristić

INTRODUCTION

The first UN Tribunal established so as to prosecute war crimes, crimes against humanity, and genocide in former Yugoslavia, was officially closed in 2018. Left behind is a Mechanism for Criminal Tribunals (IRMCT) mandated to deal with the unfinished cases, and a contested legacy across the region. One of the last judgments issued by the ICTY, in the case of *Prlić et al.*, which concerned crimes committed by the Croatian army in south-western and central Bosnia and Herzegovina, ended in the public suicide of one of the accused, Slobodan Praljak. Praljak's dramatic suicide came as a final, and most tragic expression of the 'will for innocence', which was shared by the majority of the accused, who found sanctuary and shelter solely within their own states. For many of the convicted war criminals, return from prison implied public rallies, and celebrations, which in turn received a fair share of intense media coverage.[1] This chapter examines the public discourses on war crimes trials that enabled such acceptances, and which created a space of security, moral righteousness and comfort for convicted war criminals.

The ICTY was established in the midst of the war in former Yugoslavia, on 25 May 1993. For more than forty years, 25 May had been celebrated as 'Youth Day' which marked Josip Broz Tito's birthday. It was routinely accompanied by 'a relay of Yugoslav youth running through the country with a white baton, symbolizing the country's unity'.[2] The last white baton was

---

[1] K. Ristić, 'The Media Negotiations of War Criminals and their Memoirs: The Emergence of the "ICTY Celebrity"', *International Criminal Justice Review*, vol. 28(4), 2018, pp. 391–405. See also J. Mihajlović Trbovc, 'Homecomings From "The Hague": Media Coverage of ICTY Defendants After Trial and Punishment', *International Criminal Justice Review*, vol. 28(4), 2018, pp. 406–22.

[2] Z. Volčič, 'Yugo-Nostalgia: Cultural Memory and Media in the Former Yugoslavia', *Critical Studies in Media Communication*, vol. 24(1), 2007, p. 23.

taken through the country in 1988, and only five years later, the ICTY was established. The Tribunal was tasked with the 'restoration and maintenance of peace',[3] by bringing criminals to justice and justice to victims. The ICTY's prosecution strategy emphasized clearly, and from its very outset, that its aim was to prosecute perpetrators from all sides, thus providing justice to all victims of conflict. For many observers, this meant that the Tribunal would contribute to reconciliation; justice allocated by the Tribunal was supposed to overcome ethno-national grievances of former enemies, as it opted to operate upon the universal level of humanity and the innocence of victimhood of all peoples.

Just like the official 'brotherhood and unity' ideology that underlined the 'Day of Youth' and the 25 May celebrations in former socialist Yugoslavia, the Tribunal's mission clashed with ethnic nationalism within its receiving countries. The ethnic nationalism that arose in Yugoslavia from the mid-1980s onwards led to three wars and millions of victims throughout the region; to expulsions, ethnic cleansings, and mass murders. In hindsight, both the Yugoslav states and the Tribunal bitterly underestimated the power of ethnic nationalism and widespread nationalist mobilization. Initial willingness to die for one's homeland during the war, translated after the war into a willingness to defend the purity of the state and the alleged defensive nature of the war just waged – to an almost unlimited extent. This visceral desire to protect the state's alleged defensive ethos often resulted in a rejection of the Tribunal's judgments, coupled with a vehement defence of its convicted war criminals. Granted these general similarities, within each country, this defence adopted a somewhat different form, depending largely on the concrete political circumstances, and the hitherto existent narrative about the war in each country. Criminal charges, the military or political ranks of the accused, and the overall prosecution strategy of the Tribunal, also played their parts in consecrating these differing perspectives. In the following pages, a special emphasis is paid to the way media coded, weighted and signified the war crime trials in Serbia, Bosnia-Herzegovina and Croatia, and how it contributed to their transformation into sites of national memory.

Existing literature has pointed to the limitations inherent to processes aimed at dealing with the past in the former Yugoslavia. It has highlighted the tendency to resort to the 'hijacking of justice' by political elites,[4] the problematic attitudes towards The Hague Tribunal,[5] the prevalence of nationalism in media

---

[3] UNSC Res. 827, 25 May 1993, at preambular para. 6.
[4] J. Subotić, *Hijacked Justice: Dealing with the Past in the Balkans*, Ithaca, NY: Cornell University Press, 2009.
[5] V. Dimitrijević, *Stavovi prema ratnim zločinima, Haškom tribunalu i domaćem pravosuđu za ratne zločine*, Beograd: Beogradski centar za ljudska prava, 2004–9.

reporting,[6] and the reticence with which the ex-Yugoslav states cooperated with the Tribunal.[7] Building further on this literature, this chapter looks at how court proceedings were used to create collective memory, which topics were selected as publicly relevant, which trials were commented on in the media – in what way and for what purpose.

The unfolding of the notions of memory within the different ex-Yugoslav countries requires a brief theoretical introduction of the concept of collective memory and its two correlating sub-types: national memory and transnational memory. These two types embrace not only different scales at which memory is performed, but also different moral obligations of communities: while the former blindly disregards any responsibility for the crimes committed by its own group members while glorifying its own victims, the latter focuses also on atrocities committed by its own members and acknowledges the victimhood of others thus incorporating them into the war's more general memory. The chapter then examines the usage of war crime trials as sites of memory, and how these were appropriated by the dominant national memory in Croatia, Bosnia and Serbia, leading to the formulation of 'victims' memory' in Bosnia, 'victor's memory' in Croatia, and 'memory of the defeated' in Serbia. Finally, the chapter explores the emergence of transnational, reflexive memory in the regional human rights networks, which entails a critical encounter with the past and an acceptance of the Tribunal's rulings.

WAR, WAR CRIME TRIALS, AND NATIONAL MEMORY

When creating collective memory, few events can measure up to war as the 'fundamental crash of experience' and a real 'crisis of memory', in terms of the strength of its psychological impact.[8] Wars seem to constitute the nodal points of national memory, providing a source of endless inspiration and moral

---

[6] A. Džihana and Z. Volčič (eds.), *Media and National Ideologies*, Sarajevo: Mediacentar Sarajevo, 2011.

[7] V. Peskin, *International Justice in Rwanda and the Balkans: Virtual Trials and the Struggle for State Cooperation*, Cambridge: Cambridge University Press, 2008.

[8] W. Höpken, 'Memory Politics and Mourning: Remembering World War II in Yugoslavia', in C. Sighele and F. Vanoni (eds.), *Bad Memories: Sites, Symbols and Narrations of the Wars in the Balkans*, Rovereto: Osservatorio Balcani e Caucaso, 2008, pp. 27–33.

obligation for society's members. As Idith Zertal observes with regard to the formation of national identity in Israel:

> Where memory and national identity meet, there is a grave, there lies death. The killing fields of national ethnic conflicts, the graves of the fallen, are the building blocks of which modern nations are made, out of which the fabric of national sentiment grows.[9]

Stories of fallen soldiers, victorious battles and bitter defeats are translated into the 'biography of nation', which narrates its immortality through the remembrance or the forgetting of the dead as 'our own'.[10]

War crime trials, to the extent to which they address the past, also contribute to the creation of collective memory, constituting specific 'sites of memory'.[11] For Nora, a 'site of memory' marks a break in historical continuity, an embodiment of memory, which no longer preserves real environments of memory: '*lieux de mémoire* are fundamentally remains, the ultimate embodiments of a memorial consciousness that has barely survived in a historical age that calls out for memory because it has abandoned it'.[12]

But trials are more than silent sites of memory, in the sense of a symbolical embodiment of meaning, since unlike flags and anthems, they produce meanings of their own. In judgments, legal institutions decide about the past, challenge or confirm existing narratives of the war, deciding about the role of the warrior and the victims. International tribunals, or rather their judgments, become yet another memory actor, offering particular interpretation of the past.

Until recently, memory scholars mainly privileged the nation-state as a dominant territorial regime for memory production. Collective memory was seen as an outcome of national 'memory entrepreneurs' who engage in the production of new meanings, bringing the past into the present with new interpretations, intentions and expectations.[13] The primacy of state agents in memory production is seen in their investment in national identity construction, creating feelings of belonging, social cohesion and symbolic borders, all guided so as to legitimize claims of one's own truthfulness. A constant threat

---

[9] I. Zertal, *Israel's Holocaust and the Politics of Nationhood*, Cambridge: Cambridge University Press, 2005, p. 9.
[10] B. R. Anderson, *Imagined Communities: Reflections on the Origin and Spread of Nationalism*, London: Verso, 2006, p. 206.
[11] P. Nora, 'Between Memory and History: Les Lieux de Mémoire', *Representations*, no. 26, 1989, pp. 7–24.
[12] Ibid., p. 12.
[13] E. Jelin, *State Repression and the Labors of Memory*, Minneapolis: University of Minnesota Press, 2003.

of oblivion guides this intensive work on memory production through 'sites of memory',[14] or markers of memory,[15] in forms of commemorations, the erection of monuments and memorials, museums, and in public debates. Collective memory preserves the knowledge of the group. Its main power derives from its capacity to reconstruct, reframe, reject or transform narratives of the past into usable identity sources. The selectiveness of memory is a token of the power behind the discourse. If collective memory production can be understood as a process of discourse configuration which attempts to create shared frames of remembering, where individuals can meaningfully interpret their personal memories and historical processes – it then becomes clear why it is the nation-state which has drawn memory scholars' closest attention.

Nevertheless, the national scale is not the sole *niveau* at which memory negotiations unfold. International tribunals are a case in point. By legally deciding to charge individuals for the commitment of atrocities, these tribunals provide new interpretations of the past that are beyond the control of the political power of any of the receiving states. By doing so, tribunals hereby shift the *niveau* within which the meaning of the past is determined – from the national to the transnational scale. Tribunals thus create alternative interpretations of the past, both by accusing central military and political actors and metamorphosing them into war criminals, and by ascribing a specific ontological weight to their crimes by tagging them with legal qualifications such as 'genocide' or 'crimes against humanity'. At the same time, trials offer a podium for victims to testify about their past and the suffering they endured – providing a space where their witnessed experiences can be ventilated.

In this interplay between different actors, who operate at different levels of memory production, two different kinds of memory habitually emerge: national and transnational memory. National memory refers not only to the dominant scale at which memory actors operate, but also to a specific type of the self-rightfulness narrative, focusing on grievances against the 'other' and the victimhood experiences pertaining to members of its own ethno-social group. This sort of memory has been prevalent throughout the history of nation-states. Victimhood of other group is usually played down, or in the worst cases denied outright, as victims from the other group cannot appear as 'grievable lives',[16] and are constantly reduced to the stature of 'unworthy victims'.[17]

---

[14] Nora, 'Between Memory and History', p. 12.
[15] Jelin, *State Repression and the Labors of Memory*.
[16] J. Butler, *Frames of War: When Is Life Grievable?*, London: Verso, 2009, p. 15.
[17] E. Herman and N. Chomsky, *Manufacturing Consent: The Political Economy of the Mass Media*, New York: Pantheon Books, 1988, p. 37.

Transnational memory, on the other hand, operates beyond the nation-state scale, at the same time including a reflexive, critical stand towards all perpetrators, based on the 'shared acceptance of responsibility for wrongs one's own nation has done to others'.[18] Levy and Sznaider introduced the concept of 'cosmopolitan memory', assessing that the globalization of the Holocaust's memory has triggered the creation of new cosmopolitan sensibilities. Executed primarily through the usage of a global media, 'cosmopolitan memory' gave rise to a new and critical narrative of the past, which privileges past injustices of one's own nation, while recognizing the history of the other. This critical narrative sees reconciliation as a 'central mnemonic event' in its building upon the 'never again' dictum as a new moral imperative. Hence, conclude Levy and Sznaider, 'the transposition of Holocaust over genocide sensibilities was a foundation for cosmopolitan memories as a self-reflective form of global memory'.[19]

Back when it was established, it was largely believed that the Tribunal would contribute to reconciliation, since the justice allocated by the Tribunal was supposed to surpass ethno-national grievances of former enemies, as it opted to operate upon the universal level of humanity and the innocence of victimhood of all peoples.

Nevertheless, and despite the ICTY's clear universalist approach to war crimes, once these trials entered the national levels of the newly established states of the former Yugoslavia, they took on a vehemently nationalistic facet. Within each particular country, the trials were viewed and filtered through ethnic lenses, stressing the accused's ethnicity. The trials gradually came to be perceived as 'accusatory' when the accused turned out to be a member and national of that country. Conversely, the trials were perceived as 'consolatory' as soon as they recognized the pain and suffering of that country's nationals thus confirming the victimization of that group.

The following analysis examines the particular way in which The Hague's war trials were interpreted within the receiving nation-states and their respective end-communities. It ponders how war crimes were coded, weighted and narrated by – and within – national media outlets.

---

[18] A. Assmann and U. Frevert, *Geschichtsvergessenheit, Geschichtsversessenheit: vom Umgang mit deutschen Vergangenheiten nach 1945*, Stuttgart: Deutsche Verlags-Anstalt, 1999, p. 168.

[19] D. Levy and N. Sznaider, 'The Holocaust and the Formation of Cosmopolitan Memory', *European Journal of Social Theory*, vol. 5(1), 2002, p. 99.

COLLECTIVE MEMORY IN POST-WAR YUGOSLAVIA

Contrary to the Tribunal's universalist legal approach, indictments and judgments were retold as national grievances, as 'our victimhood' against 'their atrocities'. Rather than justice for the victims of all sides so as to facilitate reconciliation, nationalist media successfully transformed the trials into narratives of nationalist memory, thus leading the general public debate into a symbolic battle for the recognition of 'our victims' *versus* 'their atrocities'. In all the countries discussed, the creation of memory was primarily led by the need to stabilize a national identity and produce usable positive self-images. Correspondingly, legal narratives were accepted only to the extent that they coincided with, or conformed to, a flattering image of the nation, while being attacked, rejected or marginalized when offering evidence to the contrary. The media discourses were created around distinctly non-legal meanings and interpretations of the trials, as they encoded *individual criminal responsibility* into *collective guilt*, and crimes into national historical catastrophes.

BOSNIA AND HERZEGOVINA – THE MEMORY OF THE VICTIMS

In the case of Bosnia,[20] Bosniak victimhood received its ultimate vindication from the unmatched rate of consolatory legal narratives handed down by several of the ICTY's verdicts. With Srebrenica serving as the central measure of Bosnian national collective trauma, and the Tribunal's pronouncement that *genocide* was indeed committed, in not one but several of its judgements (*Krstić*,[21] *Popović et al.*,[22] *Tolimir*,[23] *Karadžić*[24] and *Mladić*[25]), Bosniak *vic-*

---

[20] The Dayton Agreement formed two political entities in post-war Bosnia: Republika Srpska (RS) and the Federation of Bosnia-Herzegovina. The following analysis relates primarily to Bosniak media in the Federation.

[21] ICTY, Judgment of 2 August 2001, *Prosecutor v. Krstić*, Case No. IT-98-33-T, at para. 634, available at http://www.icty.org/x/cases/krstic/tjug/en/krs-tj010802e.pdf.

[22] ICTY, Judgment of 10 June 2010, *Prosecutor v. Popović et al.*, Case No. IT-05-88-T, at para. 1180, available at www.icty.org/x/cases/popovic/tjug/en/100610judgement.pdf.

[23] ICTY, Judgment of 12 December 2012, *Prosecutor v. Tolimir*, Case No. IT-05-88-T, at para. 791, available at www.icty.org/x/cases/tolimir/tjug/en/121212.pdf.

[24] ICTY, Judgment of 24 March 2016, *Prosecutor v. Karadžić*, Case No. IT-95-5/18-T, at para. 5998, available at www.icty.org/x/cases/karadzic/tjug/en/160324_judgement.pdf.

[25] ICTY, Judgment of 22 November 2017, *Prosecutor v. Mladić*, Case No. IT-09-92-T, at para. 5130, available at www.icty.org/x/cases/mladic/tjug/en/171122-4of5_1.pdf.

timhood received its official and ultimate international vindication. Public discourses focused on narrating, evaluating and weighting the genocide, and its meaning, for Bosniak identity, the state, for politics and for the society's future. Consonant to genocide's dominance as *the* topic in public focus, Bosniak politicians unanimously embraced it as the most salient mnemonic event in the creation of collective memory – now substantiated by the ICTY's numerous verdicts which pronounced the commission of this crime.

Bosniak media focused on the victims-witnesses' testimonies in and beyond the trial, and reported the victims' stories, while adopting the victim's perspective in these reports. Pursuant to Radoslav Krstić's entry of his 'not guilty plea' at the Tribunal, the media reported upon the inner monologue of Hasan Nuhanović, a Srebrenica survivor. Pondering on Krstić's thoughts at the moment he entered his not guilty plea, Nuhanović questioned whether he remembered:

> ... the entire group of thousand, and the second thousand ... of Muslims, lined up next to each other ... Did Krstić enjoy this scene? Bursts of machine guns, bodies fallen slain in the freshly dug graves ... caterpillars of bulldozers crumbling the bodies, now buried under hundreds of tons of soil and mud while they were still breathing and looked with their eyes open.[26]

Nuhanović 'recalled' an image of a child with his grandfather standing before the execution squad, moments before its shots were fired:

> A twelve-year-old boy called out to his mother ... A beardless boy standing with his eighty years old grandfather, holding his hand, and waiting for the outburst of shots ... Did Krstić see this image, which played out in front of his eyes four and a half years ago?[27]

The narration here is one of emotional engulfment in the victim's experience. He expresses the need to depict the crimes he personally witnessed in detail, to break them down into the individual victim's image as standing in front of the execution squad, to emotionally feel the pain of the victims, narrated now through the words of a survivor. Factually, though, Nuhanović *was not* a first-hand witness to these crimes. His recollection, which is a *second-hand* story-telling, nevertheless does not reduce the persuasiveness or even truthfulness of his statement. As a Srebrenica survivor who lost his entire family, Nuhanović's account pertains to a moral position, regardless of the *factual* secondary nature of his statement. Such accounts, which build upon facts now globally well-known about the Srebrenica genocide, and which dovetail with

---

[26] 'Dobri Bože uzmi i mene', *Dani bh. nezavisni news magazin*, 15 July 2011.
[27] Ibid.

other testimonies of mass killings, allow personal, emotional engulfment with the victims' suffering.

Another set of actors who played a key role in the formulation of Bosniak memory within the sphere of the public debates about The Hague trials and their interpretation, were victims' organizations. In due course, their members eventually became frequent commentators on the trials in the media, especially with regards to the contested issue of war-criminal fugitives who managed to escape international authorities, following their official indictment at The Hague. For years, the ICTY's inability to apprehend high-ranking fugitives such as former President of the Republika Srpska Radovan Karadžić and its army commander Ratko Mladić, was taken as a visible token of the Tribunal's inability to deliver justice to the victims. Cases in which perpetrators were brought to trial thanks to the delivery of the suspects to the Tribunal were welcomed by victims' organizations. These, however, were harshly criticized if and when the judgment rendered by them did not conform to the perceived sense of injury which the victims' organizations harboured. The Tribunal's judgment in *Popović et al.*,[28] which convicted Popović[29] and Beara[30] of genocide in Srebrenica and sentenced them to life imprisonment, while sentencing Nikolić[31] to 35 years in prison, Borovčanin[32] to 17 years, Pandurović[33] to 13 years, and Gvero[34] to 5 years is a case in point. In its reaction to these verdicts, the well-known victims' organization the 'Mothers of Srebrenica' chose to focus its attention on the lenient sentences delivered by the Tribunal to Gvero and Pandurović, as opposed to Popović and Beara's life sentences. As noted by Hatidža Mehmedović from the Mothers of Srebrenica organization, these judgments were:

'an insult over injury' and provided 'additional humiliation' given that 'monsters are rewarded with freedom', while we still look for our children in mass graves.[35]

In addition to perceived inadequate sentences, Bosniak victims' organization criticized the failure of the ICTY to prosecute other atrocities committed in Western Bosnia in 1992, which were perceived as genocide. Victims'

---

[28] ICTY, Judgment of 10 June 2010, *Prosecutor v. Popović et al.*
[29] Ibid., p. 832.
[30] Ibid., p. 833.
[31] Ibid., p. 834.
[32] Ibid., p. 835.
[33] Ibid., pp. 837–8.
[34] Ibid., pp. 836–7.
[35] 'Beari i Popoviću doživotni zatvor', *Oslobođenje*, 11 June 2010.

groups lobbied for years for the legal qualification of 'genocide' to be attributed to these atrocities:

> If every piece of the mosaic would ever be put together, about the terrible things which happened in the region of Prijedor, it would be proved that genocide over Bosniaks was also executed in Krajina.[36]

Although the ICTY Prosecutor included the charges for genocide in six municipalities in the final indictment in the trials of Karadžić and Mladić, the Tribunal's judges dismissed these charges. This dismissal triggered a sense of resignation and dissatisfaction among the victims. Victims' organizations protested vocally against these judicial outcomes, as they consider that 'Prijedor was the beginning of genocide',[37] showing that the process of memory creation is led by the trauma, rather than by the actual content of the final judgments rendered by the tribunal.

This focus on the victims' narratives, and victims' perspectives in the media contributed to 'victims' memory' – pursuant to Aleida Assmann's understanding. The two main linguistic strategies used to create this 'victims' memory' were (1) the usage of consolatory legal narratives as building blocks of memory, and (2) a justification and explanatory strategy in response to the accusatory legal narratives in favour of indicted Bosniak war criminals. The crimes committed by the Bosniak armed forces, as prosecuted in the *Orić*, *Delić* or *Halilović* trials were acknowledged, albeit excused and justified through a referencing of the harrowing living conditions and existential threats writ large, as generally experienced by many Bosnians during the war.

Although crimes committed by the Bosnian army were described in minute details, following stringently the charges enumerated in the Tribunal's indictments, they were always connected with the personal memories of survivors, of hunger and desperation within Srebrenica's 'safe area':

> Naser Orić was a commander of the Srebrenica Defence, accused by Tribunal in The Hague for the beating of eleven and the murder of seven Serbian prisoners, for the unnecessary plunder of villages, for plunder of private and collective property in fifteen primarily-Serbian villages in the surrounding of Bratunac. In Srebrenica – Naser Orić was bigger than life, bigger than himself, he played a bigger role than he could have ever imagined playing. His facing of a trial is the price he would have to pay.[38]

---

[36] 'Prijedorski genocid', *Dnevni avaz*, 9 January 2009.
[37] 'Prijedor je bio početak genocida', *Oslobođenje*, 23 November 2017.
[38] 'Suđenje većem od života', *Dani bh. nezavisni news magazin*, 4 April 2003.

The main feature of media discourse on the *Orić* case is the presence of an overarching, dominant framework of Bosnian victimhood, transforming Orić's crimes into a tragic *necessity* of the conflict. The Bosnian media's perception of the Tribunal's charging of Orić is seen as an attempt to equate criminality and guilt, by ascribing the same quota of responsibility for the war to all sides of the conflict.[39] The equation of guilt to all parties is rejected not only due to the far lower number of atrocities committed by Bosnians, but more importantly due to the parties' different ideologies and their goals for the war. Unlike their Serbian and Croatian counterparts, crimes committed by Bosnians were not premised upon a political-military doctrine of ethnic cleansing, which was invariably bent upon the extermination of other ethnic groups.[40]

The readiness and easiness with which the Bosnian public turned a blind eye towards victims of the other side, underlies the viewing of the emergent Bosnian memory as a nationalist rather than a reflective one. Notwithstanding, and against this nationalist memory stratum, several victims' groups and individuals in Bosnia did promote a critical memory of the war. These efforts are addressed in the last part of this analysis.

CROATIA – THE MEMORY OF VICTORS

The second, and more challenging view of the ICTY trials as sites of memory, concerns the case of Croatia. Here, the 'Homeland War' narrative completely dominated the media's public portrayal of the trials of Croatian war crime perpetrators. In this case, consolatory legal narratives were used so as to promote the Homeland War narrative. This was executed through the positive portrayal of Croatian leaders, generals and soldiers defending the homeland. Unlike the reluctant and sporadic military defence actions undertaken by Bosnian fighters, Croatian military and political leaders emerged as heroes from the war. The ICTY's charges against them clashed with a common aspect of Croatian heritage, namely: the heroism of its leaders and the moral purity of the state they established through the war. Despite the significant number of consolatory legal narratives which could have been observed in the *Milošević*, *Mrkšić et al.*, *Perišić* or *Strugar* trials, Croatian public attention actually focused on the *Gotovina et al.* trial, which directly challenged the focal point of the Homeland War narrative. This narrative interpreted 'Operation Storm' (the Croatian offensive against Serbs) as a defensive operation in liberation of parts seen as integral to the Croatian state. This narrative contrasted sharply

---

[39] 'Ostavite Bosanske heroje, tragajte za zločincima!', *Oslobođenje*, 28 April 2003.
[40] 'Ličnost u fokusu – Rasim Delić', *Dani bh. nezavisni news magazin*, 25 February 2005.

with the ICTY's pronouncement in *Gotovina*, which framed Operation Storm in war crimes' terms, as it ascribed criminal responsibility to the Croatian military and political leaders. These contrasting ICTY narratives were hectically debated in the Croatian media and bitterly rejected. In turn, the alleged moral, political and legal aspects implicit in Operation Storm's objectives were defended:

> 'The Storm' was a morally legitimate military operation in accordance with international law. . . . 'The Storm' was a magnificent action of recovering conquered territory, and was supported by leading world powers, such as the United States, and its positive effect was the collapse of the neighbouring para-state of Karadžić in Bosnia and Herzegovina, which, after four years of bloodshed, halted, at least temporarily, the attempt to create a Greater Serbia.[41]

Prime Minister Jadranka Kosor repeated this interpretation only four months after the Trial Chamber's verdict, which convicted the defendants Gotovina[42] and Čermak[43] to 24 years and 18 years respectively, of imprisonment:

> The operation 'Storm' was a struggle for freedom and justice, fighting for Croatia, honouring Vukovar, Škabrnja, and Dubrovnik – a tribute to the thousands of wounded and killed. We will never accept being resented for our victories, victories of democracy and freedom from the yoke of Greater Serbia and Milošević's policy of aggression, destruction and hatred.[44]

By far the most disturbing issue was the Trial Chamber's conclusion that the Croatian war President, Franjo Tuđman, was a member of what the Tribunal named 'a joint criminal enterprise'.[45] The public's rejection of this judgment by the ICTY in fact served to further reinforce Croatian social cohesion and strengthen its decisiveness to defend the state and its heroes from the Tribunal's alleged defamation:

> Franjo Tuđman is for a large number of Croatian people truly the 'Father of the Nation', as General Ante Gotovina is the hero of the war. What is left for that majority of the Croatian people, the Croatian authorities and the opposition after the verdict in the Hague, is to unite to rescue the reputation of the process in which the

---

[41] 'Previsoka kazna koja bi mogla utjecati na novu radikalizaciju društva', *Nacional Dnevno online izdanje*, 15 April 2011.
[42] ICTY, Judgment of 15 April 2011, *Prosecutor v. Gotovina et al.*, Case No. IT-06-90-T, p. 1340, available at www.icty.org/x/cases/gotovina/tjug/en/110415_judgement_vol2.pdf.
[43] Ibid., p. 1341.
[44] 'J. Kosor s kninskog stadiona pozdravila Gotovinu i Markača', *Večernji List*, 5 August 2011.
[45] ICTY, Judgment of 15 April 2011, *Prosecutor v. Gotovina et al.*, at para. 2316.

state was created after the liberation of the occupied territories, and to honour those who, like Tuđman and Gotovina, have participated in the realization of the dream of the Croatian people of an independent state.[46]

In this heroization of accused generals, Ante Gotovina became the symbol of the Homeland War, his conviction by the ICTY Trial Chamber's judgment turned into a celebration of a Croatian martyrdom. Gotovina was seen not only as a war hero, but also as an innocent victim now sacrificed for the sake of Croatian independence. His sacrifices became a symbol of 'Croatian martyrdom', comparable with the sacrificial lamb and Jesus Christ in Croatia's Catholic ethos:[47]

> In the Gotovina case, all the symbolic elements of the sacrificial paradigm are present. The innocent victim pays the toll because he has been proclaimed guilty from the beginning, but the guilt derives from the sins committed by others.[48]

Public screenings of the Gotovina judgment, projected on the main squares of cities throughout Croatia demonstrated the despair and anger with which the judgment was received by Croatians who followed the trial.

Two years later, Gotovina and Čarmak were acquitted of all charges by the ICTY Appeals Chamber.[49] Croatia celebrated this acquittal with public rallies, concerts and fireworks, while the generals appeared on the stage in Zagreb, accompanied by the President and the Prime Minister, as they addressed one of the most spectacular mass gatherings in the newly born country. According to the Homeland War narrative, which saw the Croatian state as the real victim of Serbian aggression, this state was now defended and secured thanks to the victorious battle that was Operation Storm. Under such a victorious and heroic narrative, individual victims were only sporadically included. The public's central gaze was oriented towards the celebrations of the war's veterans. Croatian voices of victimhood were thus subjugated before the narrative glorious victory. Correspondingly, the most prominent groups who featured in Croatia's memory-creation process were not victims' organizations but rather veterans' organizations. Despite their omnipresence in the public debates, and

---

[46] 'Pokrenimo prijatelje ako ih poslije svega imamo u svijetu!', *Večernji list*, 16 April 2011.

[47] V. Pavlaković, 'Croatia, the International Criminal Tribunal for the Former Yugoslavia, and General Gotovina as a Political Symbol', *Europe-Asia Studies*, vol. 62(10), 2010, pp. 1707–40.

[48] 'Izručenje i suđenje Anti Gotovini slično Isusovom', *Jutarnji List*, 28 May 2009.

[49] ICTY Appeals Chamber, Judgment of 16 November 2012, *Prosecutor v. Gotovina et al.*, Case No. IT-06-90-A, available at www.icty.org/x/cases/gotovina/acjug/en/121116_judgement.pdf.

in public rallies that protested the arrests of Croatian war criminals,[50] even as they garnered a role in the state's apparatus as in the ministry of defence, veterans' organizations were constantly requesting further vindication from the public. As they lamented that the 'defenders are ignored and the importance of the war is depreciated', the Croatian veterans' organizations vociferously advocated for the obligation to 'honour the heritage of the Homeland War and its dignity'.[51]

In Croatia, the discrepancy, and even cognitive dissonance, between the ICTY's war crimes charges against Gotovina and others, and the perceived trauma of Croatians who undoubtedly suffered during the war, was even greater than that in Bosnia. From a Croatian perspective, the Serb war crimes committed against Croatian civilians in Vukovar merited the title of 'genocide'. What Croats saw as Serb-perpetuated genocidal acts against them, were neither charged as such by the ICTY, let alone established. And state aggression as such was not even included as one of the major criminal offences within the Tribunal's Statute. Hence, to Croatian eyes, the legal narratives which the ICTY did pronounce against Serbs, concerning the crimes against Croats, seemed bitterly inadequate and an insufficient response to Croatian national suffering. While the ICTY's judgments against Croats in their anti-Serb actions were contextualized, and the court's authority was still recognized, the judgments themselves were viewed as different examples of the ICTY's seemingly permanent judicial inadequacy.

The Homeland War narrative thus clashed with the ICTY's judgments in both the consolatory and accusatory Croatian legal narratives. Consolatory legal narratives, as in a recognition of Croats' suffering, failed to provide the much-needed acknowledgement of trauma sought by Croatian memory entrepreneurs. The Hague's accusatory legal narratives, as in the Trial Chamber's guilty verdict on Gotovina, ran counter to the very nature of the Croatian war narrative and the ethos of Croatia's defenders, thus bringing about a strong rejection and political mobilizations in favour of the dismissal of The Hague's charges against Gotovina. The rendering of the accused as heroes who achieved Croatia's legitimate war goal, as in the defence, propagated the creation of a 'winner's memory' – now carried forwards by the veterans' organizations. The 'memory of the winner' was created by celebrating the victory in Operation Storm by Croatian veterans as defenders, now seen as heroes, while simply

---

[50] A. Ljubojevic, 'Croatian War Veterans: Coup de Théâtre or Coup d'État?', *London School of Economics and Political Science blog*, 6 July 2017, available https://blogs.lse.ac.uk/lsee/2015/06/12/croatian-war-veterans-coup-de-theatre-or-coup-detat/.

[51] 'O dignitetu Domovinskog rata trebaju brinuti braniteljí', *Jutarnji List*, 4 August 2006.

dismissing the Tribunal's accusatory legal narratives against Croat actions in Operation Storm.

SERBIA – THE MEMORY OF THE DEFEATED

In Serbia, the ICTY's sheer amount of accusatory legal narratives and the charging of so many Serbs of war crimes, all pointed to criminal responsibility which if adopted, might have led to a 'perpetrator's memory'. However, the public's efforts to minimize the importance of the Tribunal's judgments effectively resulted in a tendency towards the intensification of Serbian denial. Genocide charges were by and large ignored. The first *Kristić* judgment was hardly mentioned in the Serbian press, and no evaluation, or attempt to assign particular meaning to this verdict was undertaken. Four years after the first genocide judgment in *Krstić*, the public in Serbia still debated whether genocide actually happened in Srebrenica in the first place. As Dr Smilja Avramov put it:

> No genocide was committed against Bosnians in Srebrenica because there was no intention to exterminate them.[52]

Dr Milan Bulajić was somewhat more nuanced. Stressing that 35 000 Bosnians were *spared* in Srebrenica, that is *not* killed, against the recognized number of over 7000 deaths there, Bulajić thus concurred that no *genocide* was committed. Instead, Srebrenica was encoded as just another 'simple' massacre – *à la guerre comme à la guerre*. On the whole, Serbian public opinion opted to simply ignore the ICTY's verdicts on this matter and refused to make reference to them even as simple sources of reliable evidence or general knowledge concerning the atrocities that actually took place.

One might ponder the depth of the intellectual efforts to assign a distinction between 'massacre' and 'genocide', so vehemently defended in the Serbian media, and the seemingly false moral gain that this entails. The answer to this question lies in the nature of premeditation. The massacre, explains Avramov, is a *spontaneous* act, which happens in all wars. Genocide is a planned intentional atrocity aimed at *a priori* annihilating another group. Avramov stresses that there was no evidence indicating that the Serbian side

---

[52] 'Masakr ili genocid? Pravnici i dalje podeljeni povodom zločina u Srebrenici', *Večernje novosti*, 5 July 2005.

planned the genocide. The spontaneity attributed to Serb crimes is premised upon strong and sudden feelings and desires for revenge and vengeance:

> the crime (in Srebrenica) was incited by revenge. . . . 142 Serbian villages – from Kravice to Višnjice – had been previously destroyed.[53]

The normalization of Srebrenica as a massacre – tragic, albeit nothing out of the ordinary – then serves to equate the crimes of both sides and their number of casualties, leading to the normalization of the conflict as nothing more than a 'normal' civil war. The asymmetry of *genocide* as the absolute epitome of evil must be avoided at any cost, be it through the denial of facts, the avoidance of references to the Tribunal's judgments, or the removal of the victims from the public eye. Rather than a one-off event, the refusal to recognize that something fundamentally different than a simple massacre took place in Srebrenica, soon became entrenched within the Serbian public psyche. Reporting on the ICTY's conviction of general Momčilo Perišić (former Chief of Staff of the Yugoslav army) of aiding and abetting Srebrenica's Serb *génocidaires*, B92 journalist Ljubica Gojgić managed to avoid any mention of 'genocide' in her dispatch from The Hague. Instead, Gojgić referred to 'that which happened in Srebrenica', to 'everything that was happening in Srebrenica' and to 'all that was happening'.[54]

Importantly, the Serb struggle with the meaning of the crimes committed in Srebrenica was geared almost exclusively towards the avoidance of attribution of any particular or special moral weight to what took place there. Fearful of the *stigma* associated with genocide and concerned with the eventuality whereby the transfer of Srebrenica's guilt to all Serbs would result in an image of Serbs as a 'nation of *génocidaires*', Srebrenica's atrocity was now defined as a massacre – a 'normal' part of the atrocities of war. Public references to *genocide* were to be avoided at any cost. Illustrative of this attempt is a commentary by Slobodan Antonić, who acknowledged the crimes, but rejected the moral weight of genocide, and its political consequences:

> The existence of mass atrocities is *per se* a sufficiently terrible fact which we should not deteriorate further. It is unreasonable to insist on calling it genocide as in WWII. It is wrong to equate Srebrenica with Auschwitz, or Dachau with Ovčara. . . . Following the claim that a genocide occurred in Srebrenica, the Republika Srpska is denounced as a genocidal creation, and then its abolition is demanded. This does not contribute to dealing with the crimes.[55]

---

[53] Ibid.
[54] *News Program Vesti B92*, 6 September 2011.
[55] 'Prekršaj', 8 December 2006, available at https://pescanik.net/prekrsaj.

In other words, dealing with the past, which postulates the moral requirement to recognize the victims and acknowledge atrocities, was now equated with the *political* aim of the dissolution of the Republika Srpska – the Serbian constitutional entity within Bosnia-Herzegovina. The moral demand which required the acknowledgement of genocide, and the request to provide dignity to its victims, was now seen as a moral over-masking of the Bosnian 'true' realpolitik objective which was to undercut Serb legitimacy in Bosnia-Herzegovina.

The asymmetry between the crimes committed by Bosnians and those committed by Serbian forces in Bosnia was confirmed by the ICTY. Nevertheless, Serbian media continuously maintained a view as to the symmetry of crimes allegedly committed by all three parties. This falsely perceived symmetry manifested itself through the 'Civil War' thesis adopted by Serb media.

The Civil War thesis postulated that the wars in both Croatia and Bosnia were in fact a struggle between three different, *albeit equal* parties, thus relieving Serbs from their major stake in the general burden of responsibility for the carnage in the former Yugoslavia. It established a moral symmetry between crimes, matching those committed in Vukovar by Serbian forces with the ones committed by Croatian forces in Operation Storm. Victims in Srebrenica were equated with victims in Kravica and Bratunac. This Civil War thesis which assumed an equal distribution of responsibility and guilt among all three sides, led to the expectation that the ICTY would press equal charges against all three leaders in the conflict. The impunity which the Tribunal seemed to have eventually granted to the Croatian president Franjo Tuđman and Bosnian president Alija Izetbegović contrasted starkly with Slobodan Milošević's harsh indictment. To Serbian media, this merely confirmed the ICTY's alleged wholesale bias against Serbia, as it 'buried law, justice and morality'.[56]

The Tribunal's selectivity in pressing charges more so against Serbs than others, and the high-ranking positions of the Serb accused led to the tautologous conclusion that 'Serbs are guilty because they are Serbs.'[57] If *victims* in Bosnia and *veterans* in Croatia dictated the general tone of their media outlets' reports on the war crime trials back in The Hague, in Serbia these trials took on primarily political garb. As with Srebrenica, where the *political* consequences of the Tribunal's pronouncement that genocide had been committed was the main concern, so did the Tribunal's other verdicts metamorphose into the *political* battle between Serbia and the West. The ICTY – representing the latter – now evolved into Serbia's main enemy. Demonized as a 'kangaroo court' or the 'court of inquisition', Serb media maintained that the Tribunal's trials and sentencing were uniquely reserved for Serbs. This perception of the

---

[56] 'U Hagu su sahranjeni pravo, pravda i moral', *Politika*, 8 April 2008.
[57] 'Srbi krivi što su Srbi', *Večernji novosti*, 7 April 2008.

Tribunal as critically biased against Serbs, and the view that the court ICTY was in fact little more than a *political* international tool, eventually prevailed amongst most of the Serb population. The strong public condemnations of its proceedings – and the general rejection of any kind of justice it produced – followed suit.

The few consolatory legal narratives pronounced by the Tribunal, as in *Gotovina*, in *Haradinaj* and in the *Orić* trials, which all ended up with bitterly contested acquittals, merely confirmed the public sentiment in Belgrade that there was no justice for Serbian victims in the Tribunal, as noted by President Nikolić in the UNGA thematic debate on the role of international criminal justice in reconciliation, in April 2013.[58] The Serb temptation to exaggerate the crimes of acquitted Croats such as Gotovina, and reinterpret any war crime they allegedly committed into *genocide* was also salient, thus creating an abysmal rift between *perceived* and *confirmed* atrocities – between what was imagined, and what actually took place. For example, in the news on the arrest of Gotovina, as covered by the Serb national television channel RTS, the number of victims, which in the Tribunal's indictment of Gotovina stood at 150 Serbs killed during Operation Strom, was inflated to 1922 killed or disappeared, with expellees amounting to 220 000. Thus, in the Serb news coverage of *Gotovina*'s first judgment, journalists broadened the scope of crimes from what was stated in the judgment, quoting instead the victims' organization 'Veritas'. This gradual increase in the number of victims reached its climax in the Serb news coverage of Gotovina's acquittal. The television channel simply announced that in Croatia 'there were no Serbs left'.[59] To Serb media who constantly increased the quoted figures of Gotovina's Serb victims, the systematic nature of his alleged atrocities, for which he was nonetheless acquitted by the Tribunal, rendered this court's decision as tantamount to a legal pardon for what was seen as Gotovina's plan to annihilate Serbs in Croatia. In the final account, in the Serb national memory, the ICTY's charges and judgments against Serbian perpetrators were perceived as ungrounded draconian punishments, rendered down by a politically biased tribunal, which could render these allegedly biased judgments only because of Serbia's military defeat. To the false Serb psyche, the atrocities committed by Serbian perpetrators were simply no different from all other atrocities during 'the civil war'. Serbia was militarily defeated. A Serb memory of the defeated thus correspondingly emerged.

---

[58] 'Nikolić: Haški sud inkvizicija, bez pravde za srpske žrtve', *Vesti Online*, 10 April 2013, available at https://vesti-online.com/Vesti/Srbija/305367/Nikolic-Haski-sud--inkvizicija-bez-pravde-za-srpske-zrtve.

[59] 'Dnevnik', *RTS*, 16 November 2012.

TRANSNATIONAL, REFLEXIVE MEMORY OF WARS

Nevertheless, not all memory in the former Yugoslavia was nationalist. In contrast to state-based media, human rights NGOs and circles of oppositional media contributed to the view of the ICTY trials as sites of an emergent reflexive memory. Focusing primarily on denial and silencing within their own community, human rights NGOs and alternative media quickly obtained the status of 'traitors' and 'enemy agents', and they suffered constant attacks by right-wing and radical politicians and their press agents. Notwithstanding their marginalization, these reflexive memory voices were never silenced, as their proponents continued to promote a de-ethnicized vision of justice for victims throughout the former Yugoslavia.

The cynical position of a nationalist one-sided vision of justice – hypersensitive to its 'own' victims, yet cruelly indifferent towards the suffering of others – was a constant topic in writings of journalists. It is *against* this type of writing that alternative journalists such as Boris Dežulović, Dejan Anastasijević, Drago Hedl, Tanja Tagirov and others came to labour. Dežulović often disguised the ethnicity of the victims until the very end of his dispatches. This enabled him to encode the immorality of crimes as violations against human beings as such, and avoid the ethnicized victimhood, as he appealed to the universalist moral sentiments of his readers beyond their own specific ethnic community.

Several human rights NGOs in Croatia, Serbia and Bosnia-Herzegovina who were dedicated to transitional justice goals repeatedly insisted on the importance of recognition for all crimes, as they stressed the need to put the accused on trial and to punish all perpetrators, regardless of their ethnic denomination. The monitoring of domestic trials, the collection of transcripts and the issuance of yearly reports on transitional justice were only a small part of the activities undertaken by these organizations, as they tried to push up against the pro-accused inertia of their own states' institutions. A number of Croatian human rights NGOs such as Documenta, the Centre for Peace, Non-violence and Human Rights (Centar za mir, nenasilje i ljudska prava), the Civic Committee for Human Rights (Civilni odbor za ljudska prava), and the Youth Initiative for Human Rights in Croatia regularly reported about the trials in The Hague, thus reminding the public about the crimes against civilians which were not subject to prosecution. Throughout the post-war period, these organizations argued in favour of justice for victims and vigorously defended the ICTY Trial Chamber's guilty verdict in *Gotovina*, notwithstanding the routine collective denial they faced.

Rather than dissuading their efforts, the ICTY Appeals Chamber's judgment which exonerated Gotovina galvanized these pro-accountability NGOs even further, and brought them to formulate a request for *domestic* criminal prosecution. Zoran Pusić, the president of the Civic Committee for Human Rights, called for the politicians to show generosity in victory, and to abandon the politics which:

> have polluted the liberation with ideas of ethnic cleansing and actions to achieve it, to offer people who were victims of these acts words which will show that the current Croatian official policy is not insensitive to their sufferings and that these words are followed with deeds which will offer concrete help.[60]

Similarly, in Serbia, a number of NGOs voiced calls for the adoption of responsibility by the Serbian political and military *élites* for the crimes committed in Croatia, Bosnia-Herzegovina and Kosovo, as they argued in favour of the ICTY's objectivity and the soundness of its judgments. Nationalist media who interpreted the conviction of Serbian leaders by the Tribunal as an insult to the Serbian nation were confronted with reminders about the crimes committed by these leaders, and the innocent civilians they victimized, thus morally condemning these war criminals in public. In the weekly *Vreme* and the daily *Danas*, as well as on the web portal Peščanik and E-novine, readers could find victims' testimonies about the crimes and the Tribunal's corresponding judgments against the Serbian leaders who perpetrated them, in addition to the demand that *domestic* criminal guilt be ascribed to the Tribunal's convicted war criminals.

One of the 'lost opportunities' for dealing with the past in Serbia was the direct outcome of such activism by the NGO Humanitarian Law Centre. During the Milošević trial, in June 2005, the video of the cold-blooded murder of six Bosnian captives in Trnovo, in July 1995, was played in the ICTY courtroom.[61] Nataša Kandić, the executive director of the Humanitarian Law Centre was the person who actually got hold of this tape and provided it to the ICTY Prosecutor. After the video was played in the courtroom, Kandić shared the tape with the media. The news made headlines across the globe in the press and TV outlets. Equally importantly, the tape made the headlines in Serbia, leading to the immediate arrest of the perpetrators, coupled with a strong condemnation by politicians who now demanded justice for the victims. A few months later, Boris Tadić, Serbia's President, received representatives of the victims'

---

[60] Z. Pusić, 'Kako izbjeći da nas presuda ne osudi na sukob', *Sense News Agency*, 26 November 2012, available at http://www.crocc.org/hrvatski/news/print.asp?id=29455.

[61] V. Petrović, 'A Crack in the Wall of Denial: The Scorpions Video in and out of the Courtroom', in D. Zarkov and M. Glasius (eds.), *Narratives of Justice In and Out of the Courtroom: Former Yugoslavia and Beyond*, Cham: Springer, 2014, pp. 89–109.

organization 'Mothers of Srebrenica', thus further confirming the Serbian population's wholesale condemnation of that crime.

Nevertheless, nationalist media sentiments prevailed and it did not take long before Srebrenica's cold-blooded murders were transformed into an incident of no particular relevance for the Serbian war memory.[62] With that said, the Humanitarian Law Centre nevertheless continued to challenge these official narratives of denial, issuing its reports on crimes, supporting victims in their domestic war crime trials and collecting testimonies from victims.[63] Women in Black and the Helsinki Committee for Human Rights continued with their public activities against denial and forgetting, while youth organizations such as the Youth Initiative for Human Rights (YIHR) organized a number of protests and actions demanding that the crimes committed by Serbian forces be acknowledged. Upon the return of Serbian war criminals, and with their celebrity status now public,[64] activists of YIHR protested against the normalization of the entry of convicted war criminals into public life, through interruptions of their press conferences and their public discussions.[65] In Bosnia-Herzegovina, a number of human rights NGOs actively promoted a vision of a de-ethnicized transnational justice for victims.[66] Operating on a regional scale, these organizations and like-minded media created a network of institutions, NGOs, and activists which remained dedicated to the goals of dealing with the past, using the ICTY judgments as the basis for a mutually shared narrative of war. At the same time, their uncompromising struggle for the criminal punishment of the accused clashed with the ICTY judgments, especially in cases where very questionable acquittals took place (e.g. Gotovina, Stanišić and Simatović, Perišić). These acquittals, while causing much distress did not, however, diminish their generally supporting attitude towards the Tribunal.[67]

---

[62] K. Ristić, 'Our Court, Our Justice – Domestic War Crime Trials in Serbia', *Südost-Forschungen*, vol. 75(1), 2016, pp. 165–85.

[63] K. Ristić, *Medijski diskursi o domacim sudjenjima za ratne clocine*, Beograd: Fond za Humanitarno pravo, 2014.

[64] K. Ristić, 'The Media Negotiations of War Criminals and their Memoirs: The Emergence of the "ICTY Celebrity"', *International Criminal Justice Review*, vol. 28(4), 2018, pp. 391–405.

[65] O. Fridman, '"Too Young to Remember Determined Not to Forget": Memory Activists Engaging With Returning ICTY Convicts', *International Criminal Justice Review*, vol. 28(4), 2018, pp. 423–37.

[66] O. Fridman and K. Ristić, 'Online Transnational Memory Activism and Commemoration: The Case of the White Armband Day', forthcoming in A. Sierp and J. Wüstenberg (eds.), *Agency in Transnational Memory Politics*, New York: Berghahn Books.

[67] B. Ivanišević, 'Falling Out of Love With the Hague Tribunal', *BalkanInsight*, 11 June 2013, available at https://www.ceas-serbia.org/en/external/1279-falling-out-of-love-with-the-hague-tribunal.

Misinterpreted either as traitors siding with enemy propaganda, or as cold-hearted persons unable to sympathize with their own society's victims, the human rights NGOs were generally regarded as a threat to the national unity in each of the former Yugoslav societies, as opposed to what they aspired to become – human rights memory activists. In Serbia, the term 'auto-chauvinist' was coined to capture this constant preoccupation with crimes committed by one's own nation, perceived in turn as an expression of 'hatred toward one's own people'.[68] From public attacks to police arrests and court fines, these individuals were exposed to the constant tyranny of nationalist media, political and institutional actors.

CONCLUSION

In all three cases of nationalist memory, legal narratives were incorporated into the shared memory when these facilitated a positive self-image and a stable identity fabrication. The expectation that accusatory legal narratives were going to be used to confront the past did not materialize in any of the former Yugoslav Republics. Instead, actors who laboured for the deconstruction of the existent war narratives and fought for the acknowledgement of crimes and their responsibility, were attacked and later silenced with a constant proliferation of nationalist narratives of the past. The dissonance between the imagined nationalist narratives and the concurrent legal narratives that – coming from the ICTY – pertained to a much higher degree of objective truthfulness – was washed aside. The facts that were established by the Tribunal, as well as the disturbing victims-witnesses' testimonies rarely made it to the public eye in the media portrayal of the trials. Similarly, the portrayals of the accused were routinely in conformance with the strategy of discursive victory – more dominantly heroic in the winners' memory case (Croatia) and more martyr-like in the victims' memory (Bosnia), or in the memory of the defeated (Serbia). In short, a positive portrayal of war criminals across all three countries remained an equally constant feature.

Such an outcome could be interpreted as a confirmation that political power, 'controlling the means of symbolic production',[69] has remained the prevalent factor in determining national memory of the former warring parties. And yet, the failure to transfer universalist legal narratives pursuant to reflexive memory practices certainly *did not* belong exclusively to the domestic actors.

---

[68] A. Omaljev, *Discourses on Identity in 'First' and 'Other' Serbia: Social Construction of the Self and the Other in a Divided Serbia*, New York: Columbia University Press, 2016.

[69] J. C. Alexander, *Trauma: A Social Theory*, Cambridge: Polity Press, 2012, p. 36.

At the end of the day, reflexive memory was associated with transitional justice as part of a broader humanity-led discourse. Contrary to nationalism, which is naturalized in a self-evident perception of reality, especially in post-conflict communities in the midst of establishing their nation-states, reflexive memory and abstract humanity could not provide the emotional and existential bonds of nationalist discourse.

Legal proceedings are complex and multi-layered events, with different potential outcomes and ambivalent meanings. In the case of the former Yugoslavia, the potential usage of the ICTY's trials to trigger a process of dealing with the past incorporated in transnational, reflexive memory failed. The calling for moral obligations towards victims, which would follow Hannah Arendt's dictum of 'universal responsibility',[70] clashed with the political needs and realities of the receiving states. Changes in political circumstances, a generational change, or new political projects in the future, might nevertheless provoke a new wave of memory production, which would result in a substantially different, if not reconciliatory, memory of the past. For this new memory, an important source could be the ICTY archive, which, in the end, might prove to be the long lasting legacy of the Tribunal in the region.

---

[70] H. Arendt, *Essays in Understanding, 1930–1954: Formation, Exile, and Totalitarianism*, ed. J. Kohn, New York: Harcourt, Brace and Co., 2005, pp. 121–32.

8. The rise and demise of the ICC relationship with African states and the AU
Erika de Wet[*]

INTRODUCTION

In June 2014 African states adopted the so-called Malabo Protocol which intends to introduce an African Criminal Chamber (ACC) into the yet-to-be-established African Court of Justice and Human Rights.[1] Once established, the ACC will have the competence to investigate and prosecute international crimes in African member states that will *inter alia* include those states currently covered under the Statute of the International Criminal Court (ICC).[2] This author has elsewhere elaborated on the potential overlap or conflicts between the respective jurisdictions of the ACC and the ICC, while also suggesting potential legal avenues for cooperation.[3] Yet, it has to be acknowledged that the adoption of the Malabo Protocol symbolizes a severe disenchantment of African states with the ICC. The clause on immunity in particular may be interpreted as an overt attempt to undermine the ICC, as Article 46A *bis* of the Malabo Protocol determines that the ACC will not have

---

[*] This research was supported by the South African Research Chairs Initiative of the Department of Science and Technology and National Research Foundation of South Africa (Grant No. 98338).

[1] See Protocol on the Amendments to the Protocol on the Statute of the African Court of Justice and Human Rights, 27 June 2014 (hereinafter 'Malabo Protocol'), available at https://au.int/en/treaties/protocol-amendments-protocol-statute-african-court-justice-and-human-rights. This Protocol amended the Protocol on the Statute of the African Court of Justice and Human Rights of 1 July 2008, available at https://au.int/en/treaties/protocol-statute-african-court-justice-and-human-rights.

[2] Malabo Protocol, Art. 28A.

[3] E. de Wet, 'Concurrent Jurisdiction of the International Criminal Court and the African Criminal Chamber in the Case of Concurrent Referrals', in C. Jalloh, K. Clarke and V. Nmehielle (eds.), *The African Court of Justice and Human and People's Rights*, Cambridge: Cambridge University Press, 2019.

jurisdiction over serving heads of state or senior state officials.[4] This sweeping acknowledgement of immunity based on official capacity is in stark contrast to Article 27 of the ICC Statute, which states the exact opposite.[5]

An attempted side-lining of the ICC may also be deduced from the complementarity principle enshrined in the Malabo Protocol. Article 46H of the Malabo Protocol (like Art. 17 of the ICC Statute) acknowledges that prosecutions should first and foremost be undertaken by the national courts of state parties that have jurisdiction over the crime, unless they are unwilling or unable to do so. In addition, Article 46H of the Malabo Protocol provides for complementarity in relation to the courts of the African regional economic communities (RECs), where those are specifically provided for.[6] Thus, while Article 46H of the Malabo Protocol envisages cooperation with regional courts on the basis of the complementarity principle, it does not foresee (at least not explicitly) such cooperation with the ICC.

While a prominent manifestation of the deteriorating relationship between African states and the ICC, the adoption of the Malabo Protocol was not the only instance. In fact, several events in recent years suggest that the African Union (AU) and several of its member states are in practice increasingly rejecting cooperation with the ICC, even though thirty-three African states

---

[4] Malabo Protocol, Art. 46A *bis* determines: 'No charges shall be commenced or continued before the Court against any serving AU Head of State or Government or anybody acting or entitled to act in such a capacity, or other senior state officials based on their functions, during their tenure of office.'

[5] Art. 27(1) of the Rome Statute of the International Criminal Court (17 July 1998, UN Doc. A/CONF.183/9) determines: 'This Statute shall apply equally to all persons without any distinction based on official capacity. In particular, official capacity as a Head of State or Government, a member of a government or parliament, an elected representative or a government official shall in no case exempt a person from criminal responsibility under this Statute, nor shall it, in and of itself, constitute a ground for reduction of sentence.' See also M. Ssenyonjo, 'State Withdrawal Notifications from the Rome Statute of the International Criminal Court: South Africa, Burundi and The Gambia', *Criminal Law Forum*, vol. 29(1), 2018, p. 113.

[6] Art. 46H of Malabo Protocol reads: '1. The jurisdiction of the Court shall be complementary to that of the National Courts, and to the Courts of the Regional Economic Communities where specifically provided for by the Communities. 2. The Court shall determine that a case is inadmissible where (*a*) the case is being investigated or prosecuted by a state which has jurisdiction over it, unless the state is unwilling or unable to carry out the investigation or prosecution; (*b*) the case has been investigated by a state which has jurisdiction over it and the state has decided not to prosecute the person concerned, unless the decision resulted from the unwillingness or inability of the state to prosecute; (c) the person concerned has already been tried for conduct which is the subject of the complaint . . .'.

remain parties to the ICC Statute.[7] Since 2009 various African member states have refused to arrest and surrender President Bashir from Sudan when he visited these countries, despite an arrest warrant issued by the ICC in 2009,[8] subsequent to the 2005 referral of the situation in Darfur to the ICC by the United Nations Security Council (UNSC) under Chapter VII of the United Nations Charter.[9] At the time of writing, these states included Chad, Kenya, Djibouti, Malawi, Nigeria, Democratic Republic of the Congo (DRC), South Africa and Uganda.[10] These acts of rebellion essentially gave effect to repeated decisions since 2013 by the AU that its member states should not cooperate with the ICC in relation to the surrender of sitting heads of state.[11] Moreover,

---

[7] For the current status of ratification of the ICC Statute, see https://asp.icc-cpi.int/en_menus/asp/states%20parties/pages/the%20states%20parties%20to%20the%20rome%20statute.aspx.

[8] ICC Pre-Trial Chamber 1, Decision on the Prosecution's Application for a Warrant of Arrest against Omar Hassan Ahmad Al Bashir, 4 March 2009, *Prosecutor v. Omar Hassan Ahmad Al Bashir*, ICC-02/05-01/09, available at https://www.icc-cpi.int/CourtRecords/CR2009_01517.PDF.

[9] See UN Doc. S/RES/1993, 31 March 2005, at para. 1.

[10] In two decisions of 12 and 13 December 2011 respectively, Pre-Trial Chamber I rebuked Malawi and Chad for failing to comply with the cooperation requests issued by the ICC to arrest and surrender Omar Al-Bashir during his visits to their territories (ICC-02/05-01/09-139 and ICC-02/05-01/09-1). Pre-Trial Chamber II also issued a second decision on non-compliance in relation to Chad on 26 March 2013 (ICC-02/05-01/09). See also Pre-Trial Chamber II, Decision on the Co-operation of the Democratic Republic of the Congo regarding Omar Al-Bashir's Arrest and Surrender to the Court, *The Prosecutor v. Omar Hassan Ahmad Al Bashir* (ICC-02/05-01/09-195), 9 April 2014, at para. 29 (*Al Bashir (DRC)* decision); Pre-Trial Chamber II, Decision following the Prosecutor's Request for an Order Further Clarifying that the Republic of South Africa is Under the Obligation to Immediately Arrest and Surrender Omar Al Bashir, *The Prosecutor v. Omar Hassan Ahmad Al Bashir* (ICC-02/0501/09), 13 June 2015 (*Al Bashir (South Africa)* decision); and Pre-Trial Chamber II, Request by the Court for the Arrest and Surrender of Omar Al-Bashir, *The Prosecutor v. Omar Hassan Ahmad Al-Bashir* (ICC-02/05-01/09), 6 July 2017 (*Al Bashir (South Africa II)* decision); Pre-Trial Chamber II, Decision under Article 87(7) of the Rome Statute on the Non-Compliance by Jordan with the Request by the Court for the Arrest and Surrender or Omar Al-Bashir, *The Prosecutor v. Omar Hassan Ahmad Al-Bashir*, 11 December 2017 (ICC-02/05-01/09). See also F. Boehme, '"We Chose Africa": South Africa and the Regional Politics of Cooperation with the International Criminal Court', *International Journal of Transitional Justice*, vol. 11(1), 2017, p. 51.

[11] See AU, Assembly/AU/Dec. 243-267 (XIII) Rev.1 Assembly/AU/Decl.1-5(XIII), 1–3 July 2009, Doc. Assembly/AU/13(XIII), at para. 10, available at https://au.int/sites/default/files/decisions/9560-assembly_en_1_3_july_2009_auc_thirteenth_ordinary_session_decisions_declarations_message_congratulations_motion_0.pdf; AU, Assembly/AU/Dec.296(XV), 27 July 2010, Doc. Assembly/AU/10(XV), at para. 5, available at https://archive.au.int/collect/auassemb/import/English/Assembly%20AU%20Dec%20296%20(XV)%20_E.pdf; AU, Assembly/AU/

the AU has embarked on a strategy of mass withdrawal from the ICC, as *inter alia* reflected by the creation of the Open-Ended Ministerial Committee in January 2016, the purpose of which was to develop a comprehensive strategy for collective withdrawal.[12]

While this strategy has evoked mixed responses among African states,[13] Burundi has since withdrawn from the ICC Statute in accordance with Article 127(1) of the ICC Statute.[14] In 2016 South Africa and The Gambia also submitted notifications of withdrawal from the ICC Statute to the United

---

Dec.391-415(XVIII) Assembly/AU/Res.1(XVIII) Assembly/AU/Decl.1-3(XVIII), 29–30 April 2012, Doc. EX.CL/710(XX), at paras. 6 and 8, available at https://au.int/sites/default/files/decisions/9649-assembly_au_dec_391_-_415_xviii_e.pdf; AU, Ext/Assembly/AU/Dec/1, 12 October 2013, at para. 2.3, available at http://www.iccnow.org/documents/Ext_Assembly_AU_Dec_Decl_12Oct2013.pdf. See also Boehme, '"We Chose Africa": South Africa and the Regional Politics of Cooperation with the International Criminal Court', p. 51. In January 2018, the Assembly further expressed its support for requesting the UNGA to request an advisory opinion from the ICJ 'on the question of immunities of a Head of State and Government and other Senior Officials as it relates to the relationship between Articles 27 and 98 and the obligations of States Parties under International Law'. See AU, Assembly/AU/Dec.672(XXX), 28–29 January 2017, at para. 5(ii), available at https://au.int/en/decisions/decisions-declarations-and-resolution-assembly-union-thirtieth-ordinary-session.

[12] AU, Assembly/AU/Dec.588-604(XXVI) Assembly/AU/Decl.1-2(XXVI) Assembly/AU/Res.1(XXVI), 30–31 January 2016, Doc. EX.CL/952(XXVIII), at para. 10(iv), available at https://au.int/sites/default/files/decisions/29514-assembly_au_dec_588_-_604_xxvi_e.pdf; G. Naldi and K. D. Magliveras, 'The International Criminal Court and the African Union: A Problematic Relationship', in C. Chenor Jalloh and I. Bantekas (eds.), *The International Criminal Court and Africa*, Oxford: Oxford University Press, 2017, pp. 136–7; Ssenyonjo, 'State Withdrawal Notifications from the Rome Statute of the International Criminal Court', p. 66.

[13] In January 2017, 16 AU member states formally expressed reservations about the strategy. These were Benin, Botswana, Burkina Faso, Cape Verde, Côte d'Ivoire, The Gambia, Lesotho, Liberia, Madagascar, Malawi, Mozambique, Nigeria, Senegal, Tanzania, Tunisia and Zambia. See AU, Assembly/AU/Dec.621-641(XXVIII) Assembly/AU/Decl. 1-2(XXVIII) Assembly/AU/Res.1-2(XXVIII) Assembly/AU/Motion(XXVIII), 30–31 January 2017, Doc. EX.CL/1006(XXX), at para. 6 and notes 1–2. See also Ssenyonjo, 'State Withdrawal Notifications from the Rome Statute of the International Criminal Court', p. 105.

[14] Art. 127(1) of the ICC Statute determines: 'A state party may, by written notification addressed to the Secretary-General of the United Nations, withdraw from this Statute. The withdrawal shall take effect one year after the date of receipt of the notification, unless the notification specifies a later date.' On 27 October 2017, Burundi's withdrawal from the ICC Statute took effect. See AFP, 'Burundi Becomes First Nation to Leave International Criminal Court', *The Guardian*, 28 October 2017, available at https://www.theguardian.com/law/2017/oct/28/burundi-becomes-first-nation-to-leave-international-criminal-court. Burundi's notice of withdrawal is available at https://treaties.un.org/Doc./publication/cn/2016/cn.805.2016-eng.pdf.

Nations (UN) Secretary-General,[15] but subsequently withdrew their respective notifications of withdrawal before these could take effect.[16] Yet, in South Africa this was not as a result of any change in policy by the government or ruling party. Instead, it resulted from a decision of the South African High Court (Gauteng Division, Pretoria) according to which the executive had acted unconstitutionally by not seeking prior parliamentary approval for its decision to withdraw.[17] While honouring the High Court's decision by revoking the notice of withdrawal in March 2017, the (then) Zuma administration prepared draft legislation that would facilitate withdrawal.[18] While the draft legislation has since been introduced for debate in Parliament in 2018, it is unlikely that the debate will be concluded before some time in 2019. Other governments that have in principle decided to leave the ICC include Kenya and Namibia, although these states have not yet acted on these decisions.[19] These steps towards withdrawal have been accompanied by verbal attacks by individual African high-level officials that ranged from depicting the ICC as an 'abomi-

---

[15] Declaratory Statement by the Republic of South Africa on the decision to withdraw from the Rome Statute of the International Criminal Court, 19 October 2016, available at https://treaties.un.org/doc/publication/cn/2016/cn.786.2016-eng.pdf; Notice of Withdrawal of The Gambia, 10 November 2016, available at https://treaties.un.org/doc/publication/cn/2016/cn.862.2016-eng.pdf. The notifications of withdrawal were welcomed and supported by the AU, Assembly/AU/Dec.621-641(XXVIII) Assembly/AU/Decl. 1-2(XXVIII) Assembly/AU/Res.1-2(XXVIII) Assembly/AU/Motion(XXVIII), 30–31 January 2017, Assembly/AU/Dec.622(XXVIII), available at https://au.int/sites/default/files/decisions/32520-sc19553_e_original_-_assembly_decisions_621-641_-_xxviii.pdf), at para. 6. See again Ssenyonjo, 'State Withdrawal Notifications from the Rome Statute of the International Criminal Court', p. 64.

[16] For The Gambia, see https://treaties.un.org/doc/Publication/CN/2017/CN.62.2017-Eng.pdf; for South Africa, see https://treaties.un.org/doc/publication/CN/2017/CN.121.2017-Eng.pdf.

[17] South Africa High Court (Gauteng Division, Pretoria), Order of 22 February 2017, *Democratic Alliance v. Minister of International Relations and Cooperation and Others (Council for the Advancement of the South African Constitution Intervening)*, Case No. 83145/2016, *ZAGPPHC*, 2017, p. 53, 017 (3) SA 212 (GP).

[18] Implementation of the Rome Statute of the International Criminal Court Act Repeal Bill, 2016, *Government Gazette*, No. 40403, 3 November 2016, available at http://www.justice.gov.za/legislation/bills/2016-b23-RomeStatuteActRepeal.pdf.

[19] Naldi and Magliveras, 'The International Criminal Court and the African Union: A Problematic Relationship', p. 137. See the discussion below.

nation',[20] to a 'bunch of useless people',[21] to a 'political instrument targeting Africa and Africans'.[22]

These sentiments are a far cry from the support the ICC enjoyed among African states before and during the Rome conference of July 1998 when the ICC Statute was adopted. Not only did they endorse the ICC enthusiastically, but African states also played a decisive role during the negotiations.[23] The first state to ratify the ICC Statute was Senegal and the first Review Conference of the ICC Statute was hosted in Uganda in 2010.[24] As far as domestic developments in Africa were concerned, South Africa, which ratified the ICC Statute in November 2000, was particularly pro-active and became the first African country to implement the ICC Statute in its municipal law in 2002.[25] In so doing, South Africa introduced a universal jurisdiction clause that extended beyond the requirements of the ICC Statute and which has formed the basis

---

[20] I. Shinovene, 'Cabinet Affirms ICC Withdrawal', *The Namibian,* 24 November 2015, available at https://www.namibian.com.na/index.php?page=archive-read&id=144660; Naldi and Magliveras, 'The International Criminal Court and the African Union: A Problematic Relationship', p. 137.

[21] 'Walkout at Ugandan President's Inauguration over ICC Remarks', *The Guardian*, 12 May 2016, available at https://www.theguardian.com/world/2016/may/12/walkout-at-ugandan-presidents-inauguration-over-icc-remarks; Naldi and Magliveras, 'The International Criminal Court and the African Union: A Problematic Relationship', p. 137.

[22] S. Hickey, 'African Union Says ICC Should Not Prosecute Sitting Leaders', *The Guardian*, 12 October 2013, available at https://www.theguardian.com/world/2013/oct/12/african-union-icc-kenyan-president. See again Naldi and Magliveras, 'The International Criminal Court and the African Union: A Problematic Relationship', p. 115; and Boehme, '"We Chose Africa": South Africa and the Regional Politics of Cooperation with the International Criminal Court', p. 63.

[23] B. S. Brown, 'The International Criminal Court in Africa: Impartiality, Politics, Complementarity and Brexit', *Temple International and Comparative Law Journal*, vol. 31(1), 2017, p. 145, p. 164.

[24] M. Tadesse Tessama and M. Vesper-Gräske, *Africa, the African Union and the International Criminal Court: Irreparable Fissures?*, Brussels: Torkel Opsahl Academic E-Publisher, Policy Brief Series No. 56, 2016, available at http://www.toaep.org/pbs-pdf/56-tadesse-graeske; Brown, 'The International Criminal Court in Africa: Impartiality, Politics, Complementarity and Brexit', p. 164; Boehme, '"We Chose Africa": South Africa and the Regional Politics of Cooperation with the International Criminal Court', p. 62.

[25] The Implementation of the Rome Statute of the International Criminal Court 2002, Act 27 of 2002, quoted by Ssenyonjo, 'State Withdrawal Notifications from the Rome Statute of the International Criminal Court', p. 65 and Boehme, '"We Chose Africa": South Africa and the Regional Politics of Cooperation with the International Criminal Court', p. 62.

of national prosecutions.[26] The government at the time thus reflected a very positive stance towards the ICC.

The question arising is how it was possible that a predominantly positive relationship between the newly created AU, its member states and the ICC could deteriorate so dramatically within the span of a decade. Stated differently, what motived the region with the largest group of ICC members to rebel openly against the ICC in a tone that is unusually unbecoming in diplomatic circles? The following sections attempt to provide insight into some of the key events, the combined effect of which significantly contributed to this downward spiral.

THE HISTORY OF ALIENATION

As is well known, all ICC cases pursued beyond the preliminary investigation stage have thus far originated from Africa. While some cases resulted from self-referrals at a time when the ICC was still in good standing on the continent,[27] others were triggered by UNSC referrals of African situations to the ICC, or by the Prosecutor's *ex proprio motu* investigations. These notably resulted in indictments of a sitting head of state (President Bashir from Sudan) and a future head of state (President Kenyatta from Kenya). The subsequent analysis will reveal that the context in which the Bashir and Kenyatta indictments developed played into the hands of those African leaders that had a lot to gain from the weakening of the ICC.[28]

On a continent where sensitivities towards any form of neo-colonialism remain palpable, the timing and modalities of these indictments assisted some African leaders in portraying the ICC as a neo-colonial instrument, funded by Western powers for the purpose of controlling African leaders and their people.[29] In essence, various African politicians who personally had much to fear from ICC indictments were provided with arguments for gaining or retaining political power domestically.[30] The distrust that was created within African

---

[26] The Implementation of the Rome Statute of the International Criminal Court 2002, sect. 4(3)(c).

[27] Brown, 'The International Criminal Court in Africa: Impartiality, Politics, Complementarity and Brexit', p. 164.

[28] Ibid.

[29] Ibid., pp. 146 and 164; O. Chinedu Okafor and U. Ngwaba, 'The International Criminal Court as a "Transitional Justice" Mechanism in Africa: Some Critical Reflections', *The International Journal of Transitional Justice*, vol. 9(1), 2015, pp. 101–2.

[30] See M. du Plessis, T. Maluwa and A. O'Reilly, 'Africa and the International Court', *Chatham House International Law*, No. 1, 2013, pp. 1–13, p. 3,

societies towards the ICC was further aggravated by the fact that self-referrals have thus far resulted exclusively in the prosecution of international crimes by members of rebel (opposition) groups.[31] In certain circles, the office of the ICC Prosecutor was perceived as assisting incumbent leaders in ridding themselves of political opponents, while alleged perpetrators on the side of the government were not investigated.

THE SELECTIVE REFERRAL POLICY OF THE UNSC

Article 13(b) of the ICC Statute facilitates referrals by the UNSC under Chapter VII of the United Nations Charter to the ICC.[32] Through such referrals, states that are not parties to the ICC statute can be brought under the jurisdiction of the ICC.[33] Thus far, the UNSC has referred only two situations to the ICC, namely, that of Darfur (in Sudan) in Resolution 1593 (2005)[34] and Libya in Resolution 1970 (2011).[35] With the vision of hindsight, the UNSC referral of the situation in Darfur, which paved the way for the 2009 and 2010 ICC arrest warrants for crimes against humanity, war crimes and genocide against President Bashir,[36] marked the turning point in the relationship between the

---

available at https://www.chathamhouse.org/sites/default/files/public/Research/International%20Law/0713pp_iccafrica.pdf. They noted that early signs of alienation were already emerging in 2000, when Belgium issued an arrest warrant for the then Minister of Foreign Affairs of the DRC on the basis of universal jurisdiction. See ICJ, Judgment of 14 February 2002, *Arrest Warrant of 11 April 2000 (Democratic Republic of the Congo v. Belgium)*, *ICJ Reports* 2002, p. 3. Similarly, the 2008 execution of a French arrest warrant in Germany vis-à-vis the Chief of Protocol to the President of Rwanda in connection with the 1994 genocide was depicted by the Rwandan President as an abuse of universal jurisdiction by European states. See M. Tran, 'Rwandan President Kagame Threatens French Nationals with Arrest', *The Guardian*, 12 November 2008, available at https://www.theguardian.com/world/2008/nov/12/rwanda-france.

[31] Boehme, '"We Chose Africa": South Africa and the Regional Politics of Cooperation with the International Criminal Court', p. 63.

[32] The cooperation between the UNSC and the ICC in matters of referral is further regulated by Art. 17 of the Negotiated Relationship Agreement between the International Criminal Court and the United Nations, 4 October 2004, available at https://treaties.un.org/doc/Publication/UNTS/Volume%202283/II-1272.pdf.

[33] See *The Prosecutor v. Omar Hassan Ahmad Al Bashir*.

[34] UNSC Res. 1593, 31 March 2005, at paras. 1 ff.

[35] UNSC Res. 1970, 6 February 2011, at paras. 4 ff. See extensively A. Ciampi, 'Legal Rules, Policy Choices and Political Realities in the Functioning of the Cooperation Regime of the International Criminal Court', in O. Bekou and D. J. Birkett (eds.), *Cooperation and the International Criminal Court: Perspectives from Theory and Practice*, Leiden and Boston: Brill Nijhoff, 2016, pp. 7–57, p. 21.

[36] See ICC Pre-Trial Chamber 1, Decision on the Prosecution's Application for a Warrant of Arrest against Omar Hassan Ahmad Al Bashir.

AU, several of its member states and the ICC.[37] Within the AU, several states took the position that the indictment of a sitting head of state undermined internationally supported regional efforts to negotiate peace in Sudan.[38] Also, the fact that the UNSC thus far had only referred situations in Africa to the ICC was criticized for representing double standards and bias towards Africa.[39] In addition, the arrest warrants triggered a protracted debate about whether UNSC referrals indeed placed non-member states under the jurisdiction of the ICC in a manner that also extinguishes immunities.[40]

When considering these criticisms, there are important qualifications to be kept in mind. African members in the UNSC did not oppose the Darfur and Libyan referrals. None of the African members in the UNSC voted against the UNSC referrals in Darfur and Libya. In fact, in the case of Darfur, Benin and Tanzania voted in favour of the referral, while Algeria abstained.[41] In relation to Libya, all the African members at the time (South Africa, Gabon and

---

[37] C. Chenor Jalloh, 'Introduction', in Jalloh and Bantekas (eds.), *The International Criminal Court and Africa*, p. 1; Brown, 'The International Criminal Court in Africa: Impartiality, Politics, Complementarity and Brexit', p. 164; du Plessis et al., 'Africa and the International Court', p. 4.

[38] Jalloh, 'Introduction', pp. 2–3. The arrest warrant against the then Libyan President Gaddafi on 27 June 2011 was also not well received within the AU, which would have preferred a negotiated exit of the ex-leader. See ICC Pre-Trial Chamber I, Decision of 27 June 2011, *Warrant of Arrest for Muammar Mohammed Abu Minyar Gaddafi*, Case No. ICC-01/11, available at https://www.icc-cpi.int/CourtRecords/CR2011_08351.PDF; see also du Plessis et al., 'Africa and the International Court', p. 4.

[39] Ssenyonjo, 'State Withdrawal Notifications from the Rome Statute of the International Criminal Court', p. 73. See also H. G. van der Wilt, 'Universal Jurisdiction under Attack. An Assessment of African Misgivings towards International Criminal Justice as Administered by Western States', *Journal of International Criminal Justice*, vol. 9(5), 2011, p. 1043; H. G. van der Wilt, 'Complementarity Jurisdiction (Article 46H)', in G. Werle and M. Vormbaum (eds.), *The African Criminal Court: A Commentary on the Malabo Protocol*, The Hague: Asser Press; Heidelberg: Springer-Verlag, 2017, p. 187.

[40] For different views in literature, see *inter alia*, E. de Wet, 'The Implications of President Al-Bashir's Visit to South Africa for International and Domestic Law', *Journal of International Criminal Justice*, vol. 13(5), 2015, p. 1049; D. Tladi, 'The Duty on South Africa to Arrest and Surrender President Al-Bashir under South African and International Law: A Perspective from International Law', *Journal of International Criminal Justice*, vol. 13(5), 2015, p. 1027.

[41] UNSC Press Release, Security Council Refers Situation in Darfur, Sudan, to Prosecutor of the International Criminal Court, 31 March 2005, UN Doc. SC/8351, available at https://www.un.org/press/en/2005/sc8351.doc.htm; Ssenyonjo, 'State Withdrawal Notifications from the Rome Statute of the International Criminal Court', p. 76.

Nigeria) voted in favour.[42] Moreover, the Libyan referral occurred at a time when the Bashir arrest warrant had already been issued and African states were aware of the fact that similar indictments may result from the Libyan referral. African states, therefore, have been co-responsible for the African referrals that paved the way for indictments against high-level state officials.[43]

Nonetheless, the selective UNSC referral policy has delegitimized the ICC in the eyes of many in Africa.[44] Through its relationship with the UNSC, as embodied in Article 13(b) of the ICC Statute, the ICC is perceived as supporting the manner in which the UNSC exposes atrocities in Africa, while ignoring them elsewhere.[45] One pertinent example is the Russian and Chinese veto in May 2014 against a draft UNSC resolution that would have referred the situation in Syria to the ICC.[46] In so doing, they defied all other thirteen members of the UNSC, as well as sixty-five other states which supported the referral.[47] This example is illustrative of the extent to which permanent UNSC members will go to shield regimes with which they have close ties. While in the case of Syria the Assad regime was shielded in particular by Russia with which it has had long-standing ties, all states with strong alliances with any of the five permanent UNSC members are likely to profit from similar preferential treatment.[48]

The negative impact on the credibility of the ICC due to this reality is further aggravated by the fact that three of the five permanent UNSC members (China,

---

[42] UN Doc. SC/10187/REV.1.

[43] In fact, the AU itself has also recommended that those with the greatest responsibility for the atrocities at the highest level should be brought to account. Final Report of the African Union Commission of Inquiry on South Sudan, 15 October 2014, at para. 1142, available at http://www.peaceau.org/uploads/auciss.final.report.pdf. See also Ssenyonjo, 'State Withdrawal Notifications from the Rome Statute of the International Criminal Court', p. 77.

[44] Ssenyonjo, 'State Withdrawal Notifications from the Rome Statute of the International Criminal Court', p. 75.

[45] Declaratory Statement by the Republic of South Africa on the decision to withdraw from the Rome Statute of the International Criminal Court; Ssenyonjo, 'State Withdrawal Notifications from the Rome Statute of the International Criminal Court', p. 72.

[46] UN Doc. S/2014/348, 22 May 2014, at para. 2; UNSC Press Release, Referral of Syria to International Criminal Court Fails as Negative Votes Prevent Security Council from Adopting Draft Resolution, 22 May 2014, UN Doc. SC/11407, available at https://www.un.org/press/en/2014/sc11407.doc.htm.

[47] In February 2013, the Independent Commission of Inquiry on the Syrian Arab Republic, appointed by the UN Human Rights Council, proposed that the ICC was the appropriate venue to prosecute alleged international crimes in Syria. See UN Doc. A/HRC/22/59, at paras. 126–7.

[48] Ssenyonjo, 'State Withdrawal Notifications from the Rome Statute of the International Criminal Court', pp. 75 and 82; Naldi and Magliveras, 'The International Criminal Court and the African Union: A Problematic Relationship', p. 118.

Russia and the United States) have neither acceded to the ICC Statute,[49] nor are they likely to do so.[50] Stated differently, some of the very same states whose votes are decisive in bringing (other) non-state parties under the jurisdiction of the ICC have made it clear that they will not accept such jurisdiction themselves.[51] The ICC's choice to indict President Bashir subsequent to Resolution 1593 (2005), while it is yet to indict sitting high-level state officials outside the African continent, also strengthened the perception (whether rightly or wrongly) that the Court is the willing vehicle of a biased UNSC.[52] Some African political leaders have not hesitated to play into these inconsistencies as a reason for withdrawing from the ICC. For example, in its 2016 notice of withdrawal, the South African government stated that the ICC had lost credibility due to the perceived focus of the ICC on African states, notwithstanding clear evidence of violations by others outside the continent who also committed international crimes.[53] The Gambia's information minister at the time, Sheriff Baba Bojang, for his part described the ICC as an 'International Caucasian Court for the persecution and humiliation of people of colour, especially Africans'.[54]

The AU has further played into the negative ICC sentiments resulting from the UNSC's unwillingness to hear or act upon the AU's request to defer the proceedings against President Bashir as provided for in Article 16 of the ICC Statute.[55] This article allows the UNSC to defer a particular investigation or

---

[49] A point raised specifically in the South African Declaratory Statement.

[50] Ssenyonjo, 'State Withdrawal Notifications from the Rome Statute of the International Criminal Court', p. 81.

[51] Ibid., p. 82.

[52] Any investigations and other proceedings (including the issuing of arrest warrants) pursuant to UNSC referrals are undertaken and determined by the ICC itself in accordance with its Statute and the Rules of Procedure and Evidence. See also Ssenyonjo, 'State Withdrawal Notifications from the Rome Statute of the International Criminal Court', p. 77.

[53] South African Declaratory Statement; Ssenyonjo, 'State Withdrawal Notifications from the Rome Statute of the International Criminal Court', p. 72.

[54] J. Bavier, 'Gambia Announces Withdrawal from International Criminal Court', *Reuters*, 26 October 2016, available at https://www.reuters.com/article/us-gambia-icc-idUSKCN12P335; President Museveni of Uganda described the ICC as a 'biased instrument of post-colonial hegemony'; see F. Makana, 'Ugandan President Yoweri Museveni Lashes Out at ICC, Wants Africa to Pull Out', *Standard*, 13 December 2014, available at https://www.standardmedia.co.ke/article/2000144601/ugandan-president-yoweri-museveni-lashes-out-at-icc-wants-africa-to-pull-out. See also D. Miriri, 'Uganda's Museveni Calls on African Nations to Quit the ICC', *Reuters*, 12 December 2014; Ssenyonjo, 'State Withdrawal Notifications from the Rome Statute of the International Criminal Court', p. 75.

[55] Ssenyonjo, 'State Withdrawal Notifications from the Rome Statute of the International Criminal Court', pp. 91–2.

prosecution for one year, where the UNSC has requested the ICC to do so in accordance with Chapter VII of the UN Charter.[56] Since the office of the ICC Prosecutor indicated its intent to request an arrest warrant against President Bashir of Sudan in 2008, the AU has on several occasions called upon the UNSC to apply Article 16 of the ICC Statute and defer the proceedings initiated by the ICC for a period of twelve months.[57] The UNSC has remained unresponsive to these requests, even though it has also remained unwilling to provide the necessary political and financial support or follow-up measures for ensuring the execution of the Bashir arrest warrant.[58] The dissatisfaction within the AU with the UNSC's response spilt over into the ICC. The AU called on its member states not to cooperate with the ICC in relation to the arrest and surrender of the Sudanese President,[59] motivating its stance with the fact that the indictment undermined peace efforts in Darfur.[60] The upshot of this conflict between the AU, the UNSC and the ICC was that President Bashir has been travelling openly across and beyond Africa, in defiance of UNSC Resolution 1593 (2005) and the resulting indictment.[61]

---

[56] Art. 16 of the ICC Statute reads: 'No investigation or prosecution may be commenced or proceeded with under this Statute for a period of 12 months after the Security Council, in a resolution adopted under Chapter VII of the Charter of the United Nations, has requested the Court to that effect; that request may be renewed by the Council under the same conditions.'

[57] See *inter alia* AU PSC/MIN/Comm (CXLII), 21 July 2008, at paras. 3 ff., available at http://www.iccnow.org/documents/AU_142-communique-eng.pdf; AU PSC/PR/Comm (CLXXV) Rev. 1, 5 March 2009, at paras. 4 ff., available at http://www.peaceau.org/uploads/iccarrestwarranteng.pdf; and AU Assembly/AU/Dec.334(XVI), 30-31 January 2011, Doc. EX.CL/639(XVIII), at para. 3, available at https://au.int/sites/default/files/decisions/9645-assembly_en_30_31_january_2011_auc_assembly_africa.pdf. See also M. Ssenyonjo, *op. cit.*, *supra* note 5, p. 92.

[58] Art. 115 of the ICC Statute provides for the possibility that the UN contribute to the ICC's expenses incurred due to UNSC referrals. See also ICC Twenty-Fourth Report of the Prosecutor of the International Criminal Court to the United Nations Security Council Pursuant to UNSC Resolution 1593 (2005), 13 December 2016, available at https://www.icc-cpi.int/itemsDocuments/161213-otp-rep-24-darfur_Eng.pdf, at para. 36. See also Ssenyonjo, 'State Withdrawal Notifications from the Rome Statute of the International Criminal Court'; Naldi and Magliveras, 'The International Criminal Court and the African Union: A Problematic Relationship', p. 115.

[59] See *inter alia* AU Assembly/AU/Dec.245(XIII) Rev.1; AU Assembly/AU/13(XIII), paras. 9–10; Ssenyonjo, 'State Withdrawal Notifications from the Rome Statute of the International Criminal Court', p. 92.

[60] See AU Assembly/AU/Dec.245(XIII) Rev.1, Doc. Assembly/AU/13(XIII), at para. 3; see also South African Declaratory Statement. See also du Plessis et al., 'Africa and the International Court', p. 11.

[61] Ssenyonjo, 'State Withdrawal Notifications from the Rome Statute of the International Criminal Court', p. 74; see also Naldi and Magliveras, 'The International Criminal Court and the African Union: A Problematic Relationship', p. 115.

Requests for a UNSC deferral in terms of Article 16 of the ICC Statute were also made in relation to the investigations and prosecutions concerning Kenya's President Kenyatta and Deputy President Ruto.[62] In these instances, the indictments resulted from *ex proprio motu* investigations initiated by the ICC Prosecutor, as will be illuminated in the following section. As in the case of President Bashir, the requests for deferral could not muster sufficient support within the UNSC and were also strongly contested by civil society groups.[63] In the wake of the UNSC's unwillingness to engage with the AU on deferring the investigations and prosecutions of President Bashir, President Kenyatta and Deputy President Ruto, South Africa (on behalf of the AU) unsuccessfully suggested to amend the ICC Statute, so as to allow the UN General Assembly to invoke the deferral clause in Article 16 of the ICC Statute when the UNSC failed to do so.[64]

Furthermore, Kenya for its part lobbied the East African Legislative Assembly in April 2012 to request the ICC 'to transfer the case of the accused four Kenyans facing trial in respect of the aftermath of the Kenyan general elections to the East African Court of Justice'.[65] In practice, any such transfer

---

[62] Letter dated 23 March 2011 from the Permanent Representative of Kenya to the United Nations addressed to the President of the Security Council, 29 March 2011, UN Doc. S/2011/201, available at https://www.securitycouncilreport.org/atf/cf/%7B65BFCF9B-6D27-4E9C-8CD3-CF6E4FF96FF9%7D/Kenya%20S%202011%20201.pdf; M. Ssenyonjo, 'The Implementation of the *Proprio Motu* Authority of the Prosecutor in Africa', in Jalloh and Bantekas (eds.), *The International Criminal Court and Africa*, p. 54. See *inter alia* AU Assembly/AU/Dec.419(xix), 15–16 July 2012, Doc. EX.CL/731(XXI), at para. 4, available at https://au.int/sites/default/files/decisions/9651-assembly_au_dec_416-449_xix_e_final.pdf; AU Ext/Assembly/AU/Dec.1, October 2013, at para. 10(ix), available at http://www.iccnow.org/documents/Ext_Assembly_AU_Dec_Decl_12Oct2013.pdf; UNSC Press Release, UNSC Draft Resolution Seeking Deferral of Kenyan Leaders' Trial Fails to Win Adoption, with 7 Voting in Favour, 8 Abstaining, 15 November 2013, UN Doc. SC/11176, available at https://www.un.org/press/en/2013/sc11176.Doc.htm.

[63] C. Maina Peter, 'Fighting Impunity: African States and the International Criminal Court', in E. A. Ankumah (ed.), *The International Criminal Court: One Decade On*, Cambridge: Intersentia, 2016, p. 25, p. 30.

[64] Ssenyonjo, 'State Withdrawal Notifications from the Rome Statute of the International Criminal Court', p. 94.

[65] See East African Community, East African Legislative Assembly, Resolution of the Assembly Seeking the EAC Council of Ministers to Implore the International Criminal Court to Transfer the Case of the Accused Four Kenyans Facing Trial in Respect of the Aftermath of the 2007 Kenyan General Elections to the East African Court of Justice and to Reinforce the Treaty Provisions, 26 April 2012, available at http://www.eala.org/Documents/view/seeking-to-try-kenya-2007-general-elections-aftermath-accused-persons-at-ea; see also Ssenyonjo, 'State Withdrawal Notifications from the Rome Statute of the International Criminal Court', p. 55.

is highly unlikely, despite the support of the East African Community of Heads of State on 28 April 2012 to extend the mandate of the East African Court of Justice (EACJ) to include international crimes.[66] Not only has the EACJ not yet been constituted to facilitate criminal trials,[67] but any future granting of criminal jurisdiction would be unlikely to have a retroactive effect.[68] Furthermore, as will be indicated in the following section, the trials against President Kenyatta and the Deputy President have been discontinued.

BIASED EXERCISE OF PROSECUTORIAL DISCRETION

The criticism of prosecutorial bias concerned both the manner in which the office of the ICC Prosecutor managed self-referrals, as well as the initiation of investigations *proprio motu*. Self-referrals mean that the states in question brought the cases to the ICC for investigation of their own accord. The procedure was not explicitly provided for in the ICC Statute, but has in practice been developed and acquiesced in by state parties. African countries over which the ICC gained jurisdiction via self-referral include the Central African Republic (CAR), the DRC, the Comoros, Gabon, Mali and Uganda.[69] However, these states have been criticized for using self-referral as a way of targeting rebel groups.[70] The ICC for its part has come across as a willing partner in this endeavour. It allowed incumbent governments to use the ICC as a vehicle for ridding itself of rebel leaders, while not cooperating when it came to the investigation and/or prosecution of government officials or others acting on their behalf.[71] It is rather telling that President Yoweri Museveni of Uganda initially referred cases involving the Lord's Resistance

---

[66] EAC, Communiqué of the 10th Extraordinary Summit of the Heads of State, 28 April 2012, at para. 20, available at http://en.igihe.com/spip.php?page=mv2_article&id_article=2254.

[67] B. C. Olugbuo, 'Operationalizing the Complementarity Principle: The Case for a Differentiated Standard in Kenya's Post-Electoral Violence', in Jalloh and Bantekas (eds.), *The International Criminal Court and Africa*, p. 79.

[68] M. Ssenyonjo, 'The Implementation of the *Proprio Motu* Authority of the Prosecutor in Africa', p. 56; Olugbuo, 'Operationalizing the Complementarity Principle', p. 79.

[69] Ssenyonjo, 'State Withdrawal Notifications from the Rome Statute of the International Criminal Court', p. 85; Brown, 'The International Criminal Court in Africa: Impartiality, Politics, Complementarity and Brexit', p. 146; see also Ciampi, 'Legal Rules, Policy Choices and Political Realities', pp. 17 ff.

[70] Ssenyonjo, 'State Withdrawal Notifications from the Rome Statute of the International Criminal Court', p. 85; Brown, 'The International Criminal Court in Africa: Impartiality, Politics, Complementarity and Brexit', p. 146.

[71] Ibid. and du Plessis et al., 'Africa and the International Court', p. 2.

Army to the ICC, but thereafter took a leading role in the AU campaigns against the ICC.[72] The perception that the office of the ICC Prosecutor has allowed African governments to manipulate the international criminal justice system for their own political purposes has harmed the credibility of the ICC within African societies, including amongst the victims of international crimes.[73]

Equally (if not more) controversial is the manner in which the office of the ICC Prosecutor exercised its discretion in relation to the *proprio motu* proceedings provided for in Article 15 of the ICC Statute.[74] The controversy concerns in particular the counter-productive management of the investigations in Kenya, which constituted the first instance in which the ICC Prosecutor exercised *proprio motu* powers.[75] In addition, African countries have perceived the use of *proprio motu* investigations exclusively in Africa between 2009 and 2015 as another reflection of the bias towards the continent.

Subsequent to the violence that erupted in the aftermath of the December 2007 Kenyan elections, an Independent Commission of Inquiry concluded that the root causes of the post-election violence included the manner in which (ethnic) violence was utilized by politicians as a means to gain power.[76] This conclusion was also endorsed by the AU Panel of Eminent African Personalities, which in 2009 provided supporting materials to this effect to the ICC Prosecutor.[77] By this time, Kenyan law makers had on two occasions rejected draft legislation proposing the establishment of a special tribunal for

---

[72] du Plessis et al., 'Africa and the International Court', p. 2.

[73] Ibid.; Ssenyonjo, 'State Withdrawal Notifications from the Rome Statute of the International Criminal Court', p. 85; Brown, 'The International Criminal Court in Africa: Impartiality, Politics, Complementarity and Brexit', p. 146.

[74] Art. 15(1) of the ICC Statute determines: 'The Prosecutor may initiate investigations *proprio motu* on the basis of information on crimes within the jurisdiction of the Court.'

[75] Kenya acceded to the ICC Statute on 15 March 2015 and incorporated its provisions by enacting the International Crimes Act of 2008 (entered into force 1 January 2009; available at http://www.ilo.org/dyn/natlex/natlex4.detail?p_lang=&p_isn=82568&p_classification=01.04); see also Ssenyonjo, 'The Implementation of the *Proprio Motu* Authority of the Prosecutor in Africa', p. 45.

[76] See Report of the Commission of Inquiry into Post-election Violence (CIPEV), 2008, pp. 356 ff., available at https://reliefweb.int/sites/reliefweb.int/files/resources/15A00F569813F4D549257607001F459D-Full_Report.pdf; Ssenyonjo, 'State Withdrawal Notifications from the Rome Statute of the International Criminal Court', p. 86; Ciampi, 'Legal Rules, Policy Choices and Political Realities', pp. 31 ff.

[77] ICC Press Release, ICC Prosecutor Receives Sealed Envelope from Kofi Annan on Post-Election Violence in Kenya, 9 July 2009, ICC-OTP-20090709-PR436, available at https://www.icc-cpi.int/Pages/item.aspx?name=pr436.

Kenya.[78] Claiming that there was a reasonable basis to believe that crimes against humanity had occurred in Kenya in the context of the post-electoral violence in 2007 and 2008, the ICC Prosecutor sought permission from Pre-Trial Chamber II to initiate a *proprio motu* investigation in Kenya in November 2009.[79] This request was granted by Pre-Trial Chamber II in March 2010, paving the way for the indictment of five high-ranking Kenyan government officials for crimes against humanity.[80]

Two of these government officials included Uhuru Kenyatta and William Ruto, who already held cabinet positions at the time they were charged, in 2012. Subsequently, during the March 2013 presidential elections, they were elected to President and Deputy President of Kenya, respectively. Ironically, both these individuals very effectively used anti-ICC rhetoric as a campaign vehicle in their rise to the highest office of the land.[81] Furthermore, once they took office and tightened their grip on the state apparatus, the intimidation and bribing of witnesses were the order of the day.[82] The ultimate result was the collapse of the Kenyatta and Ruto cases, due to insufficient evidence.[83] Similarly, the charges against two other Kenyan accused were also aban-

---

[78] Ssenyonjo, 'The Implementation of the *Proprio Motu* Authority of the Prosecutor in Africa', p. 45.

[79] ICC, Request for Authorisation of an Investigation Pursuant to Article 15, 26 November 2009, ICC-01/09, available at https://www.icc-cpi.int/CourtRecords/CR2009_08645.PDF; Jalloh, 'Introduction', p. 2.

[80] See ICC Pre-Trial Chamber II, Decision Pursuant to Article 15 of the Rome Statute on the Authorization of an Investigation into the Situation in the Republic of Kenya, 31 March 2010, ICC-01/09, available at http://www.refworld.org/cases,ICC,4bc2fe372.html. However, see Dissenting Opinion of Judge Hans-Peter Kaul, ibid., at para. 4. He was not convinced that the crimes that were committed were in an 'attack against any civilian population, pursuant to or in furtherance of a state or organizational policy to commit such an attack'. See also Ssenyonjo, 'The Implementation of the *Proprio Motu* Authority of the Prosecutor in Africa', pp. 39 and 46.

[81] Brown, 'The International Criminal Court in Africa: Impartiality, Politics, Complementarity and Brexit', p. 158.

[82] Ssenyonjo, 'State Withdrawal Notifications from the Rome Statute of the International Criminal Court', pp. 85 and 90; Peter, 'Fighting Impunity: African States and the International Criminal Court', p. 37.

[83] ICC Trial Chamber V(B), Decision on the Withdrawal of Charges Against Mr Kenyatta, 13 March 2015, *The Prosecutor v. Uhuru Muigai Kenyatta*, ICC-01/09-02/11, available at https://www.icc-cpi.int/CourtRecords/CR2015_02842.PDF; ICC Trial Chamber V(A), Decision on Defence Applications for Judgments of Acquittal, 5 April 2016, *The Prosecutor v. William Samoei Ruto and Joshua Arap Sang*, ICC-01/09-01/11, available at https://www.icc-cpi.int/CourtRecords/CR2016_04384.PDF. See Peter, 'Fighting Impunity: African States and the International Criminal Court', p. 25.

doned.[84] These developments raised questions about the handling of the investigations leading up to the indictments. In particular, the question arose as to why the office of the ICC Prosecutor did not take more care in obtaining and securing the necessary evidence before the confirmation of charges against high-profile government officials within a government that was clearly opposed to cooperating with the ICC.[85]

The fall-out of the collapse of the Kenyan cases did not only constitute considerable embarrassment to the ICC, but placed victims and witnesses in acute danger of persecution.[86] Furthermore, on 5 September 2013 the majority of the Kenyan National Assembly approved a motion to withdraw from the ICC and to repeal the International Crimes Act (16 of 2008).[87] While Kenya is yet to submit a notice of withdrawal to the UN Secretary-General, it has effectively discontinued cooperation with the ICC.[88]

The second *proprio motu* proceedings initiated by the ICC Prosecutor concerned Côte d'Ivoire, in the wake of the post-electoral violence of 2010 and 2011.[89] In this instance, the exercise of *proprio motu* competencies in Côte d'Ivoire resulted from the voluntary acceptance of the ICC's jurisdiction under Article 12(3) of the ICC Statute.[90] The most prominent individuals charged

---

[84] Ssenyonjo, 'The Implementation of the *Proprio Motu* Authority of the Prosecutor in Africa', p. 47.

[85] Ibid., p. 49; see extensively also Brown, 'The International Criminal Court in Africa: Impartiality, Politics, Complementarity and Brexit', pp. 157 ff.

[86] Brown, 'The International Criminal Court in Africa: Impartiality, Politics, Complementarity and Brexit', p. 158.

[87] Ssenyonjo, 'The Implementation of the *Proprio Motu* Authority of the Prosecutor in Africa', p. 56; see also 'Kenya Votes to Quit ICC, Days before Deputy President's Trial', *The Irish Times*, 5 September 2013, available at https://www.irishtimes.com/news/world/africa/kenya-votes-to-quit-icc-days-before-deputy-president-s-trial-1.1517567.

[88] Ssenyonjo, 'The Implementation of the *Proprio Motu* Authority of the Prosecutor in Africa', p. 58.

[89] See ICC Pre-Trial Chamber III, *Corrigendum* to Decision Pursuant to Article 15 of the Rome Statute on the Authorization of an Investigation into the Situation in the Republic of Côte d'Ivoire, 15 November 2011, ICC-02/11, available at https://www.icc-cpi.int/CourtRecords/CR2011_18794.PDF; M. Ssenyonjo, 'The Implementation of the *Proprio Motu* Authority of the Prosecutor in Africa', p. 39; Naldi and Magliveras, 'The International Criminal Court and the African Union: A Problematic Relationship', p. 118.

[90] While the country at the time was not a state party to the ICC Statute, it accepted jurisdiction of the ICC on 18 April 2003, 14 December 2010 and 3 May 2011. See ICC Pre-Trial Chamber III, *Corrigendum* to Decision Pursuant to Article 15 of the Rome Statute on the Authorization of an Investigation into the Situation in the Republic of Côte d'Ivoire, at paras. 10 ff. See also Ssenyonjo, 'State Withdrawal Notifications from the Rome Statute of the International Criminal Court', pp. 86–7.

in the aftermath of the civil conflict concerned the former President, Laurent Gbagbo, and his wife Simone, who were charged with involvement in crimes against humanity.[91] Unlike in the case of President Kenyatta and President Bashir, neither the AU nor the country in question requested the UNSC for a deferral in terms of Article 16 of the ICC Statute.[92] However, this might very well relate to the fact that Laurent Gbagbo was the political rival of incumbent President Quattara.[93] It is also striking that thus far no ICC arrest warrants have been made public against any pro-Quattara forces, despite evidence of international crimes having been committed on all sides.[94] This in turn suggests that the *proprio motu* proceedings in Côte d'Ivoire might have been utilized for internal political purposes, not unlike in the cases of self-referrals.

The perception of bias on the part of the office of the ICC Prosecutor in its handling of *proprio motu* investigations and prosecutions was exacerbated by the fact that until 2015, Article 15(1) of the ICC Statute was invoked exclusively in relation to situations in Africa. By contrast, the office of the ICC Prosecutor remained reluctant to exercise these powers in conflict-ridden member states in other regions, such as Iraq and Afghanistan, to name but two, despite persistent allegations of war crimes having been committed during the armed conflicts in question.[95] Only by 2015 did the office of the ICC Prosecutor commence *proprio motu* investigations in jurisdictions outside of Africa, including Georgia, and thereafter also Afghanistan, Colombia, Iraq, Palestine, the Philippines, Venezuela and Ukraine.[96] However, it remains to be seen whether any of these investigations will be undertaken even-handedly and rigorously and whether they will be pursued beyond the preliminary investigation stage.[97] As it stands, the past reluctance of the office of the ICC

---

[91] See ICC Pre-Trial Chamber III, Warrant of Arrest for Laurent Koudou Gbagbo, 23 November 2011, ICC-02/11, available at https://www.icc-cpi.int/CourtRecords/CR2015_05372.PDF; and Warrant of Arrest for Simone Gbagbo, 29 February 2012, ICC- 02/11-01/12, available at https://www.icc-cpi.int/CourtRecords/CR2012_03549.PDF.

[92] At the time of writing, the trial against Laurent Gbagbo was ongoing, while Simone Gbagbo was still at large.

[93] Ssenyonjo, 'The Implementation of the *Proprio Motu* Authority of the Prosecutor in Africa', p. 55.

[94] Ibid., pp. 60–61.

[95] Ibid., p. 41.

[96] An overview is available at https://www.icc-cpi.int/pages/pe.aspx; see also Ssenyonjo, 'State Withdrawal Notifications from the Rome Statute of the International Criminal Court', p. 87.

[97] At the time of writing, the *proprio motu* proceedings in Georgia were the only ones outside of Africa that had proceeded to the investigation stage. See Ssenyonjo, 'State Withdrawal Notifications from the Rome Statute of the International Criminal Court', p. 116.

Prosecutor to do so has caused claims that it acted independently of all political considerations to ring hollow.[98]

CONCLUSION

In conclusion it is fair to state that the blame for the deterioration in the relationship between the ICC, the AU and some of its member states can be placed at the door of all key actors. First, the commitment of many African states to the ICC may not have been as strong as their formal membership may have suggested.[99] In some instances, the ratification of or accession to the ICC Statute might have had less to do with a true commitment to hold perpetrators of international crimes responsible than a strategic choice for enhancing the possibility of obtaining development aid.[100] In addition, in those instances where African governments did support investigations by the ICC within their jurisdictions, this – at least to some extent – served the purpose of neutralizing political rivals or rebel movements, rather than forming part of an even-handed process of accountability. The office of the ICC Prosecutor for its part has – in particular during the tenure of the first Prosecutor – made grave errors in judgement, suggesting that its communication with African states and the AU at the time left much to be desired.[101] Furthermore, its systemic errors have ranged from (perceived) bias in prosecuting self-referrals, to the (perceived) biased use of the *proprio motu* proceedings. This perception of a particular African bias was aggravated by the selective referral practices of the UNSC and the resulting indictments of African heads of state.

Last but not least, the Assembly of State Parties failed to hold the first ICC Prosecutor to account for the very significant role his office played in the above

---

[98] See statements by: L. Moreno-Ocampo, 'The International Criminal Court: Seeking Global Justice', *Case Western Reserve Journal of International Law*, 40(1), 2007–2008, p. 215, p. 221; P. Smith, 'Interview: Luis Moreno-Ocampo, ICC Prosecutor', *African Report*, 21 September 2009, available at http://www.theafricareport.com/News-Analysis/interview-luis-moreno-ocampo-icc-prosecutor.html009; F. Bensouda, 'Statement at a Press Conference in Uganda: Justice Will Ultimately Be Dispensed With for LRA Crimes', *Relief Web*, 27 February 2015, available at https://reliefweb.int/report/uganda/statement-prosecutor-international-criminal-court-fatou-bensouda-press-conference.

[99] See also Brown, 'The International Criminal Court in Africa: Impartiality, Politics, Complementarity and Brexit', p. 169; Naldi and Magliveras, 'The International Criminal Court and the African Union: A Problematic Relationship', p. 113.

[100] Ssenyonjo, 'State Withdrawal Notifications from the Rome Statute of the International Criminal Court', p. 104.

[101] du Plessis et al., 'Africa and the International Court', p. 2; Brown, 'The International Criminal Court in Africa: Impartiality, Politics, Complementarity and Brexit', p. 156.

developments. In fact, with the vision of hindsight it is fair to question whether these negative developments could have been prevented if the Assembly of State Parties had recalled Louis Moreno Ocampo, after he had been found guilty of abuse of power towards an ICC staff member by an international administrative tribunal in July 2008.[102] As of that point, it was very difficult to argue that Mr Acampo lived up to Article 42(3) of the ICC Statute which *inter alia* requires the Prosecutor to be of high moral character.[103] While this issue in principle is separate from the focus of the current analysis, it has a direct bearing on it. First of all, most of the key developments in the break-down of the relations between the AU and the ICC have taken place since 2009, that is after Mr Ocampo had been found guilty of misconduct. Therefore, it is fair to ask whether at least some of the grave errors in judgement committed by his office could have been prevented if the Assembly of State Parties had recalled him in July 2008. Second, the unwillingness of the Assembly of State Parties to recall a prosecutor found guilty of abuse of power by an independent judicial body – therefore by implication not acting in accordance with Article 42 of the ICC Statute – was in and of itself an immense blow to the credibility of the ICC.

The combination of all these unfortunate developments resulted in a highly damaged relationship between the AU, many of its member states and the ICC.[104] Even if the sullied relationship does not result in a mass withdrawal by African states from the ICC Statute, passive resistance in the form of non-cooperation is the order of the day in several African jurisdictions. Creating trust and rebuilding the relationship will not be easy, although there is still support for the ICC across the continent.[105] A first step could be for the ICC to engage with African governments about strengthening national and regional capacity for prosecuting international crimes on African soil, while

---

[102] International Labour Organization Administrative Tribunal, 9 July 2008, *CP v. the International Criminal Court*, Case No. 2757, at para. 19, available at https://www.ilo.org/dyn/triblex/triblexmain.showList?p_lang=en&p_org_id=19&p_and_or=AND&p_page=2.

[103] Art. 42(3) of the ICC Statute determines: 'The Prosecutor and the Deputy Prosecutors shall be persons of high moral character, be highly competent in and have extensive practical experience in the prosecution or trial of criminal cases. They shall have an excellent knowledge of and be fluent in at least one of the working languages of the Court.'

[104] Naldi and Magliveras, 'The International Criminal Court and the African Union: A Problematic Relationship', p. 113.

[105] See also du Plessis et al., 'Africa and the International Court', p. 8.

simultaneously reinvigorating the principle of complementarity in the ICC Statute.[106]

This process can include a discussion about potential alternatives to the African Criminal Chamber as foreseen by the Malabo Protocol, notably within the RECs. Whatever the deficits of the Malabo Protocol may be, it does provide a starting point for exploring the role of regional courts in the prosecution of international crimes. Given the greater level of homogeneity and capacity within some of the RECs than within the AU, it is worth considering if and to what extent they may be willing and able to facilitate international criminal prosecution in a way that also enables meaningful cooperation with the ICC. In the final analysis, if there is to be a strong future for the ICC in Africa, all stakeholders will have to take a pro-active stance about how to avoid a repetition of past mistakes and how to embed this institution more strongly within national and regional accountability mechanisms.[107]

---

[106] Ibid., p. 2; Brown, 'The International Criminal Court in Africa: Impartiality, Politics, Complementarity and Brexit', p. 156.

[107] Okafor and Ngwaba, 'The International Criminal Court as a "Transitional Justice" Mechanism in Africa', p. 106.

Index

Abi Saab, Jeorges 9, 11
Abkhazia 28
Adorno, Theodor 94
Africa 4, 5, 9, 22, 27, 29, 30
    African states 190–210
African Court of Justice and Human
    Rights 190
African Criminal Chamber (ACC) 190
African regional economic communities
    (RECs) 191
African Union (AU) 190–210
    African Personalities 205
An Agenda for Peace 3
Agenda for Sustainable Development,
    2030 75, 80
Alamuddin, A. 165
Al-Qaeda 65
Anand, Ram Prakash 12
Antonić, Slobodan 183
apartheid 136, 137, 141, 144, 148, 150
arbitral awards 62
Arendt, Hannah 190
armed conflicts 39–40, 161–4
    civil war 183
    international armed conflict (IAC)
        105
    non-international armed
        conflict (NIAC) 103,
        105, 106, 123, 124, 126
Asia 27
Al-Assad, Bashar 200
Al-Bashir, Omar Hasan Ahmad 193, 198,
    199
Assmann, Aleida 177

Austria–Hungary 28
auto-chauvinist 189
Avramov, Smilja 182

Badinter Arbitration Committee 29
Balkanization 30
Balkans 23, 25, 33, 35, 36, 38, 40
Baron of Rio Branco 8, 9
Beijing Declaration 71
Belt and Road Initiative 73
Benenson, Peter 55
Benjamin, Walter 94
Berlin Blockade 128
Berlin isalah 19
Berlin Wall 12
Bernadotte, Folke 113
Bloch, Marc 18
Bojang, Sheriff Baba 201
Bolsheviks 26
Bosnia 168–89
    memory of victims 173–7
    Muslim population 158
Boutros-Ghali, Boutros 3
Brazil 8
Brexit 84, 93, 100
Brezhnev Doctrine 28
Bulajić, Milan 182
Burundi 194
Butterfield, Herbert 85, 94

Cahen-Salvador, Georges 105, 108, 109,
    119–26, 131
Cairo 5
Carbonnier, Jean 25

213

Cassese, Antonio 37
Cassirer, Ernst 92
central mnemonic event 173
Charter of Fundamental Rights 85–6
Chechen War (First) 58
Chechen War (Second) 58
China 58, 59, 66, 71, 73–5, 81
Clinton administration 59
Cold War 49, 50–54, 114
colonialism
 counter colonialism 5
 decolonization 50–4
 neo-colonialism 197
common article 3 103, 105, 119–27, 131, 133
complementarity (ICC) 192, 211
Crawford, James 11
Crimea 28, 40, 42
crimes against humanity 139–41
 apartheid 142–50
 forced pregnancy 150–53
Croatia 168–89
 memory of victors 178–82
Cullen, Anthony 126
Cyprus 38

Dallaire, Romeo 134
Dayton Agreement for Peace 36
De Búrca, Gráinne 97–9
Declaration on the Right to Development 51
Democratic People's Republic of Korea (DPRK) 148
Dunant, Henry 26

East African Court of Justice (EACJ) 203
Eastern Galicia 30
Eastern Ukraine 28
Eichmann, Adolf 108
Environmental Modification Convention (ENMOD) 161
environmental protection 138, 160–63

ethnic cleansing 39
ethnic violence 204
Europe
 East-Central Europe 23, 33, 37, 40–42
 Eastern Europe 23–9, 31, 33, 35, 37, 39–41
 Eastern vs. Western Europe 24–6
 European pentarchy 25
 Northeastern Europe 23
 Northern Europe 24
 Southeastern Europe 23, 30
 Southern Europe 22
 Western Europe 24–7
European Union (EU) 82, 92, 95
 see also Charter of Fundamental Rights, Treaty on European Union (TEU)
 European Court of Justice (ECJ) 57, 86–9, 95–6, 98
 internal market 49, 57, 80, 81, 98–9, 101
 human rights narratives 82–101
European Convention on Human Rights (ECHR) 88, 94
European Court of Human Rights (ECtHR) 64, 89
European Economic Community (EEC) 82, 99
European Political Cooperation (EPC) Treaty 98
European Stability Mechanism (ESM) Treaty 90
eurozone crisis 90

Falk, Richard 149
financial and economic crisis 91
Fisch, Jörg 29
forced pregnancy 137, 150–53, 159
Foucault, Michel 97
Franck, Thomas 36
free trade agreements (FTAs) 78–81

free market 49, 57, 80, 81, 98–9, 101
Fukuyama, Francis 2, 4

Gambia 194
Gbagbo, Laurent 208
General Agreement on Tariffs and Trade (GATT) 48–51, 59
  Article XX 60
  Article XXIV 78
  Enabling Clause 51
Geneva Convention for Civilians (fourth) of 1949 ('GC-IV') 103–34
  see also common article 3
Geneva Convention on the Treatment of Prisoners of War of 1929 (GC-III) 106
genocide 23, 30, 36, 39, 40, 135–8, 140, 152–60, 164, 166, 182, 183
  Srebrenica genocide 175
Genocide Convention
  Article 2 155
  Article 9 154
Germany 24, 26, 28, 33
Gojgić, Ljubica 183
Gotovina, Ante 180, 186
Gros, André 17

Habsburg 24, 33
Hague Academy of International Law 13–14
Hague Regulations concerning the Laws and Customs of War on Land of 1907 110
Hallstein, Walter 95
Hart, Herbert 101
Havana Charter for an International Trade Organization 45–9
Hedl, Drago 186
Helsinki Accords 52, 55
Herzegovina 174–8
holocaust 136, 140
  holocaust's memory 173

Horkheimer, Max 94
Huber, Max 120, 121, 134
Hudson, Manley 95
humanitarian intervention 25
human rights 44–101
  bridging existing divides 70–77
  categories 46, 47
  China's collectivist conception of 71
  China's human rights diplomacy 81
  'effectiveness' crisis of 62–5
  emergence, international relations 50–53
  European Court of Justice (ECJ) and 86–7
  Eastern Europe and 26–8
  historical developments 67–9
  indicators 68
  international investment law, parallel legitimacy crisis 65–7
  language 65
  NGOs 65
  narratives in the EU 83–100
  supremacy and autonomy of EU law and 87–91
  theory and practice, division 54–9
  trade, investment and development 78–80
  World Conference on Human Rights 71
Human Rights Council (HRC) 63, 64

individual criminal responsibility 174
International Committee of the Red Cross (ICRC) 26, 104–8, 110, 113, 115, 118, 120, 123, 125–7, 129, 131–4
International Court of Justice (ICJ) 5, 9, 11, 41, 154
International Covenant on Civil and Political Rights (ICCPR) 47, 53

International Covenant on Economic, Social and Cultural Rights (ICESCR) 47
international crimes 135–67
  origins of 136–41
International Criminal Court (ICC) 58, 135, 142, 144, 145, 164, 191
  African states and AU, relationship 191–211
  prosecutorial discretion 204–8
  self-referrals 197, 198, 204, 208–9
  United Nations Security Council referral policy 198–204
  see also Rome Statute of the International Criminal Court
International Criminal Tribunals for the former Yugoslavia (ICTY) 39, 158, 168–90
  Croatia, Bosnia and Serbia, legacy 168–90
  prosecution 186
international investment law 44, 67
  arbitral awards 62
  Multilateral Agreement on Investment (MAI) 61
International Law Commission 157
International Monetary Fund 59
international terrorism 34–5
  September 11 attacks 62, 65
  war against 65
international trade law 44
  legitimacy crisis 65–7
International Trade Organization (ITO) 48
  see Havana Charter for an International Trade Organization
interpretation of treaties 9, 11, 18–20
  hermeneutics 19
investor-state dispute settlement (ISDS) 62, 79
Izetbegović, Alija 184

Jacob, Andrée 107
jus cogens 56

Kandić, Nataša 187
Kant, Immanuel 85
Kelsen, Hans 86
Kenyatta, Uhuru 197, 203, 204, 206
Khmer Rouge 138, 148, 156
Kirby, Michael 148
Korovin, Evgeny A. 12
Koskenniemi, Martti 39, 97, 99
Kosor, Jadranka 179
Kosovo 29
  Kosovo Liberation Army 38
  Kosovo War 39
  Socialist Autonomous Province of Kosovo 29

Ladurie, Le Roy 19
Lamarle, Albert 111–13, 121, 125, 126
Latin America 4–9, 22, 25
  Brazil's declaration of independence 6
law of treaties 11, 13, 15, 17
  pacta sunt servanda 14
  rebus sic stantibus 10
  see also interpretation of treaties, Vienna Convention on the Law of Treaties
Lemkin, Raphael 35, 153
Lenin, Vladimir Ilyich 26, 129
Levy, D. 173
Libya 198
Lisbon Treaty 98
  see also European Union and Treaty on European Union
Lorca, Becker 25

Maastricht Treaty, 1992 57
  see also European Union (EU)
Malabo Protocol 191, 192, 211
  Article 46A bis 191

Article 46H 192
Martens, Friedrich Fromhold von 31
McNair, Arnold 7
media 168–70, 173–9, 182–9
memory 22–6, 41, 168–77, 180–85, 187–9
    conflict memory 23, 41
    collective memory 170–74
    cosmopolitan memory 173
    of defeated 170, 182–5
    entrepreneurs 171, 181
    holocaust's memory 173
    in history 24–6
    of victims 174–8
    of victors 178–82
    of wars 186–9
    reflexive memory 186–9
    transnational memory 170, 172–3
Mendes-France, Pierre 121
Meron, Theodor 39
Mevorah, Nissim 34, 129, 130, 133
Millennium Development Goals (MDGs) 79
minorities
    protection of 30–35
    expulsion of 35–8
Mladić, Ratko 176
Monnet, Jean 16
Monroe Doctrine 5
Morosov, Platon 126
Mothers of Srebrenica organization 176, 188
Moyn, Samuel 93, 94
Muscovite Russia 24
Museveni, Yoweri 204

Nansen, Frithjof 27
national identity 171
nationalism 169, 190
    ethnic nationalism 169
New International Economic Order (NIEO), failure of 50–53

Nicholas, Barry, 18
non-governmental organizations (NGOs) 54, 55, 81, 186, 187, 188, 189
non-international armed conflict (NIAC) 103, 105, 106, 123, 124, 126
Nora, Pierre 25
Nuremberg International Military Tribunal (IMT) 39
    Nuremberg Charter 154
    Nuremberg Charter Article 6(c) 140
Memorium Nuremberg Trials 26

Ocampo, Louis Moreno 209, 210
Occupied Palestinian Territories (OPT) 148, 149
Operation Storm 178–83
Operation Torch 117
Organization of African Unity (OAU) 5, 9
    see also Africa Union (AU)
Orić, Naser 177
Ottoman Empire 24–5, 27, 30, 33, 38, 129, 139

Paranhos, José Maria da Silva Jr. 8
    see Baron of Rio Branco
Paris Peace Conference of 1919 41
Pashukanis, Evgeny 12, 14
Peace of Westphalia of 1648 6, 25
Perišić, Momčilo 183
Pilloud, Claude 107, 126–9, 134
Poland-Lithuania 24
population exchange 35–8
    Hindu–Muslim exchange 37
Praljak, Slobodan 167
Prussia 24
Pusić, Zoran 186
Putin Doctrine 28

Reuter, Paul 17
Rey-Schyrr, Catherine 127
Riegner, Gerhart 105, 119–25, 131, 133

right to development 51, 71, 75, 76, 80
right to self-determination 3, 9 , 15, 16, 26–8
Rome Statute of the International Criminal Court 58, 135–8, 141, 142, 144, 146, 147, 149, 150–54, 157–60, 162–7
    Article 7(1)(g) 137, 150
    Article 7(1)(h) 145
    Article 7(1)(j) 144
    Article 7(1)(k) 145, 146
    Article 7(1) 141
    Article 7(2)(h) 142, 145, 146
    Article 8(2)(b)(iv) 138, 160–62
    Article 8(2)(b)(xx) 165
    Article 12(3) 208
    Article 13(b) 198, 200
    Article 15(1) 208
    Article 15 205
    Article 16 201, 202, 203, 208
    Article 27 192
    Article 42(3) 210
    Article 127(1) 194
    Rome Diplomatic Conference 164
    withdrawal from 194, 195, 201, 207, 210
Russia
    see Soviet Union (former)
Ruto, William 203, 206
Rwanda civil war 58
    genocide 58, 121–3, 130, 133–4, 135–9

Sands, Philippe 30
Sandström, Emil 122–3
Schmitt, Carl 28, 119–20
Schuman, Robert 16, 121
September 11 attacks 62, 65
Serbia 168–90
    memory of defeated 182–5
    Serb–Albanian conflict 29
    Serb crimes 183

Sinatra Doctrine 28
sites of memory 170
Skinner, Quentin 11, 18
Smismans, Stijn 91–3
Snyder, Timothy 115
South Africa 22, 147, 193–5
South Ossetia 28
Soviet Union (former) 2, 12, 13, 16, 23, 24, 26–31, 42, 46, 52–3, 58, 74, 113–15, 130, 132
    Muscovite Russia 24
    Tsarist Russia 26, 28, 30–31, 130
Sudan (Darfur) 156, 193, 198, 199, 202
sustainable development 52
Sustainable Development Goals (SDGs) 75, 78–81
Sweden–Finland 24
Sznaider, Natan 173

Thirty Years War 6
Tiananmen Square massacre 74
Tito, Josip Broz 168
Tobar, Carlos 8
Treaty on European Union (TEU) 57
    Article 2 87, 92
    Article 6 57, 86–7, 92
    Article 49 57, 92
Truman Doctrine 118
Tuđman, Franjo 179, 184
Tunkin, Grigorii Ivanovich 13, 15–17

United Nations War Crimes Commission 141
Universal Declaration of Human Rights (UDHR) 54
    unitary design, failures of 45–9
Universal Periodic Review (UPR) 63, 77
United Nations Office of the High Commissioner for Human Rights (OHCHR) 54
uti possidetis juris 4, 5, 7, 8, 11, 29

Vienna Convention on Law of Treaties in 1969 11, 15
  see also law of treaties
  see also interpretation of treaties
Vyshinsky, Andrey 12

war crimes
  chemical weapons 163–6
  environmental protection 160–63
  trials 168–73, 184, 188
Warsaw Ghetto Uprising 135
weapons
  biological weapons 164, 165
  chemical weapons 138, 160, 163–6
Wilson, Woodrow 26
World Bank 59
World Jewish Congress (WJC) 104–5, 120, 122, 131

World Trade Organization (WTO) 2, 48, 59–60, 62, 65–7
  Dispute Settlement Understanding (DSU) 62, 67
  Doha Development Round 66
  Uruguay Round 61
World War (First) 25
World War (Second) 13, 16, 27, 45–9, 84, 103, 110, 111, 114, 119, 130, 138, 140, 160

Yugoslavia (former) 135, 137, 150, 151, 158, 168, 169, 173, 174, 184, 186, 190
  collective memory in post-war Yugoslavia 174

Zertal, Idith 171
Zuma, Jacob 195